The return of the Arab revolution
Alex Callinicos

In the winter of 1939-40 the German Marxist critic Walter Benjamin wrote a remarkable text known as "Theses on the Philosophy of History". In it he attacked the widespread belief on the left that socialism would come about inevitably, as the fruit of historical progress. "Nothing has corrupted the German working class so much as the notion it was moving with the current," he wrote. Revolution is not the appointed result of humankind's "progression through a homogeneous empty time". Rather, "it is a tiger's leap into the past," which mobilises the memories of past suffering and oppression against the ruling class. And Benjamin concluded by evoking the fact that, in the Jewish Messianic tradition, "every second of time was the strait gate through which the Messiah might enter".[1]

Revolution, in other words, is not a predictable outcome of a forward historical movement—it is a sudden, unexpected irruption into a history that is a "single catastrophe which keeps piling wreckage upon wreckage".[2] Benjamin wrote these words at a very dark historical moment, "midnight in the century", when the Hitler-Stalin pact seemed to symbolise the death of all radical hope. But they fit the revolutions that have swept through the Arab world since mid-December like a glove. Exploding apparently out

---

1:   Benjamin, 1970, pp260, 263, 266. Thanks especially to Philip Marfleet as a source of analysis and information.
2:   Benjamin, 1970, p259. For a critical discussion of the "Theses", see Callinicos, 2004, chapter 5.

of nowhere, quite unanticipated, an explosion of resentments deeply compacted over decades, they are not simply rewriting the political map of the Middle East, but have a much broader historical meaning.

In the first instance, the upheavals in Tunisia, Egypt and Libya and their reverberations elsewhere in the region mark the unforeseen return of the Arab revolution. Starting with the seizure of power in Egypt by the Free Officers Movement in July 1952, the Arab revolution gripped a Middle East still dominated by British and French imperialism. After he had emerged triumphant in the internal Egyptian struggle, Gamal Abdel Nasser didn't simply successfully confront the colonial powers and seize most of the assets of the Egyptian propertied classes. He appealed to the widespread consciousness throughout the region of belonging to a single Arab nation transcending the political boundaries dividing the various states emerging from the colonial era. In 1958 Nasser proclaimed a United Arab Republic involving a short-lived union between Egypt and Syria. He waged a prolonged proxy war with Saudi Arabia, then as now the citadel of Arab reaction, in North Yemen, and his followers played an active part in the great Iraqi Revolution of 1958-63. The pan-Arab Nasserite Movement of Arab Nationalists was a training ground for the more radical leaders of the Palestinian resistance.

Already in retreat, Nasserite pan-Arabism experienced a decisive defeat when Israel triumphed over Egypt and the other Arab states in the Six Day War of June 1967. Nasser died a broken man three years later. Arab national consciousness survived in the increasingly degenerate forms of the Ba'athist dictatorships in Iraq and Syria and, much more positively, in the solidarity shown to the Palestinian struggle. But its persisting strength has been shown in the speed with which the revolutionary virus spread from Tunis after the fall of Zine El Abdine Ben Ali on 14 January to Egypt, Yemen, Bahrain and Libya. Indeed, the ripple effects have been felt in Iran, itself an increasingly influential force in the Arab world, stimulating a revival of the Green Movement. It was to prevent the spread of this revolutionary virus that the autocracies of the Gulf Cooperation Council sent troops into Bahrain in mid-March.

But no historical repetition is ever simple. Nasser's pan-Arabism sought to unite the Arab world against both Western imperialism and the Arab private bourgeoisie and landowners. It came against the background of massive popular mobilisations in both Egypt and Iraq in the late 1940s and early 1950s that threw Britain's client regimes in these countries into what proved to be terminal crises. But it was also a project relentlessly pursued from above, in which the Free Officers, and increasingly Nasser personally, sought

International Socialism 130

Spring 2011

Contributors

Chris Bambery is the author of *A Rebel's Guide to Gramsci*.

Lee Billingham is a socialist and longstanding activist with Love Music Hate Racism.

Martin Empson is the author of the pamphlets *Marxism and Ecology* and *Climate Change: Why Nuclear Power is Not the Answer*.

Iain Ferguson is co-founder of the Social Work Action Network and the author of *Reclaiming Social Work: Challenging Neoliberalism and Promoting Social Justice*.

Keith Flett is a socialist historian and activist.

Lee Humber is a lecturer in Health and Social Care at Aylesbury Further Education college. He is writing a PhD thesis on the history of employment of people with learning difficulties.

Stathis Kouvelakis is the author of *Philosophy and Revolution: From Kant to Marx*.

Philip Marfleet is Professor of Migration and Refugee Studies at the University of East London.

Sheila McGregor is a socialist activist in east London.

Chamseddine Mnasri teaches at the University of Manouba, Tunisia.

John Newsinger is the author of *The Blood Never Dried: A People's History of the British Empire* and currently is writing books on the IWW and on the US working class in the 1930s.

David Renton is a barrister practising in London. He was a pupil at Eton College in the late 1980s.

John Ridell has compiled six documentary volumes on the revolutionary socialist movement in Lenin's time; his seventh, on the 1922 congress of the Communist International, will appear later this year. He is a member of the Greater Toronto Workers' Assembly.

Dan Swain is a postgraduate student at the University of Essex.

Lucien van der Walt works at the University of the Witwatersrand, South Africa, and is involved in union and social movement education. His books include *Black Flame: the Revolutionary Class Politics of Anarchism and Syndicalism* (with Michael Schmidt, 2009).

Andy Wynne is a socialist activist in Leicester.

to maintain control, manipulating, dividing and brutally repressing popular forces such as the Muslim Brotherhood and the Egyptian Communist movement.[3] In contrast, the Arab revolutions of 2011 have been driven by popular rebellions from below. As commentators have repeated to the point of cliché, they have not been the property of any political party or movement, and have been driven by democratic aspirations given body in the forms of self-organisation that have rapidly emerged in all these struggles.

What we are seeing is a renewal of the classical political form of revolution. Innumerable social theorists and media figures have over the past 20 years proclaimed revolution dead, whether because of the definitive triumph of liberal capitalism in 1989 or thanks to the onset of "postmodernity". At one stage it seemed it would survive only in the debased form of the "colour revolutions" through which one gang of oligarchs would depose another under the banner of democracy and with Washington's strong material and moral support.

Yet, despite all the chatter about the role played by Facebook and Twitter in the Arab upheavals (debunked by Jonny Jones elsewhere in this issue), what is striking is how much the revolutions in Tunisia and Egypt conform to a pattern first set during the English Revolution of the 1640s and the Great French Revolution of the 1790s—popular mobilisations, elite divisions at the top, battles for the loyalties of the armed forces, struggles to define the political and economic character of the successor regimes, and further, potentially more radical movements from below. In Libya at the time of writing we see an even more elemental drive by Muammar Gaddafi and the revolutionaries confronting him each to amass enough fighters and firepower to inflict a decisive victory on the other, initiating a civil war whose outcome remains uncertain and that has now been used to justify the latest imperialist intervention in the Islamic world. Revolution is a 21st century reality.

The economic crisis claims political victims

Of course, it is much too simple to say that the Arab revolutions came out of the blue. To take the most important case, Egypt, a collective study by a group of scholars from the radical left (including several contributors to this journal) published less than two years ago plotted the economic, social and political contradictions, and the rising movements of resistance pushing

---

3: See, for example, Batatu, 1978, part five, Beinin and Lockman, 1987, chapters 13 and 14, and Gordon, 1992. I have also benefited from reading a draft chapter by Anne Alexander on the interaction between the mass movements and the Free Officers in Egypt and Iraq, and am grateful for her very helpful comments.

the regime of Hosni Mubarak towards "the moment of change".[4] Marx himself insisted that "it is always necessary to distinguish between the material transformation of the economic conditions of production, which can be determined with the precision of natural science, and the legal, political, religious, artistic or philosophic—in short, ideological forms in which men become conscious of this conflict and fight it out".[5] It is one thing to identify the structural contradictions destabilising a given society, quite another to predict when and how these will fuse to detonate a political explosion.

But we are dealing here with a transnational wave of revolutions and therefore the detonating contradictions can't simply be located at the national level. Indeed, the best place to start is surely the global economic and political crisis. About a year ago Susan Watkins, the editor of *New Left Review*, wrote: "Perhaps the most striking feature of the 2008 crisis so far has been its combination of economic turmoil and political stasis".[6] "*So far*" now seems the operative part of this sentence. As we pointed out in response, severe structural crises such as the present one have to be seen as protracted phenomena, passing through a succession of different phases.[7]

A similar view has recently been expressed by two Marxist economists whose explanation of the crisis is different from that developed in this journal, Gérard Duménil and Dominique Lévy:

> A common feature of structural crises is their multiple facets and their duration. It is, for example, difficult to tell exactly how long was the Great Depression or how long it would have lasted had not preparation for the war boosted the economy. The macro-economy collapsed into the Depression itself from late 1929 to 1933. A gradual recovery occurred to 1937, when output plunged anew. The war economy, then, thoroughly changed the course of events ... Most likely the same will be true of the contemporary crisis. Once positive growth rates prevail in the wake of the contraction of output, this will mark the entrance of a new phase, but certainly not the resolution of the tensions that led to the crisis. A lot will remain to be done. Will positive growth rates be decent growth rates? When will the disequilibria of the US economy be solved? How will the government debt be paid? Will the dollar support international pressures? The establishment of a new, sustainable course of events will be a long and painstaking process.[8]

4:   El-Mahdi and Marfleet, 2009.
5:   Marx, 1971, p21.
6:   Watkins, 2010, p20.
7:   Callinicos, 2010, pp6-13.
8:   Duménil and Lévy, 2011, p22.

As we argued, "a prolonged economic crisis will put pressure on bourgeois political structures, exposing their fault lines".[9] This is precisely what has happened with the Arab revolutions. The fault lines are at once economic and political. Egypt under Mubarak and Tunisia under Ben Ali were both poster boys for neoliberalism in the region. The World Bank, in its September 2010 country brief on Tunisia, couldn't contain its enthusiasm:

> Tunisia has made remarkable progress on equitable growth, fighting poverty and achieving good social indicators. It has sustained an average 5 percent growth rate over the past 20 years with a steady increase in per capita income and a corresponding increase in the welfare of its population that is underscored by a poverty level of 7 percent that is amongst the lowest in the region.[10]

While more measured in its praise of the Mubarak regime, the bank still acknowledged its "solid track record as one of the champions of economic reforms in the Middle East and North Africa region".[11] In fact, Egypt can claim to have pioneered neoliberalism in the Global South. In 1974 President Anwar Sadat announced the policy of *infitah*, economic "opening" to foreign investment and trade, that marked a radical break with Nasser's drive to state capitalism.[12] Mubarak took this policy further, agreeing on an Economic Reform and Structural Adjustment Programme with the international financial institutions in 1991. One of its key planks was Law 96 of 1991, which repealed the rights given to tenants under the Free Officers' 1952 agrarian reform allowing the old landlords and their heirs to return and dispossess peasant households.[13]

Despite talk by the Mubarak regime during the 1990s of a "Tiger on the Nile", the Egyptian and Tunisian economies experienced no "miracle" under neoliberalism, remaining heavily dependent for foreign exchange on textile production vulnerable to Chinese competition and on tourism. Despite some growth, liberalisation brought very sharp economic and social polarisation that put pressure on the corporatist structures that had been built up under Nasser and his Tunisian counterpart, Habib Bourguiba. Anne Alexander observes that in Egypt under Nasser:

9:   Callinicos, 2010, p6.
10: http://bit.ly/worldbanktunisia/
11: http://bit.ly/worldbankegypt/
12: See, for example, Waterbury, 1983.
13: Bush, 2009.

workers were offered a social contract where in return for renouncing their political independence they could expect some gains, such as subsidised housing, education, other welfare benefits and relative job security. Nasserist rhetoric, particularly in its late phase, idealised workers for their contribution to national development. But the Nasserist state crushed independent workers' organisations and in their place built an official trade union federation which was subservient to the government.[14]

But, Alexander continues, "the reforms of the 1990s and beyond fractured the Nasserist system". On the one hand, poverty, inequality and unemployment have grown in Egypt. In 2010 the International Labour Organisation claimed that 44 percent of Egyptians lived below the international poverty line of $2 a day.[15] The previous year Ahmad El-Naggar estimated that "the total number of unemployed…amounts to 7.9 million and the true unemployment rate is now 26.3 percent, and some estimate the rate in the 15 to 29 age group is over three times that figure".[16] Rising unemployment, particularly among the young, is a regional problem. Even the World Bank's own more detailed research contradicts the upbeat headlines. A report, poignantly dated 15 January 2011, the day after Ben Ali's fall, acknowledged:

In the Middle East and North Africa, the youth unemployment rate at 25 percent is the highest in the world. But that statistic alone doesn't tell the whole story.

World Bank researchers are finding that the actual number of jobless people between the ages of 15 and 29 in the region could be much higher. Many young people who are out of school and out of work are not reflected in the statistics because they are not looking for work.

Young urban males, in particular, are at a serious disadvantage in the labour market, with many underemployed, employed in off-the-books informal work, or not working at all.[17]

On the other hand, a tiny layer of super-rich have amassed vast wealth and power. Joel Beinin writes that in Egypt "the holders of the economic

14: Alexander, 2011.
15: Al-Malky, 2010.
16: El-Naggar, 2009, p42.
17: http://arabworld.worldbank.org/content/awi/en/home/featured/youth_programs.html

portfolios" in the government of Ahmed Nazif, appointed prime minister in July 2004, "were Western-educated PhDs in the entourage of Gamal Mubarak, son of the president. They promoted a second wave of privatisation and enacted other measures to encourage foreign direct investment, such as reducing to zero the tariffs on textile machinery and spare parts".[18] The 25 January Revolution forced even the *New York Times* to acknowledge the real nature of this liberalisation:

> On paper, the changes transformed an almost entirely state-controlled economic system to a predominantly free-market one. In practice, though, a form of crony capitalism emerged, according to Egyptian and foreign experts. State-controlled banks acted as kingmakers, extending loans to families who supported the government but denying credit to viable business people who lacked the right political pedigree.
>
> Ahmed El-Naggar, director of the economic studies unit at Al-Ahram Centre for Political and Strategic Studies, said government officials sold state-owned land to politically connected families for low prices. They also allowed foreign conglomerates to buy state-owned companies for small amounts. In exchange, he said, they received kickbacks.
>
> At the same time, the government required foreign investors to form joint ventures with Egyptian firms. Families with close ties to the governing party formed the Egyptian half of the lucrative joint ventures.[19]

The symbol of Egyptian crony capitalism was Ahmed Ezz who, thanks to his friendship with Gamal Mubarak in particular, was able to buy a privatised steel firm cheaply and end up controlling two thirds of the Egyptian steel market. He also became a member of parliament and ran the thuggish campaign of the ruling National Democratic Party (NDP) in the flagrantly rigged legislative elections of November 2010. The Tunisian equivalent was provided by the Trabelsis, Ben Ali's in-laws, who used their family connections to enrich themselves. According to Transparency International, between them the Ben Alis and Trabelsis controlled 30 to 40 percent of the Tunisian economy, around $10 billion. Leila Trabelsi, the ex-president's wife, is accused of fleeing to Jeddah with 1.5 tonnes of gold bars in her luggage.[20]

18: Beinin, 2009, p77.
19: Fahim, Slackman, and Rohde, 2011.
20: Lewis, 2011.

Thus neoliberalism in the Middle East meant, not the separation of economic and political power implied in the abstract idea of the free market, but its *fusion*. This was no longer state capitalism: now political connections allowed those at the top to amass vast private wealth. The effect was to direct economic and social grievances to the pinnacle of the regimes, where the corrupt interpenetration of elites was so flagrantly on display.

The global economic crisis then tightened the screws. Juan Kornblihtt and Bruno Magro write:

> The structural weakness appeared in all its magnitude with the 2008 crisis. The springs which had enabled the small boom collapsed as a whole. If we focus on Egypt, we see that remittances from emigrants fell by 17 percent compared to 2008, tourism also went from a rise of 24 percent in 2008 to a fall of 1.1 percent in 2009 and the Suez Canal revenues fell by 7.2 percent compared to 2008, because the travel passages fell by 8.2 percent and tonnage of goods transported decreased by 9 percent. The situation in Tunisia was not very different: its growth of GDP decelerates from rising at 6.33 percent in 2007 to 4.5 percent and 3.1 percent in 2008 and 2009 respectively, while exports of goods fell by 25 percent, largely due to the decline in textiles and apparel and petroleum-related products.[21]

The crisis made itself felt in the Middle East through higher unemployment, especially among the young. But a particularly important role has been played by surges in food prices. In the lead up to the 2008 financial crash there was a sharp rise in the rate of inflation, particularly for basic commodities. Hermann Schwartz argues that this marked a turning point in the development of the crisis, when China ceased to exert downward pressure on world prices by supplying a flood of ever cheaper manufactured goods. "The Chinese export successes also implied rapid Chinese growth and, thus, increasing Chinese calls on global raw materials and in its [sic] own supplies of semi-skilled labour. Raw material prices started rising in 2004 and Chinese wages started rising in 2007. China, thus, started exporting inflation rather than deflation".[22]

The recovery from the Great Recession of 2008-9 is being accompanied by a similar rise in the rate of inflation. As Schwartz argues, increases in demand, particularly in China and the rapidly growing "emerging market" economies of Asia and Latin America, have played a role in these inflationary

---

21: Kornblihtt and Magro, 2011.
22: Schwartz, 2009, p110. See also pp164-171.

episodes, but these are massively amplified by financial speculation. Higher food prices hit the world's poor hard. According to Michel Chossudovsky:

> from 2006 to 2008, there was a dramatic surge in the prices of all major food staples including rice, wheat and corn. The price of rice tripled over a five year period, from approximately $600 a ton in 2003 to more than $1800 a ton in May 2008… The recent surge in the price of grain staples is characterised by a 32 percent jump in the FAO [United Nations Food and Agricultural Organisation]'s composite food price index recorded in the second half of 2010. [23]

The scarcity and cost of bread were, for example, an important factor in the strike wave that swept Egypt from 2006 onwards, preparing the way for the 25 January Revolution. The cost of living, along with the privileges of the elite, has been endlessly cited by street protesters across the Middle East. The potentially explosive situation that developed in the region is dramatically evoked by Larbi Sadiki, writing as the Tunisian rising, sparked by the suicide of Mohamed Boazizi, brought down Ben Ali:

> It is not the Quran or Sayyid Qutb—[the Muslim Brotherhood leader] who is in absentia charged with perpetrating 9/11 despite being dead since 1966—Western security experts should worry about. They should perhaps purchase *Das Kapital* and bond with Karl Marx to get a reality check, a rethink, a dose of sobriety in a post-9/11 world afflicted by over-securitisation.

> From Tunisia and Algeria in the Maghreb to Jordan and Egypt in the Arab east, the real terror that eats at self-worth, sabotages community and communal rites of passage, including marriage, is the terror of socio-economic marginalisation.

> The armies of "khobzistes" (the unemployed of the Maghreb)—now marching for bread in the streets and slums of Algiers and Kasserine and who tomorrow may be in Amman, Rabat, San'aa, Ramallah, Cairo and southern Beirut—are not fighting the terror of unemployment with ideology. They do not need one. Unemployment is their ideology. The periphery is their geography. And for now, spontaneous peaceful protest and self-harm is their weaponry. They are "les misérables" of the modern world. [24]

23: Chossudovsky, 2011.
24: Sadiki, 2011.

But it's important to stress that, though the economic mechanisms and the political context are different, the Middle East isn't the only region where the crisis is generating significant struggles. The spread of austerity across Europe provoked serious resistance in 2010, from the general strikes in Greece to the student explosion in Britain. The near-demolition of Fianna Fáil, the historical party of southern Irish capitalism, in the general election of February 2011, leaving Sinn Féin and the United Left Alliance as the main opposition to the new Fine Gael-Labour coalition government, is another sign that the situation isn't exactly one of "political stasis".

But one of the remarkable political developments so far this year has been the explosive emergence of a mass movement in Wisconsin seeking to block Governor Scott Walker's drive to slash public sector jobs and scrap collective bargaining rights for state workers. This is a direct consequence of the sweeping successes the Tea Party movement helped to secure the Republicans in last autumn's mid-term elections. Now right wingers like Walker are installed in state capitols—and in the Congress in Washington—and are seeking to realise the Tea Party's dream massively to shrink "Big Government". As Megan Trudell suggested might happen in our last issue, the effect has been to provoke massive social and political polarisation, not just in Wisconsin, but in other mid-Western states where similar assaults are being mounted on the public sector and organised labour.[25]

The contrast between the giant demonstrations blockading the state capitol in Madison, Wisconsin and the relative small mobilisations that the Tea Party has been able to mount in response indicate the problems that the austerity offensive—initiated by the Republicans but also embraced in more moderate terms by Barack Obama—may face. A Gallup opinion poll showed that 61 percent of Americans opposed the Walker plan, with those earning less than $24,000 a year 74 percent against, those on $24,000 to $59,000 63 percent against, those on $60,000 to $89,000 53 percent against, and only those on $90,000 and upwards 50 percent in favour. A *Washington Post* blogger commented that these figures suggest that the Republican strategy of targeting public sector workers as the new "welfare queens" may be backfiring:

I think it's fair to speculate that the focus of Walker's proposal on rolling back long-accepted bargaining rights, and the massive amount of media attention to it, may have reframed the debate and refocused the public's attention in a way that is undermining the right's previous advantage on questions involving public employees. This isn't to say the right doesn't still have the upper hand

---

25: Trudell, 2011.

in some ways. And Walker very well may win in the end. But the landscape has clearly changed in an unexpected way.[26]

Now the emerging anti-austerity movement in the United States isn't the same as the Arab risings. Not only is the margin of material survival much greater, but there exist mediating structures—in particular, the Democratic Party and the trade union bureaucracy—whose absence in the Arab world greatly restricts the ruling classes' room for manoeuvre in the face of the mass risings. Nevertheless, despite the differences in local political and social geologies, the shockwaves of the crisis are making themselves felt globally.[27]

A crisis for the West

There have been moments in history where revolution spread in a region or around the world as if it were a wildfire. These moments do not come often. Those that come to mind include 1848, where a rising in France engulfed Europe. There was also 1968, where the demonstrations of what we might call the New Left swept the world: Mexico City, Paris, New York and hundreds of other towns saw anti-war revolutions staged by Marxists and other radicals. Prague saw the Soviets smash a New Leftist government. Even China's Great Proletarian Cultural Revolution could, by a stretch, be included. In 1989, a wave of unrest, triggered by East Germans wanting to get to the West, generated an uprising in Eastern Europe that overthrew Soviet rule ... similar social and cultural conditions generate similar events and are triggered by the example of one country and then spread more broadly. That has happened in 2011 and is continuing.[28]

These are the words of no Marxist, but of George Friedman, founder of the American "strategic intelligence" website Stratfor. The scale of the revolutions and rebellions in the Arab world justifies these historical comparisons. But there is an immediate difference that sets 2011 apart from its most immediate predecessor, 1989. The revolutions that swept away the Stalinist regimes in Eastern and Central Europe strengthened Western capitalism in general and US imperialism in particular. By

---

26: Sargent, 2011.
27: David McNally argues the Great Recession is provoking a "Great Resistance", though some of the most important examples he cites—Bolivia 2000-5 and Oaxaca 2006—actually predate the onset of the crisis—McNally, 2011.
28: Friedman, 2011c.

contrast, the Arab revolutions—and above all the upheaval in Egypt—are a dagger directed at the heart of American imperialism.

The reason is well explained by Friedman:

> When Egypt was a pro-Soviet Nasserite state, the world was a very different place than it had been before Nasser. When Sadat changed his foreign policy the world changed with it. If the Sadat foreign policy changes, the world changes again. Egypt is one of those countries whose internal politics matter to more than its own citizens.[29]

Egypt is the largest country in the Arab world, Cairo its cultural capital. Egypt's pivotal geographical position, at the junction of the Maghreb, the Mashreq (Arab East), the Gulf, and sub-Saharan Africa, means that when it changes, the ripple-effects are felt over a very wide area. Nasser's revolution from above and his confrontation with Western imperialism not only launched the wave of pan-Arab nationalism, but helped to conjure into existence the Third World as a political entity—post-colonial states that (*pace* Friedman) refused to align themselves firmly with either the US or the Soviet Union in the Cold War.

Similarly, when Sadat moved Egypt rightwards in the early 1970s, the impact was felt on a very wide scale. This shift wasn't just economic—*infitah*. At least as important was the geopolitical revolution consecrated by the Peace Treaty Sadat signed with Israel in March 1979, which led to Israeli withdrawal from Sinai. In the preceding 30 years Egypt had fought four wars with Israel, the most recent of which, in October 1973, had caught Israel on the hop. Peace with Egypt protected Israel's southern flank. As Noam Chomsky puts it, "crucially, Egyptian military forces were excluded from the Arab-Israeli conflict, so that Israel could concentrate its attention (and its military forces) on the occupied territories and the northern border": a generation of peace in Sinai allowed the Israel Defence Force to wage war on Lebanon and Gaza.[30]

Egypt under Sadat and Mubarak became, along with Israel and Saudi Arabia, the basis of the system of alliances through which the US has maintained its hegemony over the Middle East. The Mubarak regime proved its value to Washington in many ways: helping to orchestrate the alliance against Saddam Hussein in the 1991 Gulf War; intelligence cooperation against the Islamists (Wikileaks cables reveal how highly the US embassy in Cairo valued Omar Suleiman, Mubarak's intelligence chief and short-lived vice-president);

29: Friedman, 2011a.
30: Chomsky, 1999, pp194-195.

renditions for torture in Egypt's prisons (Suleiman seems to have played a literally hands-on role here);[31] and maintaining the blockade on Gaza. In exchange, the Egyptian armed forces that remained the basis of the regime received their annual "strategic rent" of $1.3 billion in US military aid.

But the links between the West and the Arab dictatorships are much more extensive than the US-Egyptian axis, fundamental though it is. They have been exposed by the rich crop of scandals the revolutions are producing. The most prominent victim so far is Michèle Alliot-Marie, sacked as French foreign minister after her intimate relationship with the Ben Ali regime came to light. *Le Monde* commented (maybe rather too generously to Alliot-Marie, who had been involved in Tunisian property deals via her elderly parents):

> Viewed from Tunisia, the troubles of Michèle Alliot-Marie seem almost secondary. During the Ben Ali era, Franco-Tunisian acquaintances were, in fact, so frequent, so familiar that they became part of Tunisians' everyday landscape. There was, these last twenty years, a "French tradition of supporting the dictator", says Ridha Kéfi, editor of the online journal *Kapitalis* based in the Tunisian capital. If "MAM" has been caught out, it is because she, like plenty of others, gave way to the atmosphere of tranquil connivance that had been established between Paris and Tunis.[32]

Britain and the US, by contrast, were deeply involved in intense efforts to court a much less promising candidate for neoliberal restructuring, Libya, once Gaddafi had come to terms with them in 2003. These included the debauchment of the reputation of the London School of Economics and of the name of Ralph Miliband through the relationship developed particularly by LSE's "Centre for Global Governance" with Seif al-Islam Gaddafi.[33] Ex-LSE director and ideologue of the Third Way Anthony Giddens mused after a Libyan jaunt in 2007: "Will real progress be possible only when Gaddafi leaves the scene? I tend to think the opposite… My ideal future for Libya in two or three decades' time would be a Norway of North Africa: prosperous, egalitarian and forward-looking".[34]

But the drive to integrate the Gaddafi regime in the world economy went much further. The same year, *Business Week* reported that Michael

---

31: Soldz, 2011.
32: Beaugé, 2011.
33: Shamefully, Seif Gaddafi spoke about "Libya: Past, Present, and Future" in a "Special Ralph Miliband Event" on 25 May 2010: www2.lse.ac.uk/publicEvents/events/2010/20100525t1830vLSE.aspx.
34: Giddens, 2007.

Porter, Harvard Business School guru and author of *The Competitive Advantage of Nations*, was part of a project organised by the Boston consultancy Monitor Group "to create a new pro-business elite" in Libya. [35] Among the other American intellectual grandees mobilised by Monitor Group to make the pilgrimage to Tripoli and exchange banalities with the Gaddafis were Francis Fukuyama, Richard Perle, Robert Putnam, Joseph Nye and Benjamin Barber.[36]

The very depth of Western engagement even with the Arab dictatorship with the longest history of past confrontation with the US and his allies may help to explain the vehemence with which Barack Obama and David Cameron denounced Gaddafi once the revolt against him began—and also perhaps the speed with which Cameron was willing to run up the flag of "liberal interventionism" that had been so discredited by association with George W Bush's and Tony Blair's military adventure in Iraq. By helping to deliver the *coup de grace* to Gaddafi, the Western powers might gain some leverage in an important oil producer, but also belatedly win some credit for supporting the struggle for democracy in the Arab world.

It is remarkable how the rhetoric of humanitarian intervention and "responsibility to protect" is being pumped up, as if the disasters in Iraq and Afghanistan had never happened. The Western powers' record of closely allying themselves to the Arab dictatorships should make it amply clear that their intervention in Libya is not to support the revolution, but to rebuild their domination of the Middle East and North Africa.

But they have a big hill to climb in trying to rebuild their credibility in the Arab world. The Pew Global Attitudes Project's 2010 survey of attitudes to the US found Egypt at the bottom of the table, with only 17 percent having a favourable attitude towards America, down from 30 percent in 2006, when Egypt was first polled (interestingly, both Turkey and Pakistan also recorded the same 17 percent low).[37] Even though both the Egyptian military and the Muslim Brotherhood have promised that the Peace Treaty with Israel remains sacrosanct, any future Egyptian government that is—to place the bar as low as possible—more responsive to public opinion than Mubarak's was will be less compliant with American wishes.

Bruised by the Iraq debacle and the economic crisis, and preoccupied with China's rapid rise, US policy-makers show a rueful awareness of the limits of their power. A fortnight after Mubarak's fall Robert Gates, the

---

35: *Business Week*, 2007.
36: Pilkington, 2011.
37: Pew Research Center, 2010.

outgoing defence secretary, chose West Point, where in June 2002 George W Bush first outlined his "Doctrine" affirming America's right of pre-emptive attack, to declare:"In my opinion, any future defence secretary who advises the president to again send a big American land army into Asia or into the Middle East or Africa should 'have his head examined', as General MacArthur so delicately put it".[38]

Gates also was quick to pour cold water on Cameron's ill-briefed talk of imposing a no-fly zone over Libya. Though the Obama administration eventually backed the UN Security Council resolution authorising the use of air power against Gaddafi, it is clear that the US has no great stomach for military intervention in Libya. Obama's shift may have been intended to compensate for its acquiescence in the bloody clampdowns on protesters in Bahrain and Yemen. The Saudi-initiated intervention in Bahrain represents the collective rejection by the Gulf sheikhdoms of the policy adopted by a weakened US of welcoming the democracy movements and using them to help push through neoliberal "reforms". The *Financial Times* commented on Gates's speech:

> The US is a different country today after ten years of war, struggling with record deficits and suffering from "intervention fatigue", in the words of Richard Haass, president of the Council on Foreign Relations think-tank.

> In such a context, Mr Gates's statement about the madness of dispatching US ground troops overseas simply seems like common sense. "It is a very rare admission of something that is all too true but very rarely articulated by someone of that stature," said Aaron David Miller, a former state department official.[39]

US caution contrasts with panic in Israel, whose strategic position is potentially very seriously compromised by the 25 January Revolution. After Mubarak's fall the head of an Israeli think tank admitted:"Our whole structure of analysis just collapsed".[40] Ari Shavit, a columnist in the supposedly liberal daily *Haaretz*, was positively incandescent with rage...at Washington:

> The West's position reflects the adoption of Jimmy Carter's worldview: kowtowing to benighted, strong tyrants while abandoning moderate, weak ones... Carter's betrayal of the Shah [during the Iranian Revolution of 1978-9]

38: Gates, 2011.
39: McGregor, 2011.
40: Gardner, 2011b.

brought us the ayatollahs, and will soon bring us ayatollahs with nuclear arms. The consequences of the West's betrayal of Mubarak will be no less severe. It's not only a betrayal of a leader who was loyal to the West, served stability and encouraged moderation. It's a betrayal of every ally of the West in the Middle East and the developing world. The message is sharp and clear: The West's word is no word at all; an alliance with the West is not an alliance. The West has lost it. The West has stopped being a leading and stabilising force around the world.

The Arab liberation revolution will fundamentally change the Middle East. The acceleration of the West's decline will change the world. One outcome will be a surge towards China, Russia and regional powers like Brazil, Turkey and Iran. Another will be a series of international flare-ups stemming from the West's lost deterrence. But the overall outcome will be the collapse of North Atlantic political hegemony not in decades, but in years. When the United States and Europe bury Mubarak now, they are also burying the powers they once were. In Cairo's Tahrir Square, the age of Western hegemony is fading away. [41]

In the rapids of revolution

The very shrillness of Shavit's denunciation betrays the fear of a client state that one day it too may be "betrayed" by the imperial power. Tariq Ali expresses a much more measured judgement: "American hegemony in the region has been dented but not destroyed. The post-despot regimes are likely to be more independent, with a democratic system that is fresh and subversive and, hopefully, new constitutions enshrining social and political needs. But the military in Egypt and Tunisia will ensure nothing rash happens". [42]

Assessing this judgement requires us to pay closer attention to the revolutions themselves. In what sense can these upheavals be described as revolutions at all? Trotsky in the preface to his great *History of the Russian Revolution* famously writes: "The history of a revolution is for us first of all a history of the forcible entrance of the masses into the realm of rulership over their own destiny". [43] By this criterion, the events in Tunisia, Egypt and Libya all thoroughly qualify as revolutions. All were driven by mass initiatives from below: in Egypt above all the magnificent self-organisation in Tahrir Square was on display to the world.

To say that these revolutions have been based on the self-organisation

---

41: Shavit, 2011.
42: Ali, 2011.
43: Trotsky, 1967, volume 1, p15.

of the masses isn't the same as describing them as purely spontaneous, as Chamseddine Mnasri does in his article on Tunisia elsewhere in this issue. Predictably enough, the strongest version of the latter claim has been made by Michael Hardt and Toni Negri:

> Even calling these struggles "revolutions" seems to mislead commentators who assume the progression of events must obey the logic of 1789 or 1917, or some other past European rebellion against kings and tsars... The organisation of the revolts resembles what we have seen for more than a decade in other parts of the world, from Seattle to Buenos Aires and Genoa and Cochabamba, Bolivia: a horizontal network that has no single, central leader. Traditional opposition bodies can participate in this network but cannot direct it...the multitude is able to organise itself without a centre—that the imposition of a leader or being co-opted by a traditional organisation would undermine its power.[44]

Although Hardt and Negri are eager to proclaim the novelty of what they therefore refuse to describe as revolutions, a remark that Antonio Gramsci made in 1930 fully applies to their argument: "it must be stressed that 'pure' spontaneity does not exist in history... In the 'most spontaneous' movement it is simply the case that the elements of 'conscious leadership' cannot be checked, have left no reliable document".[45] In fact, it is quite possible to demonstrate "the elements of 'conscious leadership'" present in the Arab revolutions. Thus in Tunisia, even though the leadership of the Union Générale Tunisienne du Travail (UGTT) were locked into the Ben Ali regime, affiliated and regional unions had become increasingly restive during the 2000s, took part in the developing uprising as it spread across the country, and forced the executive to call a general strike on 14 January. [46]

The Egyptian 25 January Revolution was prepared for by a decade of movements—in solidarity with the second Palestinian *intifada*, against the Iraq War, for democracy in Egypt itself, and culminating in a strike wave described by Beinin as "the largest social movement Egypt has witnessed in over half a century. Over 1.2 million workers and their families have engaged in some form of action".[47] The initial "day of rage" on 25 January was organised by activists who had been involved in these different movements—human rights campaigners, liberals, left Nasserites and revolutionary socialists. Once the

---

44: Hardt and Negri, 2011.
45: Gramsci, 1971, p196.
46: Temlali, 2011.
47: Beinin, 2009, p77.

confrontation developed in Tahrir Square, they were joined by youth cadres of the Muslim Brotherhood, even though the official leadership still held back.

Of course, the fact that the 25 January Revolution was initiated and organised by very narrow circles of activists doesn't explain why the demonstrations in late January unleashed a mass rising when the numerous earlier protests called by the same milieu attracted a few hundred or, at best, thousands. The sheer accumulation of grievances and the example of Tunisia may help to explain the difference, as may also the impact of the November 2010 elections, so flagrantly rigged that the opposition Islamists and Nasserites represented in the previous parliament withdrew from the second round in disgust. But the sheer unpredictability of revolution is nothing new: notoriously, the fall of the tsar in February 1917 took Lenin by surprise. The dynamics of the Egyptian upheaval reveal, not the lyrical insurgency of the centre-less multitude, but rather what Gramsci called "a dialectical process, in which the spontaneous movement of the revolutionary masses and the organised and directing will of the centre converge".[48]

In the case of the initial Egyptian uprising, the "centre" was at once quite small and politically heterogeneous. The one respect in which Hardt's and Negri's theory of the multitude fits the Arab revolutions is that the movements that have driven them were, to begin with at least, relatively undifferentiated socially and politically. But once again this is a common feature of the early stages of revolutions. So too was the limited content of the upheavals—the removal of autocratic rulers and of the regimes over which they presided.

Trotsky wrote: "History has known…not only social revolutions, which substituted the bourgeois for the feudal regime, but also political revolutions which, without destroying the economic foundations of society, swept out an old ruling upper crust (1830 and 1848 in France, February 1917 in Russia, etc)".[49] What we have seen so far in the Arab world are political, not social revolutions, and, moreover, ones that have so far succeeded in removing rulers rather than their regimes. Hence George Friedman's initial debunking response to Mubarak's fall:

> What happened was not a revolution. The demonstrators never brought down Mubarak, let alone the regime. What happened was a military coup that used

---

48: Gramsci, 1978, p198.
49: Trotsky, 1972, p288. See, for further discussion of this distinction, Callinicos, 1991, pp50-66, and, of the related distinction between democratic and socialist revolutions, Rees, 1999.

the cover of protests to force Mubarak out of office in order to preserve the regime. When it became clear on 10 February that Mubarak would not voluntarily step down, the military staged what amounted to a coup to force his resignation. Once he was forced out of office, the military took over the existing regime by creating a military council and taking control of critical ministries. The regime was always centred on the military. What happened on 11 February was that the military took direct control.[50]

The kernel of truth in this statement is that, in Tunisia as well as Egypt, the army stepped in to remove the president and attempt to restore order. Moreover, Mubarak's fall came against the background of conflicts between him and the military over the presidential succession. In September 2008 Margaret Scobey, US ambassador to Egypt, reported in a cable released by Wikileaks:

Contacts agree that presidential son Gamal Mubarak's power base is centred in the business community, not with the military. XXXXXXXXXXXX said officers told him recently that the military does not support Gamal and if Mubarak died in office, the military would seize power rather than allow Gamal to succeed his father. However, analysts agreed that the military would allow Gamal to take power through an election if President Mubarak blessed the process and effectively gave Gamal the reigns [sic] of power. XXXXXXXXXXXX opined that after Gamal became active in the NDP in 2002, the regime empowered the reformers in the 2004 cabinet to begin privatisation efforts that buttressed the wealthy businessmen close to Gamal. In his estimation, the regime's goal is to create a business-centred power base for Gamal in the NDP to compensate for his lack of military credentials. A necessary corollary to this strategy, he claimed, was for the regime to weaken the military's economic and political power so that it cannot block Gamal's path to the presidency.[51]

Gilbert Achcar has pointed out that the power of the military as an institution gave the Egyptian and Tunisian ruling classes and the Western imperialist powers room for manoeuvre lacking in Libya. In the latter case, Gaddafi's systematic policy of hollowing out the state apparatuses and his highly personalised family autocracy have meant that his removal proved to

---

50: Friedman, 2011b.
51: http://wikileaks.ch/cable/2008/09/08CAIRO2091.html

require armed insurrection and the destruction of the existing state.[52] The Arab dictatorships embrace in fact a spectrum of political forms, ranging from quite complex and institutionalised regimes such as Egypt, which in recent years has offered some space for legitimate opposition, to much more personalised autocratic forms of rule, often combining a reigning family with a sectarian social base: the latter is to be found in Saudi Arabia, where a monarchy transferred between the ageing sons of Ibn Saud is legitimised by the Wahhabi version of Sunni Islam, and "republican" Syria, where the presidency was successfully passed from father to son, and is sustained by the minority belonging to the Alawi sect of Shia Islam.

As Libya shows, the family autocracies are likely to be particularly tough nuts to crack. The Saudi interior minister, Prince Nayef, told reformers in 2003: "What we won by the sword, we keep by the sword".[53] King Abdullah was sufficiently worried by the popular movements in neighbouring Bahrain and Yemen and the stirrings of dissent inside his own realm to announce on returning from convalescence on 23 February $36 billion of "social investment".[54] But on 14 March the Saudi National Guard moved into Bahrain, after protesters had overwhelmed the local riot police.

The differences in state form are important, as are the divisions within individual regimes, in conditioning the possibilities for change in different countries. But they do not alter the fact that the decisive factor in the Arab revolutions has been, to repeat Trotsky's words, "the forcible entrance of the masses into the realm of rulership over their own destiny". Trotsky adds:

> The masses go into a revolution not with a prepared plan of social reconstruction, but with a sharp feeling that they cannot endure the old regime... The fundamental political process of the revolution thus consists in the gradual comprehension by a class of the problems arising from the social crisis—the active orientation of the masses by a method of successive approximations.[55]

Trotsky here highlights a key feature of revolutions: that while they revolve around decisive episodes where control over state power is settled, they are *processes* that unfold in time. The Russian Revolution of 1917, which took eight months from February to October, was in fact relatively

52: Talk at *International Socialism* seminar on Egypt, Tunisia, and Revolution in the Middle East, London, 22 February 2011; video at www.isj.org.uk/?id=716.
53: Gardner, 2011a.
54: Allam and Khalaf, 2011,
55: Trotsky, 1967, volume I, p16.

brief. The Great French Revolution lasted just over five years, from the storming of the Bastille in July 1789 to the Thermidorean coup in July 1794, while the German Revolution took almost as long, from November 1918 to October 1923.[56] The different phases of these processes, with their advances and retreats, victories and defeats for the forces of revolution and counter-revolution, and for left and right within the revolutionary camp, represent a learning process for the masses. The "successive approximations" onto which they latch in pursuit of a solution to their problems can lead to the progressive radicalisation of the masses and a decisive transfer of political power that inaugurates a social revolution.

But there is nothing inevitable about this outcome. The closest equivalent to such a process in the Arab world, the Iraqi Revolution of 1958-63, started with the overthrow of the monarchy by nationalist army officers led by General Abd al-Karim Qasim, but, very differently from Egypt in 1952, gave rise to a massive popular radicalisation that mainly benefited the Communist Party, which won considerable support within the army itself. But in May 1959 the party leadership backed away from making a bid for power, in part because of pressure from Moscow, which regarded Qasim, like Nasser, as an ally in the Cold War. The resulting demobilisation and fragmentation gave the initiative to the Ba'ath, which staged a coup with CIA support in February 1963 that toppled Qasim and subjected the Communists themselves to bloody repression.[57]

There is a strong case for saying that Mubarak was removed by the US and the military to prevent a deepening radicalisation taking place. A comparison with the other great revolutionary process in the modern Middle East, the Iranian Revolution of 1978-9, is illuminating. Confronted with a rising wave of mass protests and strikes, Shah Mohammed Reza Pahlavi clung to power, relying on increasingly savage repression. The Shi'ite tradition of commemorating the dead 40 days after their death meant, as Ryszard Kapuściński puts it, that "the Iranian revolution develops in a rhythm of explosions succeeding each other at 40-day intervals. Every 40 days there is an explosion of despair, anger, blood. Each time the explosion is more horrible, bigger and bigger crowds, more and more victims".[58]

On 8 September 1978 the shah declared martial law and his troops slaughtered thousands of demonstrators in Tehran. Mass strikes spread from

56: On the latter, see Harman, 1982, and Broué, 2006.
57: Hanna Batatu's massive account of the origins, course and consequences of the Iraqi Revolution is a historiographic masterpiece. See Batatu, 1978, pp985-986, for King Hussain of Jordan's account of the CIA's role in the February 1963 coup.
58: Kapuściński, 1982, p114.

the strategically crucial oil industry to other sectors. The cumulative effect of successive bloody mass confrontations on the streets was to erode the morale and cohesion of the army. This meant that, when the shah was finally bundled into exile in January 1979 under US pressure, mutinies spread through the army, and the generals were too weak to prevent a successful insurrection at the beginning of February, organised by radical left and Islamist guerrilla groups.[59]

This was the kind of scenario the Egyptian generals were keen to head off. During the week starting 6 February 2011 the "multitude" began to develop a sharper class profile: the Egyptian workers' movement, hitherto involved as individuals in the mass movement, but invisible as a collective, began decisively to move centre-stage, launching a strike wave that continues to the present. According to the *Washington Post,* "by midweek, confronted with growing throngs in Cairo, labour strikes and deteriorating economic conditions, top military and civilian leaders reached an apparent agreement with Mubarak on some form of power transfer". But he reneged on the deal in his television speech on 10 February, provoking a furious popular reaction. Obama responded with a statement that, in effect, called for him to go. For the *Washington Post*:

> it was a crucial shift for a White House that had been the scene of sometimes heated exchanges between aides who pressed for a strong message of support for democratic change in Egypt and others who worried that doing so could disrupt the traditional government-to-government relationship with a key ally.

> There was a discernible change in Cairo, as well. Within hours of Mubarak's speech, "support for Mubarak from [the] military dropped precipitously," said a US government official who closely tracked the events.

> "The military had been willing—with the right tone in the speech—to wait and see how it played out," the official said. "They didn't like what they saw… By the end of the day, it was clear the situation was no longer tenable."

> Mubarak was told Friday [11 February] that he must step down, and within hours, he was on his way to the Red Sea resort of Sharm el-Sheikh.[60]

But the problem facing the Supreme Council of the Armed Forces

---

59: See Marshall, 1988, chapter 2, and Poya, 1987.
60: Warrick, 2011.

that supplanted Mubarak—and behind it the Egyptian ruling class and the White House—is that, in Egypt as in Tunisia, the revolution is driven by a combination of material and political grievances that cannot be assuaged by the purely cosmetic changes on offer from the successor governments, both initially headed by prime ministers appointed by the fleeing president.

This logic became visible in Tunisia immediately after Ben Ali's fall, with continuing protests driven by the desire to get rid of the entire regime, most notably with the demand to purge the government of all members of the old ruling party, the Rassemblement Constitutionnel Démocratique (RCD). But what we have seen develop in both Egypt and Tunisia is a much broader process of what Philip Marfleet elsewhere in this issue rightly calls *saneamiento* (cleansing), after the version that developed in Portugal after the Armed Forces Movement overthrew the right wing dictatorship in April 1974.

One of the first democratic impulses after the overthrow of an authoritarian regime is the drive simultaneously to purge the state apparatus and hold it to public account. Frequently this targets the old regime's secret police—the DGS (Direcção Geral de Segurança) in Portugal, or the Stasi (Ministry of State Security) in East Germany after the 1989 Revolution. Exactly this process is unfolding today in the Arab revolutions. Thus in early March the headquarters of the State Security Investigation Service (SSIS) in Nasr City, near Cairo, was stormed, along with many of its other offices, mainly to prevent the destruction of secret documents. In Tunisia protesters simultaneously forced the interim government actually to dissolve State Security, while the RCD has been suppressed by court order. In the copycat pattern that is a striking feature of the two revolutions, as they gain encouragement from each other, the Egyptian interior minister ordered the SSIS disbanded on 15 March.

The mass movement won other victories, once again more or less simultaneously, forcing out the prime ministers inherited from the old regime in both countries. In the abstract, therefore, the thrust of these struggles has been political, seeking to push the process of democratisation much further and faster than either the Egyptian military junta or the Tunisian interim government would like. But the problem is that, because of the form that neoliberalism has taken in the Middle East, it is very hard to separate politics and economics. Tearing up the roots of the Mubarak and Ben Ali regimes will mean cutting deep into the political economy of Egyptian and Tunisian society. The Egyptian army is directly vulnerable because, in a holdover from Nasserite state capitalism, it controls an economic empire estimated at several percentage points of Egypt's national income.[61]

61: Clover and Khalaf, 2011.

There are two possible scenarios ahead for both these countries. One is · Portugal 1974-5—where the revolution was initiated by a progressive military coup, but the drive for *saneamiento* after 50 years of dictatorship promoted social and political polarisation and the radicalisation of both workers and rank and file soldiers. Portugal came closer in the 18 months after the Armed Forces Movement seized power to socialist revolution than any other Western European country since the 1930s. The left was only defeated by a Europe-wide mobilisation of reaction fronted by social democracy and orchestrated by the US. The other scenario is offered by Indonesia after 1998, where the over-throw of the Suharto dictatorship (another case of crony capitalism centred on the ruling family) at the height of the Asian economic crisis opened a new space for mass mobilisation from below, but ultimately stability was restored with the introduction of a liberal-democratic political façade.

Plainly the Western powers and the Egyptian and Tunisian ruling classes would prefer the Indonesian scenario to the Portuguese. But the fusion of economic and political power in neoliberal Egypt and Tunisia and the appalling material situation of very large sections of the population in both countries make this very hard to pull off. The economic pressures on the mass of the population—unemployment, especially among the young, the rising price of food and other basic commodities, to which must be added the disruptive effect of the revolts themselves on sectors such as tourism—are a continually destabilising factor.

Moreover, in Egypt we see the workers' movement gaining in strength and self-assertion, mounting strikes and occupations around a variety of economic and political demands. Following the initiative described by Marfleet elsewhere in this journal, a preparatory conference of the Egyptian Federation of Independent Unions met on 2 March.[62] In addition to the strikes, a plethora of protests have developed over social and economic issues ranging from rents to the price of butane gas. These economic struggles, coming as they have against the background of the 25 January Revolution, aren't in conflict with the political struggle. On the contrary, as Rosa Luxemburg pointed out in her classic analysis of the Russian Revolution of 1905, they are mutually reinforcing:

> But the movement on the whole does not proceed from the economic to the political struggle, nor even the reverse. Every great political mass action, after it has attained its political highest point, breaks up into a mass of economic strikes. And that applies not only to each of the great mass strikes, but also to

---

62: Charbel, 2011.

the revolution as a whole. With the spreading, clarifying and involution of the political struggle, the economic struggle not only does not recede, but extends, organises and becomes involved in equal measure. Between the two there is the most complete reciprocal action.

Every new onset and every fresh victory of the political struggle is transformed into a powerful impetus for the economic struggle, extending at the same time its external possibilities and intensifying the inner urge of the workers to better their position and their desire to struggle. After every foaming wave of political action a fructifying deposit remains behind from which a thousand stalks of economic struggle shoot forth. And conversely. The workers' condition of ceaseless economic struggle with the capitalists keeps their fighting energy alive in every political interval; it forms, so to speak, the permanent fresh reservoir of the strength of the proletarian classes, from which the political fight ever renews its strength, and at the same time leads the indefatigable economic sappers of the proletariat at all times, now here and now there, to isolated sharp conflicts, out of which public conflicts on a large scale unexpectedly explode.

In a word: the economic struggle is the transmitter from one political centre to another; the political struggle is the periodic fertilisation of the soil for the economic struggle. Cause and effect here continually change places; and thus the economic and the political factors in the period of the mass strike, now widely removed, completely separated or even mutually exclusive, as the theoretical plan would have them, merely form the two interlacing sides of the proletarian class struggle in Russia. And *their unity* is precisely the mass strike.[63]

Out of this dynamic interaction between economic and political struggles there is the potential that, as Trotsky put it, "the democratic revolution grows over directly into the socialist revolution and thereby becomes a permanent revolution".[64] Of course, the Egyptian ruling class is unlikely meekly to stand by in the face of this process. What methods can they use? The junta could employ the forms of direct counter-revolutionary coercion that Mubarak unsuccessfully tried against the protesters in Tahrir Square

63: Luxemburg, 1970, p185.
64: Trotsky, 1969, p278. Neil Davidson was therefore a little premature when he recently described "permanent revolution" in this journal as a "historical concept", though he contradicted himself a couple of pages later, referring to the "inherent instability" created by the uneven and combined development of global capitalism as containing "the possibilities of permanent revolution"—Davidson, 2010, pp195, 197.

at the beginning of February. The army has been quietly arresting and torturing activists, some of whom have been given five-year prison sentences by military courts. Attacks by gangs of thugs on women demonstrators on International Women's Day (8 March) and simultaneously on members of the Coptic Christian minority in Moqattam, north Cairo, were interpreted by some activists as the SSIS hitting back.[65]

A combination of repression and divide and rule may just allow Gaddafi to hang onto power in Libya, but it is unlikely to work, certainly in the short-term, in Egypt, given the proliferation of mass struggles and popular organisation there. Committees to defend the revolution have been formed in different neighbourhoods and workplaces. The alternative would be to try to develop the mediating political structures—what Gramsci called the "trench systems" forming the "very complex structure" of bourgeois democracy—that have been at best marginal in Egypt since the Free Officers decisively crushed their opponents in 1954.[66]

Egyptian liberalism—represented by Mohamed ElBaradei, Ayman Nour, and the historic Wafd Party—is almost certainly too weak a reed on which to lean. The Muslim Brotherhood is quite another matter. The object of much Islamophobic speculation in the West, the Brotherhood is in fact a highly ambiguous and heterogeneous formation that has taken a number of different forms: the mass anti-colonial movement of the 1940s and 1950s was crushed by Nasser, but the Brotherhood has revived since the 1980s as what Sameh Naguib describes as a "populist political force", building up the strong base in the universities and professional syndicates and in poor neighbourhoods that allowed it to win nearly 20 percent of the seats in the relatively open parliamentary election of 2005.[67] The Brotherhood's revival took place, incidentally, at the same time as the regime's murderously successful campaign to crush the armed jihadist groups, elements of which went on to help form Al Qaida.

The Brotherhood's solidly bourgeois leadership has been divided between advocates of the alliances with more secular opposition forces that saw it cooperate with Nasserites and revolutionary socialists in the Cairo conferences against occupation and imperialism and support the *Kifaya* democracy movement in the middle of the last decade and political quietists favouring an accommodation with the regime. The latter were in the ascendant before the 25 January Revolution, but this did not prevent

---

65: Ozman, 2011.
66: Gramsci, 1971, p235.
67: Naguib, 2009, p114.

Brotherhood activists joining the rising. The essentially bourgeois character of the Brotherhood meant that it has taken an ambivalent attitude towards the strike wave. But undoubtedly many workers have supported it in recent years as the most powerful opposition force.

The historical development of the workers' movement in Egypt in the first half of the 20th century was characterised by a combination of "workerism"—militant class organisation on economic issues—and "populism"—support for multi-class nationalism in the struggle against British imperialism. This allowed the liberal nationalist Wafd to become, as Joel Beinin and Zachary Lockman put it, "the hegemonic ideological and organisational force in the labour movement".[68] Though the Wafd's dominance was undermined by Communists and the Brotherhood after the Second World War, the strength of anti-colonial nationalism (which in their own ways both these tendencies supported), combined with a mixture of repression and economic reforms, allowed Nasser to reduce the Egyptian working class to a subaltern position in his state capitalist regime.

The situation in Egypt is very different today. Nevertheless, the Brotherhood's organisational resources and the very political and social ambiguity of its political message—"Islam is the answer"—mean that it could play a decisive role in preventing the development of independent working class politics in Egypt. The danger the Brotherhood poses is thus less the Islamist "radicalisation" obsessing the likes of Tony Blair, but its potential as a *conservative* force (though playing such a role would cause divisions in its ranks). This underlines the foolishness of rhapsodies about the "centre-less" character of the Arab revolutions. If the more radical elements in the movement refuse to organise politically, other forces are very unlikely to be so self-denying. In fact, a plethora of new Egyptian parties are being formed in the wake of Mubarak's fall, fortunately including the Democratic Workers Party.[69] The fate of particular initiatives such as this one depends on many contingencies. But, although a very small and weak force, revolutionary socialists have played an important part in the 25 January Revolution and the development of the Egyptian workers' movement. If they help Egyptian workers develop a clear political voice of their own, then dramatically greater revolutionary possibilities will open up throughout the Middle East.

68: Beinin and Lockman, 1987, p450; see generally part two. For a discussion of the dialectic of workerism and populism in the South African context, see Callinicos, 1988, especially pp191-194.

69: Shukrallah and El-Abbas, 2011.

References

Al-Malky, Rania, 2010, "In Egypt, A Fair Minimum Wage is Inevitable", *Daily News Egypt* (17 April), www.thedailynewsegypt.com/editorial/in-egypt-a-fair-minimum-wage-is-inevitable-dp1.html

Ali, Tariq, 2011, "This is an Arab 1848, But US Hegemony is Only Dented", *Guardian* (22 February), www.guardian.co.uk/commentisfree/2011/feb/22/arab-1848-us-hegemony-dented

Alexander, Anne, 2011, "The Gravedigger of Dictatorship", *Socialist Review* (March), www.socialistreview.org.uk/article.php?articlenumber=11580

Allam, Abdeer, and Roula Khalaf, 2011, "Gas Leak in the House", *Financial Times* (10 March).

Batatu, Hanna, 1978, *The Old Social Classes and the Revolutionary Movements of Iraq* (Princeton University Press).

Beaugé, Florence, 2011, "Leur ami Ben Ali", *Le Monde* (18 February).

Beinin, Joel, 2009, "Workers' Struggles under 'Socialism' and Neoliberalism", in El-Mahdi and Marfleet, 2009.

Beinin, Joel, and Zachary Lockman, 1987, *Workers on the Nile: Nationalism, Communism, Islam, and the Egyptian Working Class, 1882-1954* (Princeton University Press).

Benjamin, Walter, 1970, *Illuminations* (Jonathan Cape).

Broué, Pierre, 2006, *The German Revolution, 1917-1923* (Brill).

Bush, Ray, 2009, "The Land and the People", in El-Mahdi and Marfleet, 2009.

Business Week, 2007, "The Opening of Libya" (12 March), www.businessweek.com/magazine/content/07_11/b4025061.htm

Callinicos, Alex, 1988, *South Africa Between Reform and Revolution* (Bookmarks).

Callinicos, Alex, 1991, *The Revenge of History* (Polity).

Callinicos, Alex, 2004, *Making History* (Brill).

Callinicos, Alex, 2010, "Analysis: The Radical Left and the Crisis", *International Socialism 126* (spring), www.isj.org.uk/?id=634

Charbel, Beno, 2011, "After 50-Year Hiatus, Egypt's First Independent Labour Union is Born", *Al-Masry Al-Youm* (2 March), www.almasryalyoum.com/en/node/337515

Chomsky, Noam, 1999, *Fateful Triangle: The United States, Israel and the Palestinians* (Pluto).

Chossudovsky, Michel, 2011, "Tunisia, the IMF, and Worldwide Poverty", *Pacific Free Press* (23 January), www.pacificfreepress.com/news/1/7854-tunisia-the-imf-and-worldwide-poverty.html

Clover, Charles, and Roula Khalaf, 2011, "Egyptian Military Uneasy over Business Ties", *Financial Times* (28 February).

Davidson, Neil, 2010, "From Deflected Permanent Revolution to the Law of Uneven and Combined Development", *International Socialism 128* (autumn), www.isj.org.uk/?id=686

Duménil, Gérard, and Dominique Lévy, 2011, *The Crisis of Neoliberalism* (Harvard University Press).

El-Mahdi, Rabab, and Philip Marfleet (eds), 2009, *Egypt: The Moment of Change* (Zed).

El-Naggar, Ahmad El-Sayed, 2009, "Economic Policy: From State Control to Decay and Corruption", in El-Mahdi and Marfleet, 2009.

Fahim, Kareen, Michael Slackman, and David Rohde, 2011, "Egypt's Ire Turns to Confidant of Mubarak's Son", *New York Times* (6 February).

Friedman, George, 2011a, "The Egypt Crisis in a Global Context: A Special Report", Stratfor Global Intelligence (30 January), www.stratfor.com/analysis/20110130-the-egypt-crisis-in-a-global-context-a-special-report?

Friedman, George, 2011b, "Egypt: The Distance between Enthusiasm and Reality", Stratfor Global Intelligence (14 February), http://www.stratfor.com/weekly/20110213-egypt-distance-between-enthusiasm-and-reality

Friedman, George, 2011c, "Revolution and the Muslim World", Stratfor Global Intelligence (22 February), www.stratfor.com/weekly/20110221-revolution-and-muslim-world

Gardner, David, 2011a, "Arab Rulers Confront a New World", *Financial Times* (13 February).

Gardner, David, 2011b, "Chill Regional Winds Blow Across Israel", *Financial Times* (14 March).

Gates, Robert M, 2011, "Speech, United States Military Academy (West Point, NY)" (25 February), www.defense.gov/speeches/speech.aspx?speechid=1539

Giddens, Anthony, 2007, "My Chat with the Colonel", *Guardian* (9 March), www.guardian.co.uk/commentisfree/2007/mar/09/comment.libya

Gordon, Joel, 1992, *Nasser's Blessed Movement: Egypt's Free Officers and the July Revolution* (Oxford University Press).

Gramsci, Antonio, 1971, *Selections from the Prison Notebooks* (Lawrence & Wishart).

Gramsci, Antonio, 1978, *Selections from the Political Writings 1921-1926* (Lawrence & Wishart).

Hardt, Michael, and Toni Negri, 2011, "Arabs are Democracy's New Pioneers", *Guardian* (24 February), www.guardian.co.uk/commentisfree/2011/feb/24/arabs-democracy-latin-america

Harman, Chris, 1982, *The Lost Revolution* (Bookmarks).

Kapuściński, Ryszard, 1982, *Shah of Shahs* (Picador).

Kornblihtt, Juan, and Bruno Magro, 2011, "El norte de África en el epicentro de la crisis mundial", *El Aromo*, 59 (March-April), www.razonyrevolucion.org/ryr/index.php?option=com_content&view=article&id=1395%3Ael-norte-de-africa-en-el-epicentro-de-la-crisis-mundial; English translation by Leonardo Kosloff at www.facebook.com/notes/leonardo-kosloff/north-africa-at-the-epicenter-of-world-crisis/10150423086445720

Lewis, Aidan, 2011, "Tracking Down the Ben Ali and Trabelsi Fortune", BBC News Africa (31 January), www.bbc.co.uk/news/world-africa-12302659

Luxemburg, Rosa, 1970, *The Mass Strike, the Political Party, and the Trade Unions*, in Mary-Alice Waters (ed), *Rosa Luxemburg Speaks* (Pathfinder); also in http://www.marxists.org/archive/luxemburg/1906/mass-strike/index.htm

McGregor, Richard, 2011, "US Loses its Appetite for Job as World's Policeman", *Financial Times* (3 March).

McNally, David, 2011, *Global Slump: The Economics and Politics of Crisis and Resistance* (PM Press).

Marshall, Phil, 1988, *Revolution and Counter-Revolution in Iran* (Bookmarks).

Marx, Karl, 1971 [1859], *A Contribution to the Critique of Political Economy* (Lawrence & Wishart), www.marxists.org/archive/marx/works/1859/critique-pol-economy/index.htm

Naguib, Sameh, 2009, "Islamism(s) Old and New", in El-Mahdi and Marfleet, 2009.

Ozman, Ahmed Zaki, 2011, "The Rise and Fall of Egypt's Notorious State Security", *Al-Masry Al-Youm* (10 March), www.almasryalyoum.com/en/node/346917

Pew Research Center, 2010, "Obama More Popular Abroad Than At Home, Global Image of US Continues to Benefit" (17 June), http://pewglobal.org/2010/06/17/obama-more-popular-abroad-than-at-home/

Pilkington, Ed, 2011, "US Firm Monitor Group Admits Mistakes over $3m Gaddafi Deal", *Guardian* (4 March), www.guardian.co.uk/world/2011/mar/04/monitor-group-us-libya-gaddafi

Poya, Maryam, 1987, "Iran 1979: Long Live Revolution! ... Long Live Islam?", in Colin Barker (ed) *Revolutionary Rehearsals* (Bookmarks).

Rees, John, 1999, "The Socialist Revolution and the Democratic Revolution", *International Socialism 83* (summer), http://pubs.socialistreviewindex.org.uk/isj83/rees.htm

Sadiki, Larbi, 2011, "The 'Bin Laden' of Marginalisation", Al Jazeera (14 January), http://english.aljazeera.net/indepth/opinion/2011/01/201111413424337867.html

Sargent, Greg, 2011, "Public Employees Not Such an Easy Scapegoat After All", *Washington Post* (25 February), http://voices.washingtonpost.com/plum-line/2011/02/public_employees_not_such_an_e.html

Schwartz, Herman M, 2009, *Subprime Nation: American Power, Global Capital, and the Housing Bubble* (Cornell University Press).

Shavit, Ari, 2011, "The Arab Revolution and Western Decline", *Haaretz* (3 February), www.haaretz.com/print-edition/opinion/the-arab-revolution-and-western-decline-1.340967

Shukrallah, Salma, and Nourhan El-Abbas, 2011, "January Revolution Generates a New Egyptian Political Map", *Ahram Online* (4 March), http://english.ahram.org.eg/NewsContentPrint/1/0/6863/Egypt/0/Januaray-Revolution-generates-a-new-Egyptian-polit.aspx

Soldz, Stephen, 2011, "The Torture Career of Egypt's New Vice President: Omar Suleiman and the Rendition to Torture Program", *Dissident Voice* (31 January), http://dissidentvoice.org/2011/01/the-torture-career-of-egypts-new-vice-president-omar-suleiman-and-the-rendition-to-torture-program/

Temlali, Yassin, 2011, "Pourquoi l'UGTT a joué un rôle aussi important dans l'intifada tunisienne", *Maghreb Emergent* (25 January), www.maghrebemergent.com/actualite/maghrebine/1976-pourquoi-le-syndicat-a-joue-un-role-aussi-important-dans-lintifada-tunisienne.html

Trotsky, Leon, 1967, *The History of the Russian Revolution*, 3 volumes (Sphere), www.marxists.org/archive/trotsky/1930/hrr/

Trotsky, Leon, 1969, *The Permanent Revolution and Results and Prospects* (Merit), www.marxists.org/archive/trotsky/1931/tpr/index.htm

Trotsky, Leon, 1972, *The Revolution Betrayed*, www.marxists.org/archive/trotsky/1936/revbet/index.htm

Trudell, Megan, 2011, "Mad as Hatters? The Tea Party Movement in the United States", *International Socialism 129* (winter), www.isj.org.uk/?id=698

Warrick, Joby, 2011, "In Mubarak's Final Hours, Defiance Surprises US and Threatens to Unleash Chaos", *Washington Post* (12 February).

Waterbury, John, 1983, *The Egypt of Nasser and Sadat: The Political Economy of Two Regimes* (Princeton University Press).

Watkins, Susan, 2010, "Shifting Sands", *New Left Review*, II/61 (January/February 2010), http://newleftreview.org/?page=article&view=2817

Engels on the power of nature

The terrible earthquake and tsunami that hit Tohuku in northeastern Japan on 11 March took place as this issue of *International Socialism* was on its way to the press. The scenes in which the tsunami swept away vast swathes of human habitation are an awesome testimony to the overwhelming power of physical forces. The grinding together of tectonic plates that causes earthquakes has nothing to do with human agency, although its effects are mediated by the structures of class, wealth and power. But we know that global warming increases the frequency of extreme weather events, and therefore the likelihood that we may witness, or suffer, more catastrophes comparable to those that have recently afflicted Kashmir, Sichuan, Haiti, Chile, New Zealand and now Japan. Moreover, the nuclear meltdowns the tsunami has caused at Fukushima Daiichi power station underline the criminal folly of governments, like the British, that are relying on expanding nuclear power in order to reduce CO_2 emissions.

So it is good to remind ourselves of this passage from Frederick Engels's *Dialectics of Nature*, where he dissociates Marxism from the fantasy of human domination of nature:

> Let us not, however, flatter ourselves overmuch on account of our human conquest over nature. For each such conquest takes its revenge on us. Each of them, it is true, has in the first place the consequences on which we counted, but in the second and third places it has quite different, unforeseen effects which only too often cancel out the first. The people who, in Mesopotamia,

Greece, Asia Minor, and elsewhere, destroyed the forests to obtain cultivable land, never dreamed that they were laying the basis for the present devastated condition of these countries, by removing along with the forests the collecting centres and reservoirs of moisture. When, on the southern slopes of the mountains, the Italians of the Alps used up the pine forests so carefully cherished on the northern slopes, they had no inkling that by doing so they were cutting at the roots of the dairy industry in their region; they had still less inkling that they were thereby depriving their mountain springs of water for the greater part of the year, with the effect that these would be able to pour still more furious flood torrents on the plains during the rainy seasons. Those who spread the potato in Europe were not aware that they were at the same time spreading the disease of scrofula. Thus at every step we are reminded that we by no means rule over nature like a conqueror over a foreign people, like someone standing outside nature—but that we, with flesh, blood, and brain, belong to nature, and exist in its midst, and that all our mastery of it consists in the fact that we have the advantage over all other beings of being able to know and correctly apply its laws.[1]

References

Engels, Frederick, 1972, *Dialectics of Nature* (Progress), www.marxists.org/archive/marx/works/1883/don/ch09.htm

---

1:    Engels, 1972, p180.

The return of fear

Iain Ferguson

In 1952 Aneurin Bevan, leader of the parliamentary Labour left and health minister in the 1945-51 Clement Attlee government, wrote a book about the newly-created welfare state in Britain. He called it *In Place of Fear*.[1] It was an appropriate title. Until then, and especially during the Depression years of the 1930s, the lives of millions of working class people had been haunted by fear of unemployment, poverty, sickness and old age. The creation of a welfare state, at the heart of which was a National Health Service free to all at the point of need and not dependent on the ability to pay, went a long way towards removing that fear and providing some security against the ups and downs of the market.

Six decades on, the fear is back. Since its election in May 2010 the Conservative-Liberal coalition has launched the most savage assault on the welfare state since its creation. That assault has three faces.

First, there are the cuts. Of the £80 billion a year cut from public spending since last June, £18 billion directly affects welfare, the biggest cut since the 1920s. Few areas, including education, are left unaffected. The cuts fall into two main categories: those that directly affect people's incomes and those that affect the services they rely on. Included in the first category is the decision to link benefits and taxes to the Consumer Price Index (CPI), which excludes housing costs and council tax, instead of the currently used Retail Price Index, which does include these factors. According to

---

1:    Bevan, 1990.

Mike Brewer and James Browne of the Institute for Fiscal Studies (IFS), this measure will provide the coalition with the largest single saving—£5.8 billion a year. Since the CPI underestimates the real cost of living for most working class people, it is, as the IFS points out, "effectively an across the board cut to all benefits received by working-age adults", and as such, a direct assault on the living standards of the poorest people in Britain.[2]

On top of this there are the planned cuts in welfare benefits, again specifically targeted at the poorest and most vulnerable. The biggest losers here will be people with disabilities. Currently 2.6 million people claim incapacity benefit, 40 percent of them on account of mental health problems. The government intends to move 1.5 million of them onto the new Employment Support Allowance (ESA), paid at a much lower rate, via a test of their capacity to work. If after a year on ESA they have still not found work, despite the "assistance" provided by private agencies such as the hated Atos Healthcare to which the government has outsourced this task, they will be moved onto Jobseeker's Allowance of £65 a week.[3] The coalition's claim that this cut is justified by the increase in the number of people wrongly claiming disability benefits is refuted by research published in January 2011 by Richard Berthoud, a leading authority on benefits and welfare. According to Berthoud, "The general assumption that these are people with trivial conditions is not supported by the evidence. It is people with more severely disadvantaging conditions that have been more affected by the trend".[4]

Cuts in housing benefit will also have a massive impact on the poor. The coalition proposed six separate changes to housing benefit in its budget last June, projected to amount to £1.8 billion by 2014. According to the government's own survey, the changes will mean that more than three quarters of a million households will lose an average of £9 a week while bigger families will lose an average of £74 a week. Nor will the changes only affect unemployed people. Some 680,000 working households also claim housing benefit, 14 percent of the total housing benefit caseload.[5] As housing charity Shelter's chief executive Campbell Robb pointed out, such losses represent "huge amounts" to some of the poorest people in Britain. "Imagine if you are on Jobseeker's Allowance of just £65 a week or a pensioner surviving on £98 a week, or those on the minimum wage of £218 a week. These losses represent a significant proportion of their income. They will really

2: Brewer and Browne, 2011.
3: Brewer and Browne, 2011.
4: *Guardian Society*, 19 January 2011.
5: *Guardian Datablog*, 8 November 2010.

struggle to find the extra money they will need to keep a roof over their head".[6] Coalition plans to cap the maximum housing benefit payable are also likely to lead to a "social cleansing" of poor people from whole parts of the country, notably London and south east England, but also from large areas of cities further north, such as Manchester.

Finally, there are the cuts to local authority spending. Research commissioned by the TUC has shown that Britain's poorest 10 percent will be hit 13 times harder by cuts to services than the richest 10 percent. The research shows that the bottom tenth of the population, who depend much more on publicly provided services, will suffer reductions in services equivalent to 20 percent of their household income, while the richest tenth will lose the equivalent of just 1.5 percent through cuts that the government plans to implement by 2013. Across the income distribution, the poorer the household, the more they will lose.[7]

The second face of the assault involves the wholesale restructuring of welfare services based on a massive extension of privatisation. Involving the private sector in the provision of public services is, of course, hardly new. The Public/Private Partnerships promoted by Tony Blair and Gordon Brown were a barely-disguised version of the Private Finance Initiative first introduced by the Conservative governments of the 1990s. Academic critics such as Allyson Pollock have also highlighted the extent to which private sector consultancies and multinational healthcare firms continued to flourish and to milk the NHS following New Labour's election in 1997.[8] What is different this time round, however, is the sheer scale of the proposed privatisations. In terms of higher education, for example, while the public focus and anger have understandably been on the hike in tuition fees and the abolition of the Educational Maintenance Allowance, the proposals of the Browne Report, most of which have been accepted by the government, will essentially transform the nature and role of English universities. As Stefan Collini has argued, what Browne is proposing is that "we should no longer think of higher education as the provision of a public good, articulated through educational judgment and largely financed by public funds... Instead, we should think of it as a lightly regulated market in which consumer demand, in the form of student choice, is sovereign in determining what is offered by service providers (ie universities)".[9]

6: *Guardian*, 8 November 2010.
7: TUC, 2010.
8: Pollock, 2004.
9: Collini, 2010.

Similarly, health minister Andrew Lansley's bill to place NHS commissioning in the hands of GP practices, which will be required to purchase services from "any willing provider", will take privatisation of the NHS to new depths. As columnist Polly Toynbee has argued, the introduction of unfettered price competition at a time when the NHS is already experiencing cuts of 4 percent "will leave the NHS open to challenge and undercutting from any private company offering temporary loss-leaders. The destabilising effect on financially fragile hospitals will be devastating".[10]

Finally, the White Paper on welfare reform which will be published in the spring will mean that no area of the public sector—other than the security services and courts—will be safe from privatisation. According to David Cameron, writing in the *Daily Telegraph*: "This is a transformation: instead of having to justify why it makes sense to introduce competition in some public services—as we are now doing with schools and in the NHS—the state will have to justify why it should ever operate a monopoly".[11] Everything, in other words, will be up for grabs. Councils, like GP practices, will be forced to accept tenders from the lowest bidders—on past experience likely to be multinationals such as Cordia, Capita and Serco— as long as they promise to "protect quality". In reality, not only will quality of service be one of the first victims of these changes as private firms and charities compete to cut costs and drive down the wages and conditions of their staff, but so too will local democracy. For once these commercial contracts are in place, neither councils nor local people will have any control over them, making a mockery of the Tories' much-vaunted concern for "localism" and "empowering communities".

Both localism and empowered communities are, of course, key elements of the rhetoric of the Big Society, the ideological framework within which much of this change is taking place and the third face of the assault on welfare. Since launching the idea at the annual *Guardian* lecture in 2009, Cameron's efforts to persuade people (including his own party) that we need to rely less on the state and more on charities and self-help have been spectacularly unsuccessful. Liverpool Council, one of the "flagship" councils piloting the idea, pulled out in February 2011, arguing that the coalition's cuts had so endangered the voluntary sector in Liverpool that it could no longer deliver it. Even more ominously for Cameron and Nick Clegg, a planned national Big Society Roadshow last autumn had to be

---

10: *Guardian*, 17 January 2011; see also Allyson Pollock's excellent blog at http://bigsocietynhs. wordpress.com/2011/03/02/guest-blog-a-call-to-action-from-allyson-pollock/
11: *Daily Telegraph*, 20 February 2011.

cancelled "after there was heckling at the first event in Stockport and the mood turned ugly".[12]

One obvious reason for the failure of the idea to take off is its sheer impracticality. However much people may like the idea of more close-knit communities (in contrast to the individualism which neoliberalism has encouraged and which was identified in a study by the Joseph Rowntree Foundation as one of the main "social evils" in Britain today),[13] very few people have the time, energy or skills to do more volunteering, let alone run their local swimming pool or library. According to research published in 2008, British workers are already among the hardest working people in Europe, with only Romanians and Bulgarians putting in longer hours. British workers in full-time jobs put in an average of 41.4 hours every week, one and a half hours more than the average for the 27 members of the European Union (EU). In addition, British workers also get less annual leave than the average EU worker.[14]

Another reason for the lack of success is that charities and voluntary organisations, supposedly the backbone of the Big Society, are also among the biggest victims of the spending cuts. Across the board cuts of 28 percent this year to local authorities, one of the biggest funders of charities in the UK, mean that voluntary organisations could be hit to the tune of approximately £4.5 billion, resulting in redundancies, closures and the loss of vital services.[15]

The main reason for its failure, however, is quite simply that, despite Cameron's protests to the contrary, most people see it simply as a big con and a cover for the cuts. That does not mean the coalition will drop the idea. The emphasis on "localism and "shifting responsibility" from the state to communities and individuals is likely to remain a central theme of coalition social policy, reflected for example in the social care policy of personalisation, a policy pioneered by New Labour involving the promotion of direct payments and individual budgets as an alternative to state-provided services.[16] This is because there is a serious ideological intent behind the rhetoric of the Big Society. Under the veil of attacking "welfare dependency", the coalition is seeking to engineer a "culture shift" whereby people no longer look to the state when they become unemployed, ill, disabled or old but rely instead on family, friends and an often mythical "community". In that sense, it's an attempt to turn the clock back to the period before the welfare

12: *Times*, 24 January 2011.
13: Utting, 2009.
14: Eurofund, 2008.
15: *Charity Times*, 21 October, 2010.
16: Ferguson, 2007.

state, to the days when the minutes of Victorian charities such as the Charity Organisation Society in London could record that "when an applicant is truly starving he may be given a piece of bread if he eats it in the presence of the giver".[17]

Whether the government can succeed in this objective is, of course, a whole other question. In part, this will depend on the strength and determination of the coalition, in part on the forces of opposition ranged against it. In relation to the first aspect, there is growing concern on the right about the coalition's apparent willingness to retreat at the first hint of opposition, the most recent example being Cameron and his minister Caroline Spelman's humiliating climbdown over the proposed privatisation of Britain's forests. Clearly, unlike Margaret Thatcher's, this is a government which is for turning.

In relation to the second aspect, given that for more than a decade Blair and Brown encouraged greater private sector involvement in public services, introduced welfare to work policies and in 2010 made it clear that if elected they would also implement massive cuts, the response of the New Labour leadership to the biggest assault on welfare since the Second World War has been predictably defensive and pitiful. Shadow secretary for work and pensions Liam Byrne, for example, welcomed Ian Duncan Smith's welfare reforms as "sensible", complaining only that the coalition wasn't doing enough to create new jobs. Despite that, the absence of a credible left alternative means that the Labour Party will benefit both electorally and in terms of membership at the growing popular anger at the coalition's attacks.

It is that growing popular anger, however, rather than the feeble response of the Labour front bench, that is causing most concern to the ruling class. As the British Social Attitudes Survey Series has shown year after year, whatever their deficiencies the welfare state and the NHS in particular hold a special place in the affections and folk memory of the British working class. Cameron and Clegg have launched a full-frontal assault on every aspect of that welfare state. Hence the concern expressed by one leading Tory: "When I heard that we were starting on health reform, I knew how Hitler's generals felt when they heard he was invading Russia".[18]

They have cause to be worried. The coalition's attempts to shift the costs of the banking crisis onto the poorest sections of British society, and in the process divide and scapegoat those who depend on welfare benefits, have already provoked resistance. They have revitalised the disability

---

17: Cited in Lewis, 1995.
18: *Financial Times*, 14 January 2011.

movement and have led to the creation of militant new organisations such as Disabled People against Cuts and the Black Triangle Campaign, both of which have shown a willingness to engage in direct action. There have been huge protests in defence of education that have united school, college and university students and staff. There have been militant protests outside town halls across much of Britain and the beginnings of a revival of organisation among health workers. The energy and militancy of these struggles stand in marked contrast to the cowardice and passivity of much of the leadership of the official trade union movement. But there is still everything to play for. The weakness of the coalition on the one hand and the willingness of millions of working class people on the other to fight, if given a lead, to defend a welfare system that offers them and their families at least some protection against the hazards of life under capitalism mean that Cameron and Clegg's attempt to privatise welfare may yet prove to be their poll tax, the rock on which the coalition founders.

References

Bevan, Aneurin, 1990 [1952], *In Place of Fear* (Quartet).

Brewer, Mike, and James Browne, 2011, "Cuts to Welfare Spending" in N Yeats, T Hauw, R Jawad and M Kilkey (eds), *In Defence of Welfare: The Impacts of the Spending Review*, (Social Policy Association).

Collini, Stefan, 2010, "Browne's Gamble", *London Review of Books* (4 November).

European Foundation for the Improvement of Living and Working Conditions (Eurofund), 2008, *Annual Review of Working Conditions in the EU*, www.eurofound.europa.eu/docs/ewco/tn0802038s/tn0802038s.pdf

Ferguson, Iain, 2007, "Increasing User Choice or Privatizing Risk? The Antinomies of Personalization", *British Journal of Social Work*, 37 (3).

Lewis, J, 1995, *The Voluntary Sector, the State and Social Work in Britain* (Edward Elgar).

Pollock, Allyson, 2004, *NHS PLC* (Verso).

TUC, 2010, *Where the Money Goes: How we Benefit from Public Services* (TUC).

Utting, D, 2009, *Contemporary Social Evils* (Policy Press/JRF).

Austerity, resistance, alternatives...

MARXISM 2011 IDEAS TO CHANGE THE WORLD

Speakers include

Eyewitnesses from the Arab revolutions

Tony Benn

Tariq Ali

Len McCluskey

Laurie Penny

Stuart Christie

Iain Sinclair

Ghada Karmi

Alex Callinicos

István Mészáros

Paul Gilroy

Jeremy Corbyn MP

Michael Rosen

and many others

30 June to 4 July, Central London

A five day political festival hosted by the SWP

Over 200 workshops, discussions and debates plus music, film and more

To book, and for more information:
www.marxismfestival.org.uk
020 7819 1190   info@marxismfestival.org.uk

Tunisia: the people's revolution
Chamseddine Mnasri

On 14 January 2011 Tunisians ousted President Zine El Abidine Ben Ali after a month's revolt. Ben Ali's removal has changed our perception of revolution. Two things explain this: the change came totally from below; and the reactionary forces have failed to restore the old order. Unplanned and spontaneous, the revolution succeeded in realising the aspirations of the subaltern because it was a veritable working class response to unemployment, uneven regional development and the suppression of liberties. The regime had been in complete disarray for three weeks before it finally succumbed; it faced the protests with ruthless force but finally ceded to the will of the people on the historic day of 14 January. Ben Ali fled the country, leaving behind a history of dictatorship whose repercussions will persist for years. Yet the cleansing process has already begun, with an interim government responsible to the people to secure the path to democratic rule.

History
In 1933 the Tunisian poet Abou Kassem Chebi wrote this verse:

> *Once the people wills life*
> *Destiny must succumb*
> *No more shall reign the dark of the night*
> *No more shall we by the chains be bound* [1]

1:    Chebi, 2009, pIII.

This verse had been part of the literature of resistance to the French Protectorate imposed on Tunisia in 1883. However, literature and art seem to have exerted only weak pressure on the nationalist movement. Tunisian peasant society was more responsive to politics from above than literary expressions. Chebi's poem coincided with the foundation of the Neo-Destour Party (New Constitution Party) in 1934. The NDP represented the political ambitions of an educated elite who sought to negotiate independence by peaceful means.[2] The people's will was then drowned by the partisanship of the Neo-Destourists, and the struggle for independence assumed an ideological character which distanced Chebi's people from political life.

The 1940s saw the rise of a single leader, Habib Bourguiba, from the womb of Neo-Destourism (neo-constitutionalism). Bourguiba came to subordinate the nationalist movement to the dictates of diplomacy and negotiation with France. The Neo-Destour was the tool with which he charted the decolonisation map on the basis of an alleged protection/obedience formula. Tunisians were a peasant society mostly bound to believe that the party leader was the protector of their destiny. Bourguiba argued that he "personified his own people" and that he "fought for the cause of the people so much and so well that the course of life of the man and the people have been led to merge".[3]

In the 1940s Chebi's poem seemed to have little influence on the peasants and miners, basically because Bourguibism was thought of as the only inspiring ideology capable of decolonising the country. In the early 1950s Bourguiba's cohort manipulated the national question in favour of Neo-Destourism and denied peasant insurgency any role against French colonialism. In 1957—a year after independence—Bourguiba was anxious to court his people by adding the term "socialist" to the old name of the party; the NDP was abandoned for the Socialist Constitutional Party (SCP). Nevertheless, the term "socialist" was completely alien to Bourguiba's republic. During the struggle period he had had a strong anti-socialist agenda inspired by American liberalism. That agenda was particularly aimed against Communism.[4] Such was Bourguiba's decolonisation strategy: to approach the liberal West in the hope of exerting pressure on France to negotiate the terms of independence.

Tunisian contemporary history has been informed by Bourguibism and has addressed only in passing the role of popular uprisings against French

---

2:   For details about the foundation of the Neo-Destour, see Bourguiba, 2011.
3:   Bourguiba, 1959.
4:   Bourguiba, 1957.

occupation. Today, for instance, very few among the Tunisian people evoke the memory of the Fellaghas (1952-1954), the most significant peasant and miner movement which, in my view, made independence possible. The Fellaghas were the only organised guerrilla rebels who attacked the French soldiers and colonists. Their leader, Lazhar Chraiti, conducted operations and planned attacks, but he is generally remembered today as the enemy of Bourguiba who attempted a coup in 1962.[5]

The role of the Fellaghas has been dumped in the hitherto closed files of the National Archive Centre (NAC); their contribution to independence has remained a book with seven seals. In the decades after 1956 official history acknowledged only the role of Bourguiba. Bourguiba led no armed struggle, and was only content with what he believed to be the force of diplomacy, relying for his cause on a discourse of anti-Arabism and overt praise of the West.[6] The Bourguibist state between 1956 and 1987 was characterised by the inflation of Bourguiba's role in Tunisia's history. He received the title "Supreme Combatant" and was "voted president for life" in 1975.[7]

Nevertheless, 12 years later presidency for life seemed an impossible aspiration as the 84 year old Bourguiba began to lose control of the situation. On 7 November 1987 the minister of interior, Zine El Abidine Ben Ali, made use of the turmoil and conducted a "white coup". He decided to break with every Bourguibist element and declared in the "7 November Declaration" that there would be "no life presidency" and that a new era of "democracy" was in order.[8] However, contrary to his steadfast declaration, Ben Ali took the country down a winding path where civil society was completely devoured by the state. Ben Ali's party, the Constitutional Democratic Rally (RCD), said to have constituted a break with the past, was only the tool of a new dictatorship. The RCD was deployed by Ben Ali to transform state rule from autocracy (Bourguiba) into a veritable oligarchy (Ben Ali, his wife and her family).

Ben Ali's 23-year dictatorship confirms that Chebi's verses, still dinning in our ears, need not a diplomat, a negotiator, a charismatic leader or a politician to realise. They prove that Tunisia's history has rested on a lacuna and that the people ought veritably to "will life" and change their world rather than lament it. The events of 17 December 2010 came to confirm that the people's "will to life" can only be operated from below by whatever means.

5:   Girard, 2005.
6:   Bourguiba, 1961.
7:   Bourguiba, 2011.
8:   Ben Ali, 2006.

A young vegetable vendor sparked the change. He set himself on fire and lit the path to a second republic. Yet how could such a deeply entrenched totalitarian system crumble so quickly? A crisis theory is needed to explain this.

Façade Democracy

Ben Ali's Tunisia was a façade democracy. It depended on a politics of virtual representation that the regime celebrated for 23 years. The multiparty myth had to do with a discourse of democratisation maintained since 1987. The political situation reveals that the regime's party had completely dominated the scene. The RCD, a member of the Socialist International until 17 January 2011, long sought to work up support for Ben Ali by asking or forcing people to adhere to the party.[9] On the other hand, the Tunisian Destour (constitution) in no way mentions the separation between the state and the ruling party.[10] Ministers and government officials were forced to become members of the RCD; promotions and tenure were also dictated by membership of the party.

Second, Ben Ali's façade democracy was based on the careful selection of the opposition. The opposition is composed of two main forces: authorised and outlawed. The authorised include mainly two accessory parties and two radical parties. The former are the Unionist Democratic Union (UDU) and the Party of Popular Unity (PPU). They supported Ben Ali and adopted agendas similar to that of the RCD. They also participated in elections and ran for presidency. Statistics reveal that they participated only in the hope of giving legitimacy to the regime and getting some favours in return.[11] The authorised radical parties, however, had a clear anti-regime agenda. They include a moderate left wing movement, Attajdid (Movement for Renewal) and the secular Progressive Democratic Party (PDP). On the other hand, the outlawed parties are the Islamic Renaissance Movement (Ennahda)—with a radical Islamist agenda—and the Communist Party of Tunisian Workers (PCOT). They were rejected by the regime as fanatic and fundamentalist.[12]

The third characteristic of Ben Ali's fake "democracy" was the assault on civil and human rights. Though the list of repressed civil organisations is long, two major movements might well illustrate the violations of the

---

9:   The RCD was dismissed from the Socialist International on 17 January 2011.
10:   The RCD's official site was blocked by the interim government soon after Ben Ali had fled to Saudi Arabia: www.letemps.com.tn/pop_article.php?ID_art=18685
11:   For elections statistics, see the following links: www.arabicnews.com/ansub/Daily/Day/.../2004102606; www.allafrica.com/stories/200910260111.html
12:   The PCOT 's organ was clandestine until 14 January 2001: http://albadil.org

regime: the National Council for Liberties in Tunisia (CNLT)[13] and the Association for the Prevention of Torture (APT).[14] The CNLT was founded in 1998 in the hope of making up for the eclipse of the opposition after the official institutionalisation of the RCD by the regime in the early 1990s. The absence of a strong opposition made the CNLT assume the responsibility of wrestling with the authorities. The activities of the council increased dramatically after a 2002 referendum by which immense modifications were made to the Destour to allow Ben Ali to run again in 2004. In the aftermath of the referendum the CNLT, together with human rights organisations and civil rights movements, deplored the suppression of liberties in Tunisia and asked the regime to ease society of the oppressive policies of the government.[15] Following continual protests the CNLT was shut down in May 2007 and has since then become clandestine.[16]

The APT—working closely with the Tunisian League of Human Rights—used to investigate human rights abuses in Tunisian prisons and detention centres. Its activities were mainly based on the observation of any violations, particularly those deriving from the "Anti-terrorism Law of 2003". The anti-terrorism law is dubious and notorious. It was first passed to "combat terrorism" in the wake of the Djerba synagogue bombing in April 2002.[17] But the government applied a broader definition to the law. Anti-terrorism would also broadly include any acts considered as "disturbing public order".[18] Almost all attempts by the opposition or associations to protest against government policies or organise strikes and demonstrations were treated as signs of public disorder. The law became open to extension, and human rights activists and forces of the radical opposition were often arrested on charges of treason and conspiracy against the country.[19]

The APT countered these extensions and openly condemned the abuse of the anti-terrorism law. That resulted in severe measures against the association. APT members were not immune from torture. Defending prisoners against torture was met by categorical refusal. In 2003 Nasraoui argued that "torture has become systematic" in Tunisia and that "all those

---

13: Front Line Defenders, 2007.
14: Comité pour le Respect des libertés et des Droits de l'hommes en Tunisie (CRLDHT), 2008.
15: Front Line Defenders, 2007.
16: Front Line Defenders, 2007.
17: BBC News, 2002; see also the following link for a video of the bombing: http://wn.com/la_tunisie_la_ghriba_de_djerba
18: CRLDHT, 2008, pp 19-25
19: Black, 2008.

arrested…for political reasons pass through torture".[20] Nasraoui edited a 209-page document that discusses the anti-terrorism law and gives statistics about the number of victims, and "systematic torture, as well as "testimonies".[21] Recently, thanks to the APT, the United Nations has reported the yawning gulf between official declarations and the "reality" of "torture, secret detentions and police harassment in Tunisia under Ben Ali." The report also deplores the "abuse of the definition of terrorism" by the regime.[22]

The path to revolution

In what follows I broach three main factors that, I argue, were decisive in hastening the eruption of the revolution:

● *Unemployment*: According to the 2009 census by the Tunisian National Institute of Statistics, the unemployment rate reached 13.3 percent, the highest in the Maghreb.[23] The Ben Ali government kept promising new jobs but statistics reveal that very few jobs were secured and most of such jobs went to the daughters or sons of the people who controlled the bureaucracy. The latest World Bank estimate shows that out of a population of 10,433,000 there are around 336,000 jobless graduates, and very few have any hope of getting a job.[24]

● *Corruption*: Corruption in Tunisia was determined mainly by extra-economic factors. Such factors include essentially the oligarchy and bureaucracy. The oligarchic system created a strong bureaucracy through which political life and the distribution of wealth had been controlled. It is in such a way that the regime had exploited the country for 23 years. Power abuse by Ben Ali and his wife, Leila Trabelsi, was what brought about, reinforced and expanded corruption. First, it is not difficult to observe that the major factories, companies and commercial centres are located in the Sahil region (home of the Ben Alis) and the capital, Tunis. Second, the foundation of conglomerates in these regions has been dictated either by the regional interests of the Ben Alis or the unlimited personal ambitions of the Trabelsis—relatives of Leila Trabelsi.

The Trabelsis' monopoly of wealth is far more complex than that of the Ben Alis, mainly because their exploitation of the forces of production was

---

20: Lesme Anthony, 2007.
21: CRLDHT, 2008.
22: Vermeulen, 2011.
23: National Institute of Statistics—Tunisia, 2004.
24: World Bank Report, 2011.

more flagrant. They controlled almost every industrial sector and the overall financial situation. The story of the Trabelsis reaches beyond economic profit or the abuse of the country's wealth. They tightened their grip on most state institutions. Not long ago Nicolas Beau and Catherine Graciet published *The Regent of Carthage* (2009) to examine the influence and corruption of the Trabelsi family. By "regent" the authors refer to Ben Ali's wife who literally took Ben Ali's place in ruling the country. In the book "Carthage" is a term which both refers to the presidential palace situated in the suburb of Carthage and a is symbol of the historic city founded by Queen Dido (Elissa) in 814 BC. The book ironically depicts Leila Trabelsi as the Ellisa of Tunisia.[25]

On the other hand, the relatives of the regent are described as the bloodsuckers of desperate Tunisians. They were an indispensable component of the oligarchy and used all sorts of means to control Carthage. Recently *Le Monde Diplomatique* commented on the nature of such control.[26] Their domination of the state and society had to do with the manipulation of such strong institutions as parliament and the judiciary.[27] The judiciary, in particular, had been intimidated since 2001. In their lust for money and power the Trabelsis used all means possible to expropriate factory owners, entrepreneurs and farmers and forcibly take bank loans which they never paid back. And to anticipate lawsuits, they threatened and attacked magistrates by deploying the State Security Police. Intimidation of the judiciary reached a peak in 2005 when the authorities dissolved the democratically-elected Legitimate Board of the Association of Tunisian Judges, whose task was the monitoring of the legal system in Tunisia.[28]

• *The Internet*: In Ben Ali's Tunisia the media were monitored, controlled and censored by the Ministry of Communication Technologies (MCT). Local TV stations, newspapers, magazines and papers spoke very little of the political and economic situation or the dire poverty in the interior of the country.[29] However, Tunisians found relief in the Internet, the alternative media source that was somehow underestimated by the MCT. Although the MCT established the Tunisian Internet Agency (TIA) in 1996 to watch and block the

---

25: Beau and Graciet, 2009.
26: Séréni, 2011.
27: For more on the corruption of the Trabelsis, see Monnier, 2008, and Deléan, 2008.
28: International Freedom of Expression Exchange (IFEX), 2010; for a full account of the assault on the judiciary, see www.icj.org/IMG/TUNISIA.pdf
29: Only two newspapers of the radical opposition were authorised: *Almawkef* (PDP), www.tunisiemedias.com/ecrite/almawkef.html; and *Attariq Aljadid* (Attajdid Movement), www.attariq.org. Authorities occasionally banned them on different charges.

sites considered a threat to "national security", the social media have created a fresh ground for action. Such media played a key role in pushing for the 14 January revolution. Social discontent and hostility to the regime were articulated on Twitter, YouTube, Dailymotion and, most importantly, Facebook. The use of these services had a remarkable influence on the youth. Facebook in particular was the Trojan horse of the Ben Ali regime. The social media activists (bloggers, rappers, freelance journalists and students) also had significant impact on the Tunisian people. In response to the role of cyber dissidents, the authorities, already in deep crisis, arrested a number of bloggers and rappers between 6 and 10 January 2011.[30]

The revolution

The immiseration of Tunisian society, the suppression of liberties and the influence of the social media had a powerful impact on the youth. The revolution started in the region of Sidi Bouzid when a municipal inspector slapped a street vendor, Mohamed Bouazizi, in the face and confiscated his cart. Humiliated and desperate, Bouazizi set himself on fire on 17 December 2011. He died two weeks later.[31] In consequence, demonstrations broke out in Sidi Bouzid in protest at the policy of the local council and the governor of the city. Bouazizi's death has made history and has had far-reaching implications for the future of Tunisia.

The Sidi Bouzid protests reminded the regime of similar events which had taken place in the region of Rdaeif in 2008. The Rdaeif protests had been ruthlessly crushed by the police.[32] In order to alleviate the tension and avoid another Rdaief scenario, Ben Ali sympathised with Bouazizi and promised to aid his family. However, such a step was not enough to curb the rage. The protests had already spread to the town of Menzel Bouzaien where two civilians were shot dead on 24 December.[33] In response to the riots Ben Ali delivered a speech in which he described the demonstrators as a "bandit of agitators". He vowed to quell the "violence" and warned parents that their "sons were being manipulated by agitators".[34]

Ben Ali's speech, however, did not succeed in preventing the protests spreading out to the towns of Thala and Rgeub. The events in these towns were a turning point. On 8 January the regime began the systematic cleansing of protesters. The confrontation between unarmed civilians and

---

30: Langley, 2011.
31: Reuters, 2011.
32: Reveiltunisien, 2008.
33: Al Jazeera English, 2010.
34: Pan-African News Wire, 2010.

Ben Ali's special guard (*Al Amen Arriessi*) left over 50 victims in Thala and Kasserine alone.[35] The shooting, filmed by amateurs, was later broadcast by TV stations such as Al Jazeera and France 24.[36]

On 12 January protests reached the capital Tunis, after they had spread to the South, the Sahil and Nabeul. By then the death toll had risen dramatically. Snipers shot civilians in Douz, Hammamet and Nabeul.[37] In Tunis the protests first reached the poor and densely populated suburb of Hai Tadhamen (Tadhamen quarter) where more were killed.[38] Ben Ali responded by delivering his third and last speech. He ordered the police to "stop using live bullets", and apologised to the Tunisian people,[39] but his apologies, an attempt to restore order, were too late. The following morning, 14 January, tens of thousands marched in Bourguiba Street and protested in front of the ministry of the interior—the symbol of torture. The fall of the regime seemed imminent when protesters, in a historic moment, climbed the walls of the ministry and challenged the police force.

The Tunisian General Labour Union (UGTT)

The UGTT played no central role in the Tunisian Revolution. It did not expect Bouazizi's self-immolation to trigger popular revolt across the country. Yet the Bouazizi incident, it seems to me, does not offer a thorough explanation. Historically, the UGTT was strong during Bourguiba's rule, but got systematically enfeebled under Ben Ali. It had played a significant political role between 1978 and 1985, mainly in protest against the policy of "economic liberalisation" adopted by the Tunisian government.[40] On 26 January 1978 the UGTT organised a general strike and threatened to "burn Tunis". Bourguiba refused to make concessions and ordered the police to open fire on protesters.[41] The paradox was that Bourguiba accepted strikes but crushed them while Ben Ali suppressed them altogether.

After the 1987 coup Ben Ali dwarfed the UGTT and dictated a new agenda based mainly on pay rise promises. The union's leadership was not immune to corruption and demagogy. Two secretaries-general have chaired the UGTT since 1989: Ismail Sahbani (1989-2000) and Abdesslem Jerad

---

35: Ibrahem, 2011.
36: A YouTube search for "Kasserine Thala" or "videos of Tunisians shot" reveals an astonishing amount of amateur footage of victims of the regime's violence.
37: Whitaker, 2011.
38: Kirkaptrick, 2011.
39: World Crunch, 2011.
40: Barrie, 2004.
41: Com4News, 2008.

(currently). Sahbani was entirely in support of the regime, but was ousted in 2000 on charges of corruption and financial mismanagement. Jerad, on the other hand, has certainly scored worse than his predecessor. He notoriously campaigned for Ben Ali's candidacy in 2004 and 2009 while he failed to defend the Rdaief labour activists. In December 2008 the authorities arrested 140 protesters in Rdaief, including leading activist Adnan Hajji, but the UGTT refused to condemn the regime's repressive measures.

In the context of the revolution, the UGTT stepped in only six days before the fall of Ben Ali in the hope of catching up with the unfolding events. On 8 January the UGTT spokesman, Abid Briki, declared the leadership's unconditional support for the protests and deplored the shooting of civilians. Though Briki's speech demoralised Ben Ali, it had very little effect on the demonstrators, mainly because by then they seemed too strong and steadfast to break.[42]

Nonetheless, the inconsistency of the leadership should not conceal the role of several regional unions. During the protests there was a clear rift between the UGTT's Executive Bureau and the local unions. In Sidi Bouzid, Bouzaien, Rgeub, Thala, Kasserine and later Sfax the unions acted unilaterally in support of the protesters but lacked systematic organisation. While the leadership had been gripped by undecidedness, the regional unions merged with the demonstrators. Jerad had supported Ben Ali unconditionally in two presidential elections, and was now all too cautious to turn the clock forward and risk an uncertain future. And Briki's speech was not insignificant; he intervened when he felt that the regime had already lost control of the situation.

Change from below

Social revolution is the frenzy of history. This is what the Tunisian Revolution has taught us. Hardly anyone has ever predicted a political revolution in the Arab world, let alone a popular revolt from below. Revolutions from below are rare in history. The 1791 Haitian Revolution—though social in character—was largely bound by the ideological dictates of priesthood as well as the French revolutionary tradition. The 1871 Paris Commune was an unfinished project and the Young Turk Revolution (1908) had to do more with political activism and partisanship than the aspirations of the grassroots.[43] The Iranian Revolution (1979) was conducted in the name of the Islamic sharia law, and failed to meet the

---

42: Leaders, 2011.
43: See Hanjoglu, 2001.

democratic aspirations of Iranian society. The October Revolution was wanting in the proletarian element and led to no classless society.

The Tunisian Revolution has very little in common with the above-mentioned revolutions. Its defining characteristic is the absence of an obvious leadership. It is a spontaneous movement of the masses against an oppressive regime and is informed by the aspirations of people from all walks of life. The 23-year Ben Ali rule emptied the country of any political culture, and Tunisian society, apart from a small segment, was bent on improving standards of living, education and health. Such were the fields which the regime focused on all too much in the hope of gaining credibility for itself; and such were the fields under the pretext of which liberties were suppressed.

Yet would it be appropriate to see the Tunisian Revolution as aimless and therefore contingent and without a future? The answer to this question depends on determining why such a revolution erupted in the first place. What people agree upon in Tunisia is that this revolution concerns the retrieval of "human value and dignity"; it has very little to do with bread. It occurred because the people felt dispossessed and alien to their essence. It was a battle for human dignity. In this sense it might well be understood in Marxian terms—without falling prey to the dictates of Marxist ideology. That is to say, it is the emancipation of humanity from alienation, from "the existence of the state" as such.[44]

Tunisian society was enslaved by the Ben Ali regime in the name of economic development, literacy and national security. Here the observer need not receive lessons in political history to perceive a Tunisian "false consciousness" dictated by an alleged "constructive interplay" between the people and their president. Political history has estranged people from social reality, and the politics of the "great man's history"—Ben Ali's—has dominated the country for over two decades. Such false consciousness, Marx reminds us, can only be overwhelmed when we perceive "social revolution" as "a human protest against a dehumanised life".[45]

The Tunisian people have merged Chebi's "will to life" and Marx's "human essence" to recover consciousness of the historical role of the individual. The change, unplanned and spontaneous, has come from the grassroots. No religious overtone dominated the protests and no Pan-Arabist agenda, moderate or radical, was at work. "We need a life, dignity and freedom": these were the universal principles for which Tunisians protested and got

---

44: Marx, 2000, p135.
45: Marx, 2000, p136.

killed. They demanded work, equality, freedom of speech and the right to choose their government, but were met with live ammunition.

Significantly, the spirit of the social revolution in Tunisia resides in the symbolism of the slogans chanted for over three weeks. I shall take such slogans chronologically. The first was *"Allah Akbar"* (God is Great) chanted when Bouazizi set himself on fire. This was an expected popular response to inevitable destiny. Allah would pardon Bouazizi for an act considered blasphemous by Muslims, but would also have mercy on him and punish those who pushed him to take his life. On 4 January, when Bouazizi died, the slogan *"Allah Akbar"*—very little associated with Islamism—fanned the flames of rage in Sidid Bouzid and the rest of the country. More radical slogans were introduced: "Our soul and blood are to sacrifice for the martyr." The latter confirms a sort of concord between those who die for a cause and those who are ready to sacrifice their lives for them. It symbolises the will to face up to the enemy of the people—often the regime or the coloniser.

By 8 January the protests in the Central West (Thala, Kasserine, etc) expanded into revolt and more audacious slogans were chanted by college students. Slogans included *"Kobz w mé w Ben Ali lé"* (Yes to just water and bread, and no to Ben Ali, he's dead); or *"Horia w karama watania"* (Freedom, national dignity); or *"Echogol istahkak ya isabet essorek"* (Work is a must, you the bandit of theft). These slogans sent a clear message to the regime: "We don't want the dictator"; "We want our freedom and money back, and we call upon the people of Tunisia to stand up against the Ben Ali regime." Live bullets prompted further action and more daring slogans. Ben Ali wanted to silence the students and the declassed, but the snipers failed to snuff out the crisis.

When the protests reached Tunis the slogans became uncompromising. They clearly asked the president to step down: *"Tounes hora hora w Ben Ali ala bara"* (Tunisia's free, leave Ben Ali, leave us free); *"Echaab yourid iskat ennitham"* (The people want to topple the regime); *"Ya chaabi thour thour ala dictatour"* (Rebel, my people, rebel, and quell the regime, quell). These slogans had been shouted for two days before the protests penetrated Bourguiba Street on 14 January. The Bourguiba Street slogans were succinct and powerful: *"Dégage"* (Piss off) and "Game over".

In part, the Tunisian Revolution succeeded thanks to the slogans that forcefully demoralised the regime. They forced Ben Ali to deliver his third and last speech on 13 January and call upon his guard to stop shooting people. Slogans were a social message for change not only in Tunisia but in the rest of the Arab world. The Egyptian upheaval, which started on 25 January, was operated by the same Tunisian slogans, which revealed that the power of the word might well defeat the power of the bullet.

References

Aljazeera English, 2010, "Another Tunisian Protester Dies" (31 December), http://english. aljazeera.net/news/africa/2010/12/201012317536678834.html

Barrie, Larry, 2004, "Tunisia Labour Union", *Encyclopedia.com,* www.encyclopedia.com/ doc/1G2-3424602775.html

Beau, Nicolas, and Catherine Graciet, 2009, *La Régente de Carthage: Main Basse sur la Tunisie* (Editions La Découverte).

BBC News, 2002, "Al Qaeda Claims Tunisia Attack" (23 June), http://news.bbc.co.uk/2/hi/ middle_east/2061071.stm

Ben Ali, Zine El Abidine, 2006, "November 7 1987", www.independence.tn/english/ index.php

Black, Ian, 2008, "Tunisia accused of using torture in name of anti-terrorism", *Guardian* (23 June), www.guardian.co.uk/world/2008/jun/23/humanrights.terrorism

Bourguiba, Habib, 1957, "Nationalism: Antidote to Communism", *Foreign Affairs,* 35: 4, http://www.jstor.org/stable/20031259

Bourguiba, Habib, 1959, "Une Constitution par le Peuple et pour le Peuple" (Sécretariat d'Etat à L'Information).

Bourguiba , Habib, 1961, "The Outlook for Africa", *International Affairs,* 37:4.

Bourguiba, Habib, 2011, "Biography", www.bourguiba.com/pages/biography.aspx

Chebi, Abou Kassem, 2009, *The Songs of Life* (Arabesque Editions).

Com4News, 2008, "26 Janvier le 'Jeudi Noir': la Première Grève Générale depuis L'Indépendance" (26 January), www.come4news.com/26-janvier-1978-le-jeudi-noir-la-premiere-greve-generale-depuis-lindependance-458603

Comité pour le Respect des Libertés et des Droits de l'Hommes en Tunisie (CRLDHT), 2008, *Torture in Tunisia and the Anti-terrorist Law of December 2003* (ALTT-CRLDHT), www.fidh.org/IMG/pdf/crldht-altt-torture-en-tunisie-rapport.pdf:

Deléan, Michel, 2008, "L'affaire des yachts volés refait surface", *JDD* (8 August), www.lejdd.fr/ Societe/Justice/Actualite/L-affaire-des-yachts-voles-refait-surface-125225

Front Line Defenders, 2007, "Tunisia: National Council of Liberties Shut Down by Police" (18 May), www.frontlinedefenders.org/taxonomy/term/107; www.frontlinedefenders.org/ ar/node/1030

Girard, Patrick, 2005, "Le Lion des Montagnes Arbat", www.lazharchraiti.org/journaux_ page.htm

Hanjoglu, Sukru, 2001, *Preparation for a Revolution: The Young Turks, 1902-1908* (Oxford University Press).

Ibrahem B Ahmed, 2011, "Tunisia: Death Toll Reaches 50", *Allvoices* (13 January), www.allvoices.com/contributed-news/7878994-tunisiadeath-toll-reaches-50-video

International Freedom of Expression Exchange (IFEX), 2010, "Tunisia's war on civil liberties intensifies with year's end", (22 December), http://ifex.org/tunisia/2010/12/22/yearend_ civilliberties

Kirkaptrick, David, 2011, "In Tunisia, Clashes Continue as Power Shifts a Second Time", *New York Times* (15 January), www.nytimes.com/2011/01/16/world/africa/16tunis.html

Khiari, Sadri, 2002, "The Democratic Opposition", *International Viewpoint* (September), www.internationalviewpoint.org/spip.php?article277

Langley, JT, 2011, "Tunisian Rapper and Bloggers Arrested and Missing amidst National Protest", *Ology* (10 January), http://ology.com/music/tunisian-rapper-and-bloggers-arrested-and-missing-amidst-national-protest

Leaders, 2011, UGTT: "Jerad Recu par Ben Ali" (12 January), www.leaders.com.tn/article/ugtt-jerad-recu-par-ben-ali?id=3622

Lesme Anthony, 2007, "Radhia Nasraoui: 'tous ceux qui sont arrêtés passent par la torture'", *Bakchich* (4 September), www.bakchich.info/Radhia-Nasraoui-Tous-ceux-qui-sont,01538.html

Marx, Karl, 2000, *Selected Writings* (Oxford University Press).

Monnier, Xavier, 2008, "Des mandats d'arret contre des members de la famille du président Ben Ali", *Bakchich* (29 Avril), www.bakchich.info/Des-mandats-d-arret-contre-des,03572.html

National Institute of Statistics—Tunisia, 2004, "Economic Characteristics of the population: Unemployment Distribution in the 18-59 Age Group and Unemployment Rate by Sex", *NIST*, www.ins.nat.tn/indexen.php http://www.ins.nat.tn/indexen.php

Pan-African News Wire, 2010. "Tunisia President Ben Ali Warns Protesters" (28 December), panafricannews.blogspot.com/2010/12/tunisia-president-ben-ali-warns.html

Reveiltunisien, 2008, "Lourdes Peines contre les Détenus du Bassin Minier" (31 December), www.reveiltunisien.org/spip/perso/src/moujira.blogspot.com/IMG/xls/ecrire/spip.php?article2832

Reuters, 2011, "Tunisian who sparked rare protests dies" (5 January), http://af.reuters.com/article/topNews/idAFJOE70408420110105.

Séréni, Jean-Pierre, 2011, "Le Réveil Tunisien", *Le Monde Diplomatique* (6 January), www.monde-diplomatique.fr/carnet/2011-01-06-Tunisie)

Socialist International, 2011, "Socialist International dismiss former Tunisian president's party", *Zawya* (19 January), www.internationalesocialiste.org/viewArticle.cfm?ArticleID=2085

Vermeulen, Mathias, 2011, "UN Report confirms gap between law and reality, torture, secret detentions and police harassment in Tunisia under Ben Ali", *The Lift: Legal Issues in the fight against Terrorism* (24 January), http://legalift.wordpress.com/category/tunisia

Whitaker, Brian, 2011, "Events in Tunisia, January 12", *al-bab* (12 January), www.al-bab.com/blog/2011/blog1101a.htm

World Bank Report, 2011, "For a better integration into the labor market in Tunisia", *The World Bank Group*, http://bit.ly/g3IemR

World Crunch, 2011, "Behind the Scenes of Ben Ali's Final Hours", *Le Figaro* (25 January), http://plus.lefigaro.fr/note/behind-the-scenes-of-ben-alis-final-hours-20110125-382712

Act One of the Egyptian Revolution
Philip Marfleet

Of all the startling scenes which made up Act One of the Egyptian Revolution, the events in Tahrir Square on 2 February were surely most astounding. When Mubarak sent gangs of plainclothes police to attack demonstrators, the protesters fought like demons. They first resisted, then drove back the *baltagiyya* (criminals/thugs). As news of the battle spread, people flooded in from every area of Cairo, racing to the front line to support the resistance. Even Robert Fisk of the *Independent*, who has seen conflicts worldwide, observed: "It was incredible, a risen people who would no longer take violence and brutality and prison as their lot".[1]

The episode revealed much about Egypt's upheaval. It showed how readily Mubarak turned to intense violence. Fisk, who witnessed the events, comments that introduction of the *baltagiyya* "was vicious and ruthless and bloody and well planned".[2] Mubarak and his inner circle of ministers, relatives and business associates expected that well-tried techniques would serve to break the protest movement. Their orders were to savage demonstrators—to break bones and to crush the will of the uprising. In the streets the people understood. It was a battle for their very lives: against poverty, hunger and joblessness; against fear, abuse and torture. Their numbers and their anger reached critical mass; nine days later Mubarak was gone. Unsure of the loyalties of a conscript army,

---

1: Fisk, 2011.
2: Fisk, 2011.

Egypt's generals finally pulled the plug on the dictator. As the Supreme Council of the Armed Forces they now formally hold power, guardians of a system rejected by millions who continue to agitate for radical change.

At the time of writing the focus has moved from Tahrir Square to workplaces across the country, with strikes in many of Egypt's key industries. Workers have raised a host of demands—on wages, bonuses, contracts, pensions, health insurance, union rights and recognition, and for removal of management and official trade union leaders who abused them throughout the Mubarak years. In Suez the army has seized managers accused of corruption.[3] At the Misr Spinning and Weaving Company in Mahalla Al Kubra, Egypt's largest publicly owned company and the biggest textile mill in the Middle East, strikers have demanded prosecution of managers they charge with corruption and with victimisation of union activists. A process of purging has begun—what activists of the 1974 Revolution in Portugal called *saneamiento* (cleansing). Among the first indicted was steel tycoon Ahmed Ezz, a senior official of the ruling National Democratic Party (NDP) and one of Mubarak's billionaire friends, arrested by order of the Supreme Council. Others detained included interior minister Habib al-Adly, housing minister Ahmed Maghrabi and tourism minister Zuheir Garana.

Apparatus of repression

The speed of events has been extraordinary. On 25 January 2011 the interior minister had been hailed by regime supporters as "Egypt's number one defender of human rights". In a demonstration at the Supreme Court staged for the official media they chanted: "Habib al-Adly is the hero who protects Egypt from danger" and "Habib, hit with an iron fist!"[4] Adly responded to mass protests which began the same day by mobilising the hated riot police; when they failed to clear the streets he organised the *baltagiyya*. This approach was consistent with Mubarak's attitude to popular protest throughout his presidency. On acceding to power in 1981 Mubarak imposed the Emergency Law. He suspended legal rights; banned strikes, demonstrations and public meetings of more than ten individuals; censored or closed newspapers; and introduced military courts in which there was no recourse to appeal. He massively expanded the security apparatus, encouraging police and intelligence agencies to act with impunity by seizing and incarcerating

---

3:   See "Suez Strikes"—report of 12 February on the Arabawy blog: www.arabawy. org/2011/02/12/jan25-suez-strikes-egyworkers/
4:   Afify, 2011.

suspects at will. Modest concessions were offered in order to co-opt more pliable elements within the opposition; if these proved insufficient to contain dissent, the stick was readily available and Mubarak used it freely.

The regime established a vast apparatus of repression. In addition to the civil police it mobilised the paramilitary riot force, *Amn al-Markazi* (Central Security), and multiple security/intelligence agencies.[5] These worked to suppress every form of independent political activity, pursuing even those who attempted to operate within the narrow range of activities notionally permitted by the regime. When in 2004 the mild liberal reformist Ayman Nour formed the Ghad (Tomorrow) Party and stood against Mubarak in a presidential election he was promptly framed and imprisoned.

Numerous academic assessments credit the regime with subtle means of co-optation said to have played a key role in neutralising opposition. Maye Kassem, for example, comments that Mubarak has used "a mixture of fear and rewards" to co-opt opposition parties, trade unions and professional syndicates, with the effect that his long reign has been continuously extended without major political crises.[6] This was indeed the approach adopted in the 1950s and 1960s when Gamal Abdel Nasser's radical nationalism seduced the Stalinist left—leading Communists abandoned their party to take senior positions in the bureaucracy while workers' leaders were absorbed into state-backed unions. The regime of Anwar Sadat in the 1970s also practised co-optation, modifying Nasser's monolithic single party, the Arab Socialist Union (ASU), to find space for "platforms" said to represent key opposition groups. By this means the bourgeois liberal Wafd and the remnants of communist and Nasserist organisations were given rights to organise as distinct political currents. But the changes were of limited value: the "platforms" ran offices and publications but were forbidden to organise publicly, with the result that they were in effect parties without members. Mubarak maintained these restrictions throughout his years in power. Rif'at al-Said, leader of the National Progressive Unionist Party (usually known as al-Tagammu'),[7] has commented that parties recognised by the regime "represent nothing in Egyptian politics and have no standing whatsoever with the Egyptian

---

5:   *Mabahith Amn al-Dawla* (General Directorate of State Security Investigations), *Jihaz Amn al-Dawla* (State Security Service), *Mukhabarat al-Aama* (General Intelligence and Security Service), *Mukhabarat al-Harbeya* (Military Intelligence Service) and *Jihaz al-Amn al-Qawmi* (National Security Service).

6:   Kassem, 2004, p7.

7:   Tagammu' contains the rump of the old Communist Party, officially dissolved by its own members in 1964 on the basis that Nasser had accomplished revolution in Egypt.

people".[8] None are "parties in the true sense of the term", he says: "All these are just groupings of individuals floating on the surface of society".[9]

In most authoritarian states returns from co-optation diminish greatly when it becomes clear that official bodies act as outliers of the regime or operate at its whim. In the case of Egypt, Mubarak's determination to control every area of formal politics meant that even the tamest opposition activists were denied opportunities to develop meaningful agendas and failed to develop constituencies of support. At election time, polling stations were routinely surrounded by riot police who protected officials engaged in ballot-rigging and fraud, and whose job was to guarantee huge majorities for NDP candidates. At the November 2010 parliamentary elections, *Ahram Weekly* reported:

> Footage showed people stuffing ballot boxes, attacking voting stations, opening and destroying ballot boxes, in some cases by setting them on fire. Independent watchdogs say nine people were killed in connection with the violence that erupted in dozens of constituencies across the nation.[10]

Results were often determined by Mubarak's officials in advance: before the November 2010 election the speaker of the People's Assembly (the lower house) told Muslim Brotherhood deputies they would not be returning after the poll; in the first round, as predicted, no Brotherhood candidates were elected and the organisation withdrew, furious but helpless. [11]

Alone among established opposition currents the Brotherhood has maintained some independence from the state. Founded in the 1920s, it played a leading (if inconsistent) role in anti-colonial struggles and in support of the early Palestinian resistance. Repressed by Nasser, it returned to the scene under Sadat and in the absence of other viable political alternatives grew quickly to become a mass organisation.[12] Although illegal, it has been permitted to engage in electoral activity by standing "independent" candidates known to be Brotherhood supporters. At the same time it has played by Mubarak's rules, instructing its many members not to organise collective public activity. This has not prevented successive waves of repression in which thousands of Brothers have been seized and imprisoned. In recent years

---

8:   In Hussein, Al-Said and Al-Sayyid, 1999, p77.

9:   In Hussein, Al-Said and Al-Sayyid, 1999, p77.

10: Howeidy, 2010.

11: Conversation with a leading Brotherhood activist, Cairo, January 2011.

12: For an insightful analysis of the contradictory character of the Brotherhood, see Naguib, 2009.

Mubarak has humiliated the organisation by incarcerating its most esteemed elderly leaders: still the organisation did not respond with public initiatives.

In the face of "zero tolerance" on the part of the state the organisation has retreated more and more rapidly from the political arena,[13] so that a recent analysis suggested that it was "beset by confusion and political decline...gripped by a structural and ideological crisis which has erupted into unprecedented internal disputes".[14] In 2009 a conservative group seized the leadership of the organisation: the position of the new general guide of the Brotherhood, Mohamed Badei, was described as "renunciation of violence, gradual reform, non-confrontation with the regime and other familiar stances".[15] The cost of internal conflict and public retreat has been considerable: a younger generation of supporters has been alienated from the organisation, which was conspicuous by its absence from the streets when the mass movement began its confrontation with Mubarak. It was only after days of protest that rank and file members joined the demonstrations, eventually playing a key role in resistance to the police and the thugs. These tensions are evident in factional debates currently running strongly within the organisation.

Torture and abuse

For the last 20 years Mubarak has offered few inducements to the opposition. The general crisis of political representation has become more acute; meanwhile the regime has intensified repression. In 1991 Human Rights Watch produced an extensive report on torture and detention. *Behind Closed Doors* noted that security dragnets had been cast so wide that all manner of people were detained, abused and tortured for information they did not possess.[16] The following year repression was stepped up when police and troops entered the Cairo district of Imbaba to assault radical Islamist currents which had built up large constituencies of support in the city's poorest districts.[17] The Egyptian Organisation for Human Rights recorded police sweeps followed by collective punishment of hundreds of local residents.[18] Similar assaults followed in cities of the south in which the Islamists had also

---

13: Howeidy, 2010.
14: El-Enani, 2010.
15: El-Enani, 2010.
16: Human Rights Watch, 1992, p128.
17: The targets were members of the underground organisations Islamic Jihad and *Gama'at Islamiyya* (Islamic Associations) that rejected the Brotherhood's accommodation with the regime.
18: Report of the Egyptian Organisation for Human Rights quoted by Lorenz 1993.

made gains, and in rural areas in which police and troops razed fields and villages to locate activists. Torture became common in police stations across the country. Gasser Abdel-Razek of Human Rights Watch later observed that serious forms of abuse became standard techniques of interrogation. "It became a culture," he says. "We have two generations of police who were brought up to use torture against Islamists. But if it's allowed and seen as effective, it spreads".[19] Since the 1990s torture has become an everyday practice of the police and security agencies in every area of Egypt.

In 2003 lawyers and human rights activists formed the Egyptian Association Against Torture (EAAT). They maintained that abuse had become "an oppressive policy that is adopted by the ministry of the interior and security bodies and authorities, an organised, systematic and ongoing policy used against citizens to ensure complete submission of the people".[20] Millions of Egyptians had been abused, or knew of family, friends or workmates who had been tortured: hence the success in recent years of campaigns launched by social networking sites to expose particularly notorious cases. This is the background to attacks by police and plainclothes gangs in and around downtown Cairo in early February 2011—and part of the explanation for the fightback by demonstrators. The police and security agencies not only represented *al-nizam* (the order/the system) but a sinister and cruel presence in many people's lives. The prospect of losing the Battle of Tahrir to police charged with a new campaign of revenge was unthinkable—hence the ferocious resistance and ultimately the crucial victory of Tahrir. This has been followed by numerous mass attacks on offices of state security across the country, in which demonstrators have seized police files and searched cells to find torture equipment and in the hope of releasing prisoners.

Neoliberalism
The mass movement has called for Egypt's rulers to be held to account for corruption and theft. Mubarak is widely rumoured to have seized scores of billions of dollars: even the American media notes estimates of an illicit fortune of $40 billion to $70 billion.[21] The former president is often seen as the architect of an Egyptian version of "crony capitalism"—a term favoured by neoliberal economists and global financial institutions which maintain that there are "clean" means of doing business which separate healthy

---

19: Murphy, 2007.
20: EAAT, 2003.
21: Raghavan, 2011; see also *The Week*, 2011.

private enterprise from the interests of the state. During the Asian financial crisis of the late 1990s, International Monetary Fund (IMF) managing director Michel Camdessus used the term widely to suggest that illicit relations between business people and state officials amounted to corruption and brought local and eventually global economic instability.[22] In fact, as Noam Chomsky observes, the history of capitalism is one of intimate relations between entrepreneurs and the state.[23] He observes that, from the very earliest phases of modern commercial and industrial enterprise, "merchants and manufacturers are the principal architects of government policy and they make sure their own interests are well cared for, however grievous the effects on others".[24] In the case of the independent Egyptian state, Nasser and the Free Officers Movement relegated private capital to a subordinate role throughout the 1950s and 1960s; business survived, however, and was able to use the state itself as means of advancing specific private interests.

The 1952 coup, which brought Nasser to power, was an outcome of sustained struggles against British occupation and monarchical rule. In a period of revolutionary possibilities it was also an example of revolution "deflected"—of the intervention of a radical nationalist current which used the armed forces to implement specific reforms but which also sought to control and ultimately to demobilise the mass movement.[25] Nasser and his colleagues were petty bourgeois professionals hostile to colonialism and at the same time to the mass movement itself. Their first decisive action was to suppress strikes and to order the execution of worker militants.[26] They also inveighed against peasant activism and put down efforts by *fellaheen* (peasants) to seize the lands of the great estates; instead they introduced a closely managed reform, a significant development but one which disappointed those who had struggled for years for direct access to the land.[27] The officers were initially sympathetic to the West and strongly attracted by the possibility of alliances with Europe and the United States. It was only when rebuffed by the latter, and still under strong pressure from below, that

22: See, for example, his address of 1998, describing "crony capitalism" as the outcome of situations in which "the structure of ownership is not transparent, when regulation is inadequate and unevenly applied, when too many ad hoc decisions are taken, and when market forces are prevented from playing their normal disciplining role [and] serious imbalances and deadly inefficiencies can build up"—Camdessus, 1998.

23: Chomsky, 2008.

24: Chomsky, 2008.

25: For a terse account of key developments during this period see Marfleet, 2009.

26: Mustafa Khamis and Muhammed Hassan al-Baqari were executed in August 1952 for allegedly inciting riots at the Misr Textile Company in Kafr Al-Dawwar.

27: See Bush, 2009; also Abdel-Fadil, 1975, 1980; Baker, 1978.

they adopted strategies which brought conflict with Britain over the Suez Canal and ultimately a new alignment with the Soviet Union.

The Suez episode of 1956 projected Nasser to leadership of the anti-colonial movement across the Middle East. He became the focus of radical sentiment in general and especially of pan-Arabism and of Palestinian hopes to confront Israel. Over the course of the next decade he nationalised most foreign capital and laid the basis for a welfare state in which education and health services were to be provided universally and food security was to be guaranteed. State control over the economy would, Nasser believed, build up a strong independent capitalism in Egypt. He did not suppress private capital, however. Many small businesses survived, together with powerful landed interests, which Nasser encouraged during the late 1960s as the economy became increasingly unstable. The new military elite and senior officials of the bureaucracy cohabited with private capital, so that Egypt's state capitalism was a hybrid formation in which, Malak Zaalouk observes, private capital found a place *within* the "state bourgeoisie".[28]

This was the basis for developments under Sadat, who in 1974 set about dismantling the Nasser state. His *infitah* (opening) encouraged private investment, welcomed foreign capital and reoriented Egypt from Moscow towards Washington and the market model. Building on foundations provided by private landed and commercial interests, a new network of traders, commission agents and property speculators grew rapidly—the "fat cats" of the late 1970s whose greed and conspicuous consumption infuriated many Egyptians. When Mubarak took office in 1981 he embraced this strategy and gradually increased the pace of change. Egypt was now firmly aligned with the US and with neoliberal economists whose views dominated the World Bank and the IMF, to which Mubarak repeatedly applied for loans. *Infitah* was moving too slowly for these institutions, which demanded rapid reduction of food subsidies and tariff barriers, and wholesale privatisations of state enterprise. Mubarak soon adopted their agenda, implementing the Economic Reform and Structural Adjustment Programme (Ersap) of 1991. Like Mexico, in the grip of change dictated by the North American Free Trade Agreement (Nafta), Egypt now became a laboratory for high-speed marketisation. The government prepared to sell state-owned industries and to "de-sequester" the land–to reverse Nasser's reforms by returning to landowners of the colonial era (or their families) millions of hectares that for 50 years had been cultivated by *fellaheen*. In return Mubarak obtained new loans and the Paris Club of international creditors reduced Egypt's debts by almost £30 billion.

28: Zaalouk, 1989, p41.

Clement Henry and Robert Springborg comment that by the mid-1990s Egypt was being governed by "a nexus of cronies, officers, bureaucrats and public sector managers".[29] It was difficult to discriminate between these categories. Egyptian state capitalism had long been incubating a private sector that extended into many branches of public activity. Senior state officials were already active in property, commerce and agriculture; now they advanced into industry, striking deals with incoming foreign companies for whom their influence proved invaluable. The whole process was observed closely by US, World Bank and IMF officials committed to the twin principles of demolishing the remains of the developmental state inherited from Nasser and "opening" Egypt to the world market. If Mubarak's associates were "cronies" they were at the very heart of the neoliberal project.

Inequality

At the same time Mubarak worked consistently to consolidate the central apparatus inherited from the Nasser state. He received huge sums of economic aid and foreign military assistance from the US: between 1977 and 2007 this averaged $2.1 billion a year—only Israel received more.[30] Much was spent on relatively advanced American weaponry for forces that did not engage in any actions initiated by the Egyptian state against foreign powers (Egyptian troops put in brief appearances in support of the US in the Gulf War of 1991). The uniformed establishment—the armed forces and paramilitary police—was increased to some one million men (not including civil police and security agencies).[31] Officers were indulged with all manner of special benefits: subsidised housing on modern estates, enhanced pensions, and access to dedicated social clubs and purpose-built seaside resorts. They were integral to the security of the regime, now also faced by contradictions that arose from Mubarak's success in securing vast wealth for an inner network of supporters and in supervising a historic increase in general social inequality.

Even the World Bank noted the changes: by 2005, it said, the proportion of Egyptians living in "moderate poverty" had increased significantly to a fifth of the population, some 15 million people.[32] Others who applauded the regime's commitment to neoliberalism entered anxious reservations about the consequences: the *Economist* identified a sharp increase in inequality, describing

29: Henry and Springborg, 2001, p 155.
30: Sharp, 2009, pp27-29.
31: Combined figure for the Army, Air Force, Navy and Central Security—IISS, 2007, p223.
32: World Bank, 2007. This conservative figure fails to measure real levels of deprivation and the increasing pace of immiseration. See El-Naggar, 2009.

the *nouveaux riches* as "new pharaohs" whose ostentation disturbed society at large.[33] From the late 1990s there was a huge property boom, "hot" money flooding into Egypt from the Gulf states to finance new estates for the wealthy, built largely on Cairo's desert fringe, and including gated communities, shopping malls, hypermarkets, multiplex cinemas and new private universities. Gated reservations reflected the California-style aspirations of new money and its global connections: Lakeside, Dreamland, Utopia and the rest were zones of affluence guarded by private security companies and ultimately by peasants and urban poor conscripted into the *Amn al-Markazi*. Built on state land sold at knock-down prices to property tycoons like Ahmed Bahgat (builder of Dreamland), they were provided with expressway connections to country clubs and coastal resorts which allowed the rich to bypass the inner city and the sprawling outer areas of Cairo and Alexandria, teeming with people living precariously at the margins of survival and increasingly bitter at a regime that now flaunted privilege.

From 2000 the civil police and riot police became increasingly active against new forms of collective protest. These began with widespread actions in support of the Palestinian *intifada*. Rabab El-Mahdi describes the development of "cycles of protest" which took those involved into new territory—more and more adventurous public activities which proved difficult for the state to contain.[34] In 2003 there was a massive mobilisation in Cairo against the US/British invasion of Iraq, demonstrators occupying the centre of the city in a "Tahrir *intifada*" that was to be a dress rehearsal for 2011. Gaining confidence, the following year activists initiated a series of campaigns for democratic change, organising rallies, lobbies, marches and "flash mob" protests facilitated by email networks and social networking sites. Caught unawares, the police were often absent, so that for the first time in almost 60 years extended anti-regime protests took place without harassment. Although numbers were small there was a steady growth of confidence, reflected in workplace struggles which also now emerged across all sectors of industry. In 2005 there were 202 collective labour actions; in 2006 the number rose to 222; and in 2007 to 614.[35] These included mass action at the Mahalla al-Kubra textile mill–the most important sustained strike for over 20 years, which won key concessions and acted as a green light for numerous other groups of workers. Anxious about generalising the movement, the regime hesitated to engage strikers

33: *Economist*, 2005.
34: El Mahdi, 2009.
35: Figures from the Land Centre for Human Rights, quoted in Beinin, 2009, p79.

frontally. Ministers made their usual threats but combined these with concessions and often stood off workplaces in dispute, hoping to exhaust those involved. Emboldened, other groups engaged in all manner of protests: for student rights on campus, over shortages of bread and water, against land seizures, in response to housing disasters (following numerous incidents of collapsed buildings) and against police brutality.

There was an organic growth of confidence in self-activity across society. This came as the world economic crisis was having its inevitable impacts: unemployment in Egypt rose and the prices of food and fuel rocketed. For the first time since the 1970s there were acute shortages of flour and tragic scenes in which people fighting for access to bread died in conflicts at street bakeries. The regime continued as before: hesitating over industrial struggles it nonetheless attacked democracy activists, community protesters, journalists and bloggers with renewed savagery. In the parliamentary elections of November 2010 it hardly bothered to conceal the scale of fraud and ballot-rigging. In January 2011 the Tunisian Revolution expelled Ben Ali: the dam finally broke as diverse sectors of Egyptian society unified, a mass of struggles becoming one.

Act two

The first phase of the revolution was made by a popular movement of youth, students, workers and the poor. For the first time in their lives the mass of the people experienced collective power and the means to use it for general betterment. This will not be surrendered lightly; at the same time it will need to be fought for. Egyptians removed a dictator; most now wish to remove the dictatorship. There are universal demands for an end to Emergency Law, for democratic reforms including rights to association and the creation of political parties, free elections and an end to abuse by the agencies of the state.

Notionally the armed forces hold power. At the time of writing they have not confronted the movement that removed the president. Nor, however, have they acceded to mass demands, including abandonment of the Emergency Law. Numerous groups and individuals are positioning themselves for struggles to come. A cabinet of Mubarak's men plus figures from the legal opposition, including the general secretary of the tame Wafd Party, is in formation. Among those hoping for preferment are members of a self-appointed Council of Wise Men—academics, lawyers and businessman who wish to establish a liberal capitalist alternative to the Mubarak model. This includes Ahmed Bahgat of Dreamland (also owner of the influential Dream television channel) and Naguib Sawiris, telecom billionaire and one of the wealthiest men in the Middle East, now claiming to have been appalled by the regime's corruption all along. Capitalists with a conscience should have no fear of investigations over corruption, says Sawiris: "The only ones [sic] who have done wrong should worry... Someone like me definitely has no grounds to worry... If my country needs my help in any way, I provide it".[36]

His optimism may be misplaced. A process of purging and cleansing is under way across the country, already claiming senior figures such as Adly, Cairo police chiefs involved in the *baltagiyya* offensive, and local officials arrested by the army. Numerous workforces have demanded removal of oppressive managers and officials of the state trade unions, the investigation of owners who have profited from privatisation deals, and re-nationalisation of former state enterprises. In mid-February a group of 40 strike leaders from a range of industries met to coordinate demands and to launch an independent trade union movement. Under the slogan "Revolution, freedom, social justice", they presented a "workers' programme":

> to unite the demands of striking workers that they may become an integral part of the goals of our revolution, which the people of Egypt made, and for which the martyrs shed their blood...which brings together our just demands, in order to reaffirm the social aspect of this revolution and to prevent the revolution being taken away from those at its base who should be its beneficiaries.[37]

The effectiveness of their campaign will be crucial to the revolutionary process. As Egypt's Revolutionary Socialists argued in their own statement of 6 February 2011: "The demonstrations and protests have played a key role... Now we need the workers".[38] The organisation called for the formation of revolutionary councils which combine economic and political demands.

Revolutions are invariably complex and lengthy processes. In the case of Iran, with which there are some striking similarities, protests which began in 1976 only took their full effect three years later with the fall of the Pahlavi regime. There were numerous episodes of advance and retreat of the students' movement, the petty bourgeoisie of the *bazaar*, the clerical establishment, the national minorities and the peasantry, before sustained mass strikes expelled the shah. These struggles threw up a host of forms of social organisation including local committees and workplace groups,

---

36: Stier, 2011.
37: Full statement in Appendix 1.
38: Full statement in Appendix 2.

some taking on a proto-Soviet character before they were dispersed by the Ayatollah Khomeini's offensive. There will be similar episodes in Egypt, as a movement initially animated by democratic demands addresses the possibility of further radical change—a generalisation of struggle that addresses the inequalities of the Mubarak era, the ownership of societal resources including industry and the land, and the problem of power wielded by the state itself. The entry of the workers gives cause to believe that the Egyptian Revolution is indeed "growing over" into a movement for wider and historic change—that a process of permanent revolution with global implications is under way.

Appendix 1
Statement of independent trade unionists meeting in Cairo, 19 February 2011

Revolution—Freedom—Social Justice:
Demands of the workers in the revolution
O heroes of the 25 January revolution! We, workers and trade unionists from different workplaces which have seen strikes, occupations and demonstrations by hundreds of thousands of workers across Egypt during the current period, feel it is right to unite the demands of striking workers that they may become an integral part of the goals of our revolution, which the people of Egypt made, and for which the martyrs shed their blood. We present to you a workers' programme which brings together our just demands, in order to reaffirm the social aspect of this revolution and to prevent the revolution being taken away from those at its base who should be its beneficiaries.

The workers' demands which we raised before the 25 January revolution and were part of the prelude to this glorious revolution are:

1. Raising the national minimum wage and pension, and a narrowing of the gap between minimum and maximum wages so that the maximum is no more than 15 times the minimum in order to achieve the principle of social justice which the revolution gave birth to; payment of unemployment benefit, and a regular increment which will increase with rising prices.

2. The freedom to organise independent trade unions without conditions or restrictions, and the protection of trade unions and their leaders.

3. The right of manual workers and clerical workers, peasant farmers and professionals, to job security and protection from dismissal. Temporary workers must be made permanent, and dismissed workers be returned to their jobs. We must do away with all excuses for employing workers on temporary contracts.

4. Renationalisation of all privatised enterprises and a complete stop to the infamous privatisation programme which wrecked our national economy under the defunct regime.

5. Complete removal of corrupt managers who were imposed on companies in order to run them down and sell them off. Curbing the employment of consultants who are past the age of retirement and who eat up 3 billion of the national income, in order to open up employment opportunities for the young. Return to the enforcement of price controls on goods and services in order to keep prices down and not to burden the poor.

6. The right of Egyptian workers to strike, organise sit-ins, and demonstrate peacefully, including those striking now against the remnants of the failed regime, those who were imposed on their companies in order to run them down prior to a sell-off. It is our opinion that if this revolution does not lead to the fair distribution of wealth it is not worth anything. Freedoms are not complete without social freedoms. The right to vote is naturally dependent on the right to a loaf of bread.

7. Health care is a necessary condition for increasing production.

8. Dissolution of the Egyptian Trade Union Federation which was one of the most important symbols of corruption under the defunct regime. Execution of the legal judgements issued against it and seizure of its financial assets and documents. Seizure of the assets of the leaders of the ETUF and its member unions, and their investigation.

Translated from the Arabic by Anne Alexander

Appendix 2
Statement of the Revolutionary Socialists Egypt, Cairo, 6 February 2011

Glory to the martyrs! Victory to the revolution!

What is happening today is the largest popular revolution in the history of our country and of the entire Arab world. The sacrifice of our martyrs has built our revolution and we have broken through all the barriers of fear. We will not back down until the criminal "leaders" and their criminal system are destroyed.

Mubarak's departure is the first step, not the last step of the revolution

The handover of power to a dictatorship under Omar Suleiman, Ahmed Shafiq and other cronies of Mubarak is the continuation of the same system. Omar Suleiman is a friend of Israel and America, spends most of his time between Washington and Tel Aviv and is a servant who is faithful to their interests. Ahmed Shafik is a close friend of Mubarak and his colleague in the tyranny, oppression and plunder imposed on the Egyptian people.

The country's wealth belongs to the people and must return to them

Over the past three decades this tyrannical regime corrupted [sic] the country's largest estates to a small handful of business leaders and foreign companies. 100 families own more than 90 percent of the country's wealth. They monopolise the wealth of the Egyptian people through policies of privatization, looting of power and the alliance with capital. They have turned the majority of the Egyptian people to the poor, landless and unemployed.

Factories wrecked and sold dirt cheap must go back to the people

We want the nationalisation of companies, land and property looted by this bunch. As long as our resources remain in their hands we will not be able to completely get rid of this system. Economic slavery is the other face of political tyranny. We will not be able to cope with unemployment and achieve a fair minimum wage for a decent living without restoring the wealth of the people from this gang.

We will not accept to be guard dogs of America and Israel

This system does not stand alone. Mubarak as a dictator was a servant and client directly acting for the sake of the interests of America and Israel.

Egypt acted as a colony of America, participated directly in the siege of the Palestinian people, made the Suez Canal and Egyptian airspace free zones for warships and fighter jets that destroyed and killed the Iraqi people and sold gas to Israel, dirt cheap, while stifling the Egyptian people by soaring prices. Revolution must restore Egypt's independence, dignity and leadership in the region.

The revolution is a popular revolution

This is not a revolution of the elite, political parties or religious groups. Egypt's youth, students, workers and the poor are the owners of this revolution. In recent days a lot of elites, parties and so-called symbols have begun trying to ride the wave of revolution and hijack it from their rightful owners. The only symbols are the martyrs of our revolution and our young people who have been steadfast in the field. We will not allow them to take control of our revolution and claim that they represent us. We will choose to represent ourselves and represent the martyrs who were killed and their blood paid the price for the salvation of the system.

A people's army is the army that protects the revolution

Everyone asks: "Is the army with the people or against them?" The army is not a single bloc. The interests of soldiers and junior officers are the same as the interests of the masses. But the senior officers are Mubarak's men, chosen carefully to protect his regime of corruption, wealth and tyranny. It is an integral part of the system.

This army is no longer the people's army. This army is not the one which defeated the Zionist enemy in October 1973. This army is closely associated with America and Israel. Its role is to protect Israel, not the people. Yes, we want to win the soldiers for the revolution. But we must not be fooled by slogans that 'the army is on our side'. The army will either suppress the demonstrations directly, or restructure the police to play this role.

Form revolutionary councils urgently

This revolution has surpassed our greatest expectations. Nobody expected to see these numbers. Nobody expected that Egyptians would be this brave in the face of the police. Nobody can say that we did not force the dictator to retreat. Nobody can say that a transformation did not happen in Middan el Tahrir.

What we need right now is to push for the socio-economic demands as part of our demands, so that the person sitting in his home knows that we are fighting for their rights. We need to organise ourselves into popular committees which elect their higher councils democratically, and from below. These councils must form a higher council which includes delegates of all the tendencies. We must elect a higher council of people who represent us, and in whom we trust. We call for the formation of popular councils in Middan Tahrir, and in all the cities of Egypt.

Call to Egyptian workers to join the ranks of the revolution

The demonstrations and protests have played a key role in igniting and continuing our revolution. Now we need the workers. They can seal the fate of the regime, not only by participating in the demonstrations, but by organising a general strike in all the vital industries and large corporations.

The regime can afford to wait out the sit-ins and demonstrations for days and weeks, but it cannot last beyond a few hours if workers use strikes as a weapon. Strike on the railways, on public transport, the airports and large industrial companies! Egyptian workers! On behalf of the rebellious youth, and on behalf of the blood of our martyrs, join the ranks of the revolution, use your power and victory will be ours!

Glory to the martyrs! Down with the system! All power to the people! Victory to the revolution!

References
Abdel-Fadil, Mahmoud, 1975, *Development, Income Distribution and Social Change in Rural Egypt 1952–1970: A Study in the Political Economy of Agrarian Transition* (Cambridge University Press)

Abdel-Fadil, Mahmoud, 1980, *The Political Economy of Nasserism* (Cambridge University Press).

Afify, H, 2011, "Egyptian man attempts suicide amid pro-police gathering", *Al-Masry al-Youm* (24 January), www.almasryalyoum.com/en/node/304791

Baker, Raymond William, 1978, *Egypt's Uncertain Revolution Under Nasser and Sadat* (Harvard University Press).

Beinin, Joel, 2009, "Workers' Struggles", in Rabab El Mahdi and Philip Marfleet (eds), 2009, *Egypt—the Moment of Change* (Zed).

Bush, Ray, 2009, "The Land and the People", Rabab El Mahdi and Philip Marfleet (eds), *Egypt—the Moment of Change* (Zed).

Camdessus, Michel, 1998, "Challenges Facing the Transition Economies of Central Asia", (May 27), www.imf.org/external/np/speeches/1998/052798.HTM

Chomsky, Noam, 2008, "'Black Faces in Limousines': A Conversation with Noam Chomsky", www.chomsky.info/interviews/20081114.htm

EAAT [Egyptian Association Against Torture], 2003, statement, www.aloufok.net/article.php3?id_article=484

Economist, 2005, "The New Pharaohs" (10 March), www.economist.com/node/17460568

El-Anani, Khalil, 2010, "When the Alternative is Not So Different After All", *Ahram Weekly* (28 January), http://weekly.ahram.org.eg/2010/983/op32.htm

El-Mahdi, Rabab, 2009, "The Democracy Movement", in Rabab El Mahdi and Philip Marfleet (eds), *Egypt—the Moment of Change* (Zed).

El- Naggar, A, 2009, "Economic Policy: From State Control to Decay and Corruption", in Rabab El Mahdi and Philip Marfleet (eds), *Egypt—the Moment of Change* (Zed).

Fisk, Robert, 2011, "Blood and Fear in Cairo's Streets as Mubarak's Men Crack Down on Protests", *Independent* (3 February), www.independent.co.uk/opinion/commentators/fisk/robert-fisk-blood-and-fear-in-cairos-streets-as-mubaraks-men-crack-down-on-protests-2202657.html

Henry, Clement, and Robert Springborg, 2001, *Globalisation and the Politics of Development in the Middle East* (Cambridge University Press).

Howeidy, Amira, 2010, "The Brotherhood's Zero", *Ahram Weekly* (2-8 December).

Human Rights Watch, 1992, *Behind Closed Doors* (Human Rights Watch).

Hussein, A, R al-Said and M al-Sayyid, 1999, "Twenty Years of Multipartyism in Egypt", in Mark Kennedy (ed), *Twenty Years of Development in Egypt* (The American University in Cairo Press).

International Institute for Strategic Studies (IISS), 2007, *The Military Balance 2007* (IISS).

Kassem, Maye, 2004, *Egyptian Politics: the Dynamics of Authoritarian Rule* (Lynne Reiner).

Lorenz, Andrea, 1993, "Egyptian human Rights Organisation Documents Abuses", Washington Report on Middle Eastern Affairs (June), http://amedtrust.org/backissues/0693/9306062.htm

Marfleet, Philip, 2009, "State and Society", in Rabab El Mahdi and Philip Marfleet (eds), *Egypt—the Moment of Change* (Zed).

Murphy, Dan, 2007 "As Egypt Cracks Down, Charges of Wide Abuse", *Christian Science Monitor* (10 October), www.csmonitor.com/2007/1010/p01s02-wome.html

Naguib, Sameh, 2009, "Islamisms Old and New", in Rabab El Mahdi and Philip Marfleet (eds), *Egypt—the Moment of Change* (Zed).

Raghavan, Sudarsan, 2011, "Egyptians Focus Their Attention on Recovering the Nation's Money", *Washington Post* (February 13).

Seif El Dawla, Aida, 2009, "Torture: a State Policy", in Rabab El Mahdi and Philip Marfleet (eds), *Egypt—the Moment of Change* (Zed).

Sharp, Jeremy, 2009, *Egypt-US Relations,* Brief for Congress (Congressional Research Service).

Stier, Ken, 2011, "What an Egyptian Billionaire Thinks of the New Order", *Time* (18 February), www.time.com/time/world/article/0,8599,2052116,00.html

The Week, 2011, "Hosni Mubarak's 'Stolen' $70 billion Fortune" (14 February), http://theweek.com/article/index/212105/hosni-mubaraks-stolen-70-billion-fortune

World Bank, 2007, *World Bank Country Brief: Egypt* (October), http://siteresources.worldbank.org/INTEGYPT/Resources/EGYPT-ENG2007AM.pdf

Zaalouk, Malak, 1989, *Power, Class and Foreign Capital in Egypt: the Rise of the New Bourgeoisie* (Zed).

Social media and social movements
Jonny Jones

The past few months have seen an explosion of debate, blogging, theorising and hype around the role of the Internet in today's social movements.[1] Social media—Internet applications such as Facebook, Twitter and YouTube which facilitate the creation and exchange of user-created content—have been identified as key to events as diverse as the rise of student protests in Britain at the end of 2010 and the outbreak of revolution in the Arab world.

Recent years have seen a surge of interest in appropriating new technologies for various causes. For boosters of globalisation like Thomas Friedman, the Internet was making the world a smaller place in which democracy and the market was certain to flourish. The Nobel-winning economist Paul Krugman summarised Friedman's attitude in a review of his book, *The Lexus and the Olive Tree,* saying: "We are heading for a world that is basically democratic, because you can't keep 'em down on the farm once they have Internet access".[2] Gordon Brown seized upon the communicative potential of the Internet as something that would rehabilitate the doctrine of humanitarian intervention, telling the *Guardian* in 2009: "You cannot have Rwanda again because information would come out far more

---

1:    Thanks to Robin Burrett and Dan Meyer for their input into this article. Throughout the piece I will refer to online sites, neworks and practices that may be unfamiliar to people who don't use social media but which would take up too much space to explain each and every one. If you come across one you don't understand, you can go here for answers: www.google.co.uk

2:    Krugman, 1999.

quickly about what is actually going on and the public opinion would grow to the point where action would need to be taken".[3]

The Wikileaks affair highlighted some of the problems ruling classes may face given the rise of the Internet. Wikileaks, an organisation dedicated to the release of classified documents, first came to attention when it released leaked footage of a massacre in Iraq perpetrated by US forces, in which journalists and civilians were killed.[4] In late 2010 tens of thousands of leaked US diplomatic cables shed light on the inner workings of the US State Department, sparking an international manhunt for Wikileaks founder Julian Assange.[5]

Debates about the role of the Internet in political mobilisation became increasingly polarised in the wake of the online element of Barak Obama's presidential election campaign in 2008 and the supposed "Twitter rebellion" in Iran in 2009. Increasingly, the proponents of new technologies were labelled "cyber utopians", arguing against the dinosaurs that still held to outmoded forms of organisation.[6]

In Britain the emergence of the student movement saw a proliferation of online campaigning in order to mobilise for street protests. Alongside this came a renewed preoccupation with the notion of "networks" when discussing political organisation. Writing in the *Guardian*, the journalist and activist Laurie Penny claimed that "old politics" were increasingly irrelevant:

> The young people of Britain do not need leaders, and the new wave of activists has no interest in the ideological bureaucracy of the old left. Their energy and creativity is disseminated via networks rather than organisations, and many young people have neither the time nor the inclination to wait for any political party to decide what direction they should take.

Laurie was incredulous that newspapers like *Socialist Worker* were "still being peddled at every demonstration to young cyber-activists for whom the very concept of a newspaper is almost as outdated as the notion of ideological unity as a basis for action".[7] Within a month of this article being published, the fall of Ben Ali in Tunisia and the outbreak of the Egyptian Revolution saw acres of newsprint (and server space) turned over to discussions about

---

3:   Viner, 2009.
4:   www.collateralmurder.com
5:   Davies, 2010.
6:   "Cyber-utopian" is a phrase used by Evgeny Morozov to describe those who uncritically accept the democratising nature of the Internet. See Morozov, 2010.
7:   Penny, 2010a.

how social media had sparked the return of revolution: a Google search for "Twitter Revolution" in early March 2011 turns up 203,000 results.[8]

It is, of course, unsurprising that there has been so much debate about these issues. Social media themselves engender and enable vast quantities of both amateur and professional blogging, "citizen journalism" and the like. The danger for those engaged in these debates is that they can disappear into the "data smog", that they can lose touch with the actual effects of these new technologies on people's everyday lives. To try to understand these effects, we have to grasp the changing nature of the Internet and the arguments about its application to social movements that have accompanied these changes.

"Technology is the answer, but what is the question?"

The past decade has seen an explosion in access to the Internet. The website Internet World Stats, which aggregates information from a variety of regional providers, estimates that between 2000 and 2010 the number of people with access to the Internet grew by 448.8 percent, from 360,985,492 to 1,966,514,816. This represents 28.7 percent of the world's population.[9] The most rapid areas of growth (admittedly from a low starting point, have been in Africa, where 10.9 percent now have Internet access (from 4,514,400 to 110,931,700, an increase of 2,357.3 percent) and the Middle East, where Internet access now stands at 29.8 percent of the population (from 3,284,800 to 63,240,946, an increase of 1,825.3 percent). At around 420 million, there are more Internet users in China than there are people living in the entire US.[10]

The growth of social media is equally impressive. The social networking site Facebook grew from 150 million users in January 2009 to over 500 million today. In March, Facebook announced it had reached 30 million registered users in Britain: around half the population.[11]

Claims for the radical possibilities offered by the Internet predate such expansion of the Internet and the development of social media. In 1996 an organisation called the Citizens Internet Empowerment Coalition (CIEC) was formed to campaign against sections of the US government's Communications Decency Act (CDA). The CIEC described itself as "a broad coalition of library

---

8:   Among the most ridiculous of this *oeuvre* of article was Thomas Friedman's "This is Just the Start" from the *New York Times*, which suggests that factors contributing to the revolutions included Google Earth, the example of Israeli justice and the Beijing Olympics—Friedman, 2011.

9:   www.Internetworldstats.com/stats.htm

10:   www.Internetworldstats.com/stats3.htm

11:   Barnett, 2011.

and civil liberties groups, online service providers, newspaper, book, magazine and recording industry associations, and over 56,000 individual Internet users [that] represents the entire breadth of the Internet community".[12]

The CDA was intended to impose broadcast industry-style regulations on the Internet, ostensibly with the aim of protecting children, which would have made it an offence to post "offensive" or "patently indecent" material in public forums online. However, the CIEC claimed that such regulations would mean posting text from novels such as *The Catcher in the Rye* and *Ulysses* (containing foul language) could be considered illegal. Moreover, they claimed that the CDA would endanger the Internet itself due to its "open, decentralised" nature.

In their appeal against the US Department of Justice, published as a call to action by the Internet magazine (and co-plaintiff) *Wired,* the CIEC argued that:

> during much of this century the mass media, particularly radio and television, have been characterised by a limited number of speakers transmitting programming and information to essentially passive audiences. The communications medium of the 21st century—the Internet and "cyberspace" generally—is changing that, and will allow hundreds of millions of individuals to engage in interactive communication, on a national and global scale never before possible. The public square of the past—with pamphleteering, soap boxes, and vigorous debate—is being replaced by the Internet, which enables average citizens to participate in national discourse, publish a newspaper, distribute an electronic pamphlet to the world, and generally communicate to and with a broader audience than ever before possible. It also enables average citizens to gain access to a vast and literally worldwide range of information.[13]

The Supreme Court eventually found the CDA unconstitutional, an early and important victory for online campaigning. The claims made for the Internet by the CIEC—that it would replace "the public square" as the arena for political debate—proved premature. Instead for years the Internet became synonymous with pornography, downloading music and the bursting of the dot.com bubble. But for some, this was transformed by the advent of what is known as Web 2.0.

12: www.ciec.org/more_background.shtml
13: CIEC, 1996. The subsequent line of the complaint failed to foresee the development of the ubiquitous "spam" email, stating: "while simultaneously protecting their privacy, because in this new medium individuals receive only the communications they affirmatively request".

The communications theorist Joss Hands defines Web 2.0 as:

a by now ubiquitous term that loosely refers to the proliferation of user-created content and websites specifically built as frameworks for the sharing of information and for social networking, and platforms for self-expression such as the weblog, or using video and audio sharing.[14]

Hands identifies 2006 as the year that Web 2.0 and social media made their breakthrough into the mass media, marked by *Time* magazine's decision to make "You" the Person of the Year, even going so far as having a reflective cover. Inside, Lev Grossman's article posited itself as an antidote to the "Great Man" theory of history, insisting that 2006 was:

a story about community and collaboration on a scale never seen before. It's about the cosmic compendium of knowledge Wikipedia and the million-channel people's network YouTube and the online metropolis MySpace. It's about the many wresting power from the few and helping one another for nothing and how that will not only change the world, but also change the way the world changes.[15]

Grossman argued that unlike the "overhyped dotcom Web of the late 90s…it's a tool for bringing together the small contributions of millions of people and making them matter". While the term 2.0 implied an upgrade, "it's really a revolution…an opportunity to build a new kind of international understanding, not politician to politician, great man to great man, but citizen to citizen, person to person".[16]

For Hands, "the digital, networked age is one that can be, and is, amenable to…horizontal, communicative action, and lends itself to a horizon of dissent, resistance and rebellion".[17]

It wasn't just in the realm of "people power" that Web 2.0 was to make its impact. James K Glassman, a former US state department official, told a conference organised by Facebook and Google, among others, that the social media would give the US an advantage in the "war on terror": "Some time ago, I said that Al Qaida was 'eating our lunch on the Internet'.

14: Hands, 2011, p79. Hands's book, while basing its political analysis firmly in the autonomist camp and inspired by John Holloway, Michael Hardt and Toni Negri, is a densely researched and useful guide to various forms of online activism.
15: Grossman, 2006.
16: Grossman, 2006.
17: Hands, 2011, p18.

That is no longer the case. Al Qaida is stuck in Web 1.0. The Internet is now about interactivity and conversation".[18]

What lay behind the hype? Could social media really play the kind of role that the new media boosters were hoping for? For some, the claims made for Web 2.0 were more than just hype: they represented a barrier to practical activity. Instead they represented a shortcut into "slacktivism", defined by Evgeny Morozov as "feel-good online activism that has zero political or social impact. It gives those who participate in 'slacktivist' campaigns an illusion of having a meaningful impact on the world without demanding anything more than joining a Facebook group".[19] Morozov, a specialist in social media who aims to provide advice to policymakers on spreading democracy, sees slacktivism as "the ideal type of activism for a lazy generation: why bother with sit-ins and the risk of arrest, police brutality, or torture if one can be as loud campaigning in the virtual space ?"

Jodi Dean argues that often people can "believe they are active, maybe even making a difference simply by clicking on a button, adding their name to a petition, or commenting on a blog". For Dean, this is an example of Slavoj Žižek 's notion that "the other side of...interactivity is interpassivity".[20] She explains that "when we are interpassive, something else, a fetish object, is active in our stead... The frantic activity of the fetish works to prevent actual action, to prevent something from really happening". In this account, "the circulation of communication is depoliticising, not because people don't care or don't want to be involved, but because we do!"[21]

Perhaps the best-known variant of these arguments is that put forward by the Canadian writer Malcolm Gladwell. In his article "Small Change: Why the Revolution Won't be Tweeted", Gladwell argues that social media generates networks based around "weak ties", while involvement in risky, radical action is predicated upon "strong ties". Here Gladwell is drawing a distinction between close friends and more distant friends and acquaintances. He cites research by Doug McAdam into the 1964 Freedom Summer campaign in Mississippi that found that those activists who stayed the course of the campaign were "far more likely than dropouts to have close friends who were also going to Mississippi". Gladwell goes on to claim that:

18: Cited in Gladwell, 2010.
19: Morozov, 2009.
20: Žižek , 2006, p24.
21: Dean, 2005.

This pattern shows up again and again. One study of the Red Brigades, the Italian terrorist group of the 1970s, found that 70 percent of recruits had at least one good friend already in the organisation. The same is true of the men who joined the mujahideen in Afghanistan. Even revolutionary actions that look spontaneous, like the demonstrations in East Germany that led to the fall of the Berlin Wall, are, at core, strong-tie phenomena.[22]

In one sense, this is hardly surprising. If one becomes involved in political campaigns that are not based around collective workplace organisation then it is likely that you would be introduced via friends with whom you share common interests. However, what is of particular interest in Gladwell's account at this stage is his contrast between this kind of activism and that associated with social media. For Gladwell social media like Facebook are good for "efficiently managing your acquaintances" and "keeping up with the people you would not otherwise be able to stay in touch with". Following the sociologist Mark Granovetter, Gladwell argues that our acquaintances "are our greatest source of new ideas and information", but while he considers this a good thing in itself, Gladwell notes that this form of interaction limits the usefulness of social media in promoting dissent since "weak ties seldom lead to high-risk activism". Instead, social media allow one to get large numbers of people signed-up to a campaign "by not asking too much of them". Gladwell rejects the claim made by the business consultant Andy Smith and the Stanford Business School professor Jennifer Aaker that "social networks are particularly effective at increasing motivation", arguing instead that these networks "are effective at increasing *participation*—by lessening the level of motivation that participation requires".[23]

For Micah White, a contributing editor to anti-consumerist *AdBusters* magazine, this is not simply the result of technological determinism but rather of market forces. For White there is a battle raging "for the soul of activism. It is a struggle between digital activists, who have adopted the logic of the marketplace, and those organisers who vehemently oppose the marketisation of social change".[24] White looks at the proliferation of online campaigning and advocacy groups in recent years and argues that:

22: Gladwell, 2010. The Freedom Summer Project was a campaign that saw "hundreds of Northern, largely white unpaid volunteers to run Freedom Schools, register black voters, and raise civil-rights awareness in the Deep South". Volunteers faced beatings, intimidation and police harassment. Three activists were murdered, as dramatised in the Alan Parker film *Mississippi Burning*. Around quarter of those who signed up to the programme dropped out.
23: Gladwell, 2010.
24: White, 2010.

the trouble is that this model of activism uncritically embraces the ideology of marketing. It accepts that the tactics of advertising and market research used to sell toilet paper can also build social movements. This manifests itself in an inordinate faith in the power of metrics to quantify success. Thus, everything digital activists do is meticulously monitored and analysed. The obsession with tracking clicks turns digital activism into clicktivism.[25]

White claims that these campaigns "hide behind gloried stories of viral campaigns and inflated figures of how many millions signed their petition in 24 hours" despite "the insider truth…that the vast majority, between 80 percent to 90 percent, of so-called members rarely even open campaign emails". Crucially, he argues, "ineffectual marketing campaigns spread political cynicism and draw attention away from genuinely radical movements. Political passivity is the end result of replacing salient political critique with the logic of advertising".[26]

If White is correct, the growth of Internet campaigning represents an enormous danger to the left. In order to judge the validity of the claims made for the power or danger of social media and Internet organising, it is necessary to examine some examples of its use over the past few years.

Tweeting 'bout a revolution?

Barack Obama's election campaign in 2008 was the first large-scale political attempt to harness the power of social media. David Plouffe, Obama's campaign manager, said the campaign created a "domino effect" which "used the Internet, text messaging and other forms of communication to build a now-legendary grassroots network of organisers and volunteers". On the website mybarackobama.com, the social media hub of the campaign, volunteers "created more than 2 million profiles…planned 200,000 offline events, formed 35,000 groups, posted 400,000 blogs, and raised $30 million on 70,000 personal fundraising pages".[27]

The campaign was more than just an online success: by registering volunteers online, street campaigns could be organised simply by inputting a postal code and contacting those who were registered. The Internet was used as one method among others to organise activists, not simply to engage them in clicktivism. Thomas Gensemer, one of the key players behind Obama's Internet strategy, said that the key to the campaign was "giving people real

---

25: White, 2010.
26: White, 2010.
27: Cited in Hands, 2011, pp115-116.

things to do in their neighbourhoods".[28] But it would be a mistake to see this as an example of a decentralised, grassroots campaign. As Plouffe stated after the election: "We wanted to control all aspects of our campaign... We wanted control of our advertising, and most important, we wanted control of our field operation. We did not want to outsource these millions of people, and these hundreds of thousands of full-time volunteers".[29]

The tremendous success of the Obama campaign shows that social media can play a role as an organiser. But there are important caveats. Obama's campaign tapped into enormous, widespread dissatisfaction with George W Bush and the government's handling of the economic crisis. People were optimistic about Obama's message of "Change", even if that change was undefined. Some 61 percent of registered Democrats were "enthusiastic" about their candidate, as opposed to just 35 percent of Republicans.[30] Beyond the party faithful, Obama was able to appeal to even wider layers of community activists, particularly from black and Latino communities, to join the campaign. Also, while the campaign shows that social media can be effective in mobilisation, we should not imagine that this can tell us a lot about how useful it is to socialists and working class activists who do not have millions of dollars in resources, full-time staff and corporate backing. The aim of the campaign was not to create a grassroots organisation but "to orchestrate a highly disciplined, focused and hierarchical election campaign".[31]

Closer to home both geographically and politically was the "G20 Meltdown" demonstration organised in London in April 2009. Held in protest at the assembly of the heads of the G20 states, just months after the bailout of the banks in late 2008, the protest is now best remembered for the criticisms of police "kettling" tactics and the death of Ian Tomlinson after being struck by a police officer. On the day thousands of protesters, mostly young and very angry, were kettled for hours by the police on the streets outside the Bank of England. Hands argues that "the organisation in preparation for the G20 actions followed the networked pattern, with the web functioning to orchestrate different elements and distribute information", and that, "in keeping with the distributed horizontal approach, those behind the G20 Meltdown identify themselves only as 'those associated with the April 1st Bank of England action'".[32]

However, Hands goes on to bemoan the fact that the mainstream

---

28: Hewlett, 2010.
29: Sifry, 2009.
30: Hands, 2011, p116.
31: Hands, 2011, p117.
32: Hands, 2011, p152.

media highlighted the role of Chris Knight, then professor of anthropology at the University of East London, in organising the protests and presented him as a figurehead. Hands analyses the enormous number of articles from across the journalistic spectrum, from the *Daily Mail* to the *Guardian*, and argues that they created an unsubstantiated narrative of "riots that would be probably be provoked by anarchists and their associates". He concludes "At no point did any of the articles refer to the actual substance and range of motives of the protests, only presenting accounts of their rage, of the concerns of the police, and of the potential for violence".[33]

In fact, the narrative of an enormous protest that was built up throughout the bourgeois media was the crucial element in making the protest as big and successful as it was. The media saturation, on TV and the newspapers, made the event unavoidable for weeks running up to the event. It is a common error to imagine that protesters are attracted to demonstrations purely by a set of demands—this is the same mistake made by those abstract propagandists who imagine a perfectly formed programme is necessary to build a movement, or those who stress the need to "educate" people about the real issues with the idea that this will create a rising number of socially conscious activists. In the run-up to the G20 demonstration the interplay between the Internet, figureheads like Chris Knight, and the bourgeois media established the protests as the place to be if you were angry about the bailouts and wanted to do something about it. This is something to be celebrated—the left should use every means it can to build the movement. This was equally clear, in different circumstances, during the student protests of late 2010.

The occupation of Millbank Tower on 10 November 2010 marked a significant turning point in the battle against the Tory-led coalition.[34] The return of radical student protests transformed the nature of the debate around resistance to the cuts. What is of particular interest in this context is the way in which the failure of the National Union of Students (NUS) to support the occupation saw subsequent demonstrations organised outside the structures of the NUS. But it is important to realise that there was indeed organisation. Day X—the day of protests and walkouts that took place on 24 November, two weeks after the occupation of Millbank—was first mooted several weeks before that protest at a meeting of the National Campaign against Fees and Cuts (NCAFC). It was then backed by a unanimous vote at

---

33: Hands, 2011, pp152-153.
34: For more on the dynamics and events of the student protests in late 2010, see Callinicos and Jones, 2011, and Dan Swain's article in this issue.

the Education Activist Network (EAN) conference on 31 October. It was publicised via email and Facebook, but did not take on a real momentum until after the demonstration on 10 November.

The 10 November protest—organised by the NUS and the University and College Union under the name "Demolition"—saw over 50,000 protesters take to the streets. This turnout could not have been achieved without the structures of the NUS, which invested time and money promoting the demonstration and laying on coaches. But within days of Millbank the mainstream media had picked up on the Day X protests. The newspapers highlighted the role of student activists such as EAN spokesperson and NUS executive member Mark Bergfeld, picking up on his comments about the use of "legitimate force" to "bring down the government".[35] In an echo of the G20 mobilisations, there was a reciprocal relationship between the bourgeois media, student activists and social media. In the absence of official NUS structures (or, indeed, of left wing student organisation in many parts of the country), Facebook became a way for students in disparate areas of the country to find out about what was going on, who in their area was going to protest. It was able to give school students with little or no experience of protest the confidence to get large numbers to walk out of school.

It would be a serious mistake, however, to think that the walkouts and university occupations simply emerged from horizontal networks. The schools and colleges that saw the biggest walkouts, such as Chiswick Community School and Le Swap in London, and Bury and Holy Cross Colleges near Manchester, were driven and built by socialists and radical activists. Over 30 universities went into occupation, but the "first wave" of occupations—from "University College London, School of Oriental and African Studies and King's College, to universities like Bradford, Bristol, Nottingham, York, Leeds, Edinburgh, Manchester Metropolitan University, Dundee, Sheffield and the University of East London"—were all marked by the presence of organised left wing activists and socialists.[36]

The student revolt shows us that social media can play a real role in solidifying the confidence of potential protesters in areas where the structures of the left are weakest. But the challenge for anti-capitalist activists is not to pontificate on how they can replace left wing organisation but to consider what role they can play in strengthening and rebuilding organisation. This is particularly pertinent when we look at the role played by social media in the Arab revolutions.

35: Cecil, 2010.
36: Walker, 2010.

Here it is worth remembering the Iranian protests and the "Green Movement" of 2009. Much was made of the role of social media, and particularly Twitter, in the protests that broke out after the 2009 election. US secretary of state Hillary Clinton's senior adviser for innovation, Alec Ross, claimed that "social media had played a key role in organising the protests".[37] Other were less convinced: "'Twitter's impact inside Iran is zero,' said Mehdi Yahyanejad, manager of a Farsi-language news site based in Los Angeles. 'Here, there is lots of buzz, but once you look…you see most of it are Americans tweeting among themselves'."[38]

It seems that, in reality, the use of Twitter and other social media in organising the protests was very limited:

> Analysis by Sysomos, a social media analysis company, found only 19,235 Twitter accounts registered in Iran (0.027 percent of the population) on the eve of the 2009 elections. As many sympathisers of the Green Movement began changing their Twitter location status to Tehran to confuse the Iranian authorities, it became nearly impossible "to tell whether the people 'tweeting' from Iran were in Tehran or in, say, Los Angeles ".[39]

The real strength of Twitter at this time was that those few people who were able to get information out of Iran were able to spread it far and wide.

It is understandable that the mainstream press would leap upon social media as the reason why the Arab revolutions were finally able to break out. After all, revolutions were something that belonged to a bygone age and the working class was supposed to be finished as an agent of social change. When the Egyptian working class became the decisive factor in bringing down Mubarak, however, the limits of this narrative were exposed.[40]

In an article entitled "The 'Twitter Can't Topple Dictators' Article", Jay Cohen discussed the way in which texts and interventions about the role of social media in the Arab revolutions were quickly reduced to refutations of straw-man arguments that "it *is* as simple as 'Twitter topples dictators,' or 'add Internet and you get revolution'". Such simplistic takes tended to duck the "really hard and really interesting question: how *does* the Internet affect the balance of forces in a contest between the state and people fed up with

---

37: Cited in Morozov, 2010, p18.
38: Musgrove, 2009.
39: Morozov, 2010, p15.
40: See Philip Marfleet's article elsewhere in this journal for an account of how the processes leading up to the revolution were more apparent than the media version seems to suggest.

the state?"[41] This is a problem that will not be answered decisively any time soon. But it is possible to glean some valuable lessons from recent events.

The idea that social media played a significant role in coordinating protests has been greatly exaggerated, according to the Egyptian activist Gigi Ibrahim. She points out that coordination between organisations tended to happen in face to face meetings. Facebook and emails had been used to call demonstrations in Egypt for a number of years—these protests were small. The incomparably larger mobilisations which followed 25 January were not because of some qualitative shift in the level of the Egyptian people's engagement with social media. Rather the confidence people gained from the events in Tunisia combined with the systematic work activists put into leafleting and raising slogans in areas where few people would even have access to the Internet. This was dangerous work, with activists being arrested and beaten. But it was integral to the mass mobilisations in Tahrir Square and elsewhere.[42]

Sultan Al Qassemi is a journalist based in the United Arab Emirates who extensively covered the uprisings across the region. His opinion of the role of social media is worth quoting at length:

> Social media has certainly played a part in the Arab Spring Revolutions but its impact is often exaggerated on the inside. Egypt was disconnected from the outside world for days and yet the movement never stopped...
>
> Today Libya is facing an even more severe Internet disruption, yet we continue to see the movement picking up pace. Where social media had a major impact was conveying the news to the outside world, bloggers and Twitter users were able to transmit news bites that would otherwise never make it to mainstream news media.
>
> This information has been instrumental in garnering the attention of the citizens of the world who expressed solidarity with those suppressed individuals and may even put pressure on their own governments to react.[43]

The speed at which information has travelled from continent to continent, partly propelled by activists utilising the Internet, has allowed for such images as that of the protester in Tahrir Square, surrounded by

---

41: Cohen, 2011.
42: Gigi Ibrahim is a revolutionary socialist from Egypt with a keen interest in the role of the Internet in the revolution. These observations are based on a discussion I had with her while researching this article.
43: Cited in Beaumont, 2011.

Egyptian flags, holding up a placard reading "Egypt Supports Wisconsin Workers" to be spread across the world.[44] And in Wisconsin itself, where workers have mounted huge protests against Republican attempts to roll back trade union rights, John Stavrellis, who was one of 50 people involved in the first protest, "said inspiration came from student demonstrations in Britain and protests in Tunisia and Egypt".[45] The most recent protest at the time of writing had over 100,00 people on it.

These experiences indicate that the Internet and social media are often a useful complement to the kinds of activism that the left has traditionally engaged in. Where online activism has been seen as a replacement for this kind of activity, it has been unsuccessful.[46] So there is a need for caution. For some, the explosive nature of the protests and the efficacy of the Internet have led to claims that organisation is now unnecessary. This overlooks the crucial issue of class structures that are all too often pushed into the background in discussions of the Internet.

Class 2.0

On 25 January the Egyptian regime conducted a fascinating social experiment. Egypt did "what many technologists thought was unthinkable for any country with a major Internet economy: It unplugged itself entirely from the Internet to try and silence dissent".[47] This did not have the desired effect, as protests went from strength to strength. What this futile gamble really demonstrates is the class nature of the Internet.

The idea that the Internet is a neutral space on which all sides can compete is hopelessly utopian. As Bellamy Foster and McChesney argued in a recent article on capitalism and the Internet, "technologies do not ride roughshod over history, regardless of their immense powers. They are developed in a social, political, and economic context. And this has strongly conditioned the course and shape of the communication revolution".[48] On a very basic level, you need to pay an Internet service provider (ISP)—BT, AOL, Sky, among others—just to get yourself online. These ISPs have tremendous power to prevent you from accessing the Internet. In Egypt the

44: www.good.is/post/amazing-photo-egyptians-turn-out-to-support-wisconsin-counterpartsI
45: MacAskill, 2011.
46: As anybody who has organised an event via Facebook, only to find that the number of people who say they will attend bears no relation to the number of people who eventually turn up, can bear witness to.
47: Al Jazeera, 2011.
48: Bellamy Foster and McChesney, 2011, p3.

multinational communications firm Vodafone was among a number of mobile phone providers who were ordered by the regime to shut down their network in order to prevent protesters communicating, only to reconnect in order to send pro-Mubarak messages. Naturally, they complied.[49] At the level of social media, Facebook and other social media networks are corporations that "can eject users at will and restrict the kinds of groups or communicative exchanges that occur with [their] boundaries".[50] Facebook is partially owned by the bank Goldman Sachs and JP Morgan are currently trying to purchase a 10 percent stake in Twitter.[51] Between January and March 2011 the stock market valuation of Facebook leapt from $50 billion to $75 billion.[52] Capitalism has proved itself remarkably adept at exploiting new avenues for capital accumulation, and the online world is no exception.[53]

The class nature of the Internet extends beyond these obvious facets. Open source software (OSS)—software that is openly developed and freely distributed—could be seen as a fundamentally democratic form of programming. But the reach of the market does not end at the borders of the online world. As Joseph Choonara explains in a discussion of Linux, the most successful example of OSS:

> its development is centralised through a "core-development team" to whom suggested changes to the source code must be submitted. According to one analyst, only 1,000 people contribute changes to Linux on a regular basis. An even smaller group of 100 programmers contributed 37,000 out of 38,000 recent changes all of whom were paid by their employers to work on the operating system. The main employers willing to release staff to work on Linux include Intel, IBM, Hewlett Packard and other giants. They have a vested interest in competition with Microsoft's Windows operating system, and have accumulated vast amounts of capital, allowing them to dominate the world market.

As Joseph concludes, successful OSS projects "are rapidly absorbed

---

49: BBC News, 2011.

50: Hands, 2011, p86. For details of Facebook's alleged collusion with the state to remove political groups, see Morozov, 2010, pp211-214. The Right to Work campaign's Facebook group disappeared under unexplained circumstances in late 2010.

51: *Financial Times*, 3 March 2011.

52: Swartz and Krantz, 2011.

53: Bellamy Foster and McChesney, 2011, includes a valuable and accessible account of the processes of capital accumulation on the internet.

into the capitalist market as a potential source of profit".[54] This point chimes with Nicholas Carr's recent observation that capitalists have little to fear from networks of volunteers in such fields, since "the innovations of the unpaid web-enabled masses may be 'conceived in nonmarket environments', but they ultimately create 'new platforms' that 'support commercial ventures'."[55]

Class is also a crucial consideration when it comes to considering the organisational consequences of the arguments put forward by proponents of the absolute novelty of the Internet. When Laurie Penny argues that, "in order to be properly effective, rebels have to deregulate resistance", she is accepting the typical neoliberal tropes about the working class, that "the power of organised labour was undercut across the world by building in higher structural unemployment and holding down wages, by atomising workers, outsourcing and globalising production while keeping working people tied to increasingly divided and suspicious communities".[56] There is a real danger of left wing commentators uncritically accepting such arguments, of becoming "left wing harmonies in the neoliberal chorus",[57] rather than trying to understand exactly how patterns of employment *have* changed in recent years. The waves of general strikes across Europe, the mass movement in support of trade union rights in Wisconsin and the integral role of the Egyptian working class in the revolution go a long way to showing in practice that these ideas are more informed by neoliberal ideology than they are by material reality.

This has real implications for political organisation—for one thing, the publication of a newspaper such as *Socialist Worker*. As Alex Callinicos argued in a reply to Laurie,

> *Socialist Worker* allows us to have an organised weekly dialogue with thousands of other activists. One of its advantages is precisely that it doesn't just exist in cyberspace but is a physical product that has to be sold in a specific time and space—this particular neighbourhood or workplace or picket-line or demonstration—and that involves face to face interaction.

> This allows us to develop continuing relationships with other activists that, we believe, strengthens both us and the broader struggle.[58]

54: Choonara, 2005.
55: Carr, 2010.
56: Penny, 2010b. For a thoroughgoing critique of these and related ideas, see Smith, 2007, Harman, 2007, Doogan, 2009, and Kimber, 2009.
57: Doogan, 2009, p12.
58: Callinicos, 2011. For a masterful analysis of the importance of revolutionary publications, see Harman, 1984.

When Laurie says that groups can "exchange information and change plans via Twitter and text message in the middle of demonstrations ", there's a clear problem of scale.[59] This is all well and good on a small-scale direct action. But how does it apply when hundreds of thousands march or when workers take strike action? It also runs up against problems when dealing with questions of long-term strategic thinking. The current wave of protests organised by the UK Uncut campaign has been an incredibly creative and imaginative way of bringing the issue of corporate tax avoidance to the attention of a wide audience. It conducts meetings via Twitter and is avowedly "non-hierachical". But when one member tried to set up an event in praise of the anti-union "cooperative" John Lewis, an argument ensued which was only resolved through long arguments among small numbers of people who had the time to debate the issues over multiple online mediums.[60] The idea of unstructured online decision-making may seem inclusive and democratic: it is actually unaccountable and exclusive. These problems could escalate if the campaign begins to involve much larger numbers of people, particularly if people begin to become frustrated at the failure of the protests to force either the corporations to pay their taxes or the government to change its tax policy.

In a recent *Guardian* column Newsnight economic editor Paul Mason argued that: "With Facebook, Twitter and Yfrog truth travels faster than lies, and propaganda is inflammable".[61] The obvious question is: why should truth travel faster than lies? In a world riven by class division and on an Internet that is not immune from it, how does access to social media act as an effective filter? For Mason, the answer is that strategic questions are solved through "memes"—Richard Dawkins's concept of cultural concepts that replicate and mutate as genes do in organisms. Mason argues that "ideas arise, are very quickly market-tested and then either take off, bubble under, insinuate themselves into the mainstream culture or, if they are no good, disappear". But what does Paul mean by good or bad? Does this have any bearing on how effective they are in bringing about fundamental social change? I, alongside millions of others, am fond of the very successful "watching television while eating dinner" meme. I have no illusions that this meme is going to contribute to the fight against austerity. There is a serious point behind this: the danger of deciding tactics by waiting to see what catches on opens the possibility that activism that

---

59: Penny, 2010b.
60: Seymour, 2010.
61: Mason, 2011.

is very rewarding in the short term is taken up at the expense of strategic thinking about the long-term goals.[62]

Many of the ideas the recent movements have thrown up are not especially new, even if they have a technological twist today. In early 1968 the French sociologist André Gorz argued: "in the foreseeable future there will be no crisis of European capitalism so dramatic as to drive the mass of workers to revolutionary general strikes".[63] Within months France had been gripped by the biggest general strike the world had seen up until that point, and capitalist crisis shook the continent for years afterwards. Writing about the movements that shook the US in the 1960s, Chris Harman noted that spontaneity and lack of structure could fit "situations of sudden, explosive involvement of very large numbers of students.... As they took to the streets and occupied buildings they unbalanced the authorities and did not worry unduly about strategy, tactics and organisation." But, when movements were forced to retreat, "suddenly people began to feel the need for structures and for some understanding of the forces at work in society—for an 'ideology'".[64]

Then as now, we live under a capitalist system in which workers are the source of capitalist profits; workers therefore have the collective power to stop exploitation and fundamentally change the world. Then as now, consciousness among workers is uneven. Political organisation is simply a recognition of the fact that "some people tend to break more quickly with the established ideas of existing society than others. Those who break first need to organise themselves, to win others to their ideas and to counter the manoeuvres of the ruling class and state".[65] To imagine that the Internet offers a shortcut around this is merely technological determinism. But if we understand this, we can think much more fruitfully about exactly how social media and the Internet can effectively be integrated into a political project to change the world.

62: For a critique of Dawkins's concept of memes, see Callinicos, 1996.
63: Smith, 2007.
64: Harman, 2003.
65: Harman, 2003.

References

Al Jazeera, 2011, "When Egypt Turned Off the Internet" (28 January), http://english.aljazeera.net/news/middleeast/2011/01/201112879616438o.html

Barnett, Emma, 2011, "Facebook 'used by half the UK population'", *Telegraph* (2 March), www.telegraph.co.uk/technology/facebook/8356755/Facebook-used-by-half-the-UK-population.html

BBC News, 2011, "Vodafone Network 'Hijacked' by Egypt" (3 February), www.bbc.co.uk/news/business-12357694

Beaumont, Peter, 2011, "The Truth About Twitter, Facebook and the Uprisings in the Arab World", *Guardian G2* (25 February), www.guardian.co.uk/world/2011/feb/25/twitter-facebook-uprisings-arab-libya

Bellamy Foster, John, and Robert W McChesney, "The Internet's Unholy Marriage to Capitalism", *Monthly Review* (March), http://monthlyreview.org/110301foster-mcchesney.php

Callinicos, Alex, 1996, "Darwin, Materialism and Evolution", *International Socialism* 71 (summer), http://pubs.socialistreviewindex.org.uk/isj71/darwin.htm

Callinicos, Alex, 2011, "A Reply to Laurie Penny's Reply", *Socialist Worker* website, www.socialistworker.co.uk/art.php?id=23522

Callinicos, Alex, and Jonny Jones, 2011, "The Student Revolt and the Crisis", *International Socialism* 129 (winter), www.isj.org.uk/?id=697

Carr, Nicholas, 2010, "The Unrevolution", *Rough Type* (8 November), www.roughtype.com/archives/2010/11/the_unrevolutio.php

Cecil, Nicholas, 2010, "Bring Down the Government, Says Student March Organiser", *Evening Standard* (12 November), www.thisislondon.co.uk/standard/article-23897210-bring-down-the-government-says-student-march-organiser.do

Choonara, Joseph, 2005, "Marx or the Multitude?", *International Socialism* 105 (winter), www.isj.org.uk/?id=65

CIEC, 1996, "Complaint for Declatory and Injunctive Relief", www.ciec.org/trial/complaint/complaint.html

Cohen, Jay, 2011, "The 'Twitter Can't Topple Dictators' Article", Press Think, http://pressthink.org/2011/02/the-twitter-cant-topple-dictators-article/

Davies, Nick, 2010, "Afghanistan War Logs: Story behind biggest leak in intelligence history", *Guardian* (25 July), www.guardian.co.uk/world/2010/jul/25/wikileaks-war-logs-back-story

Dean, Jodi, 2005, "Communicative Capitalism: Circulation and the Foreclosure of Politics", *Cultural Politics*, volume 1, issue 1, http://jdeanicite.typepad.com/i_cite/2005/01/communicative_c.html

Doogan, Kevin, 2009, *New Capitalism? The Transformation of Work* (Polity).

Friedman, Thomas, 2011, "This is Just the Start", *New York Times* (1 March), www.nytimes.com/2011/03/02/opinion/02friedman.html

Gladwell, Malcolm, 2010, "Small Change: Why the Revolution Will Not be Tweeted", *New Yorker* (4 October), http://www.newyorker.com/reporting/2010/10/04/101004fa_fact_gladwell

Grossman, Lev, 2006, "Time's Person of the Year: You", *Time* (13 December), www.time.com/time/magazine/article/0,9171,1569514,00.html

Hands, Joss, 2011, *@ is for Activism: Dissent, Resistance and Rebellion in a Digital Culture* (Pluto).

Harman, Chris, 1984, "The Revolutionary Press", *International Socialism* 24 (summer), www.marxists.org/archive/harman/1984/xx/revpress.html

Harman, Chris, 2003, "Autonomism For the People", *Socialist Review* (December), www.socialistreview.org.uk/article.php?articlenumber=8691

Harman, Chris, 2007, "Theorising Neoliberalism", *International Socialism 117* (winter), www.isj.org.uk/?id=399

Hewlett, Steve, 2010, "A 'new media election'?", BBC Radio 4, http://news.bbc.co.uk/today/hi/today/newsid_8606000/8606909.stm

Kimber, Charlie, 2009, "Precarious Reflections", *International Socialism 123* (summer), www.isj.org.uk/?id=564

Krugman, Paul, 1999, "Understanding Globalisation", *Washington Monthly*, volume 31, issue 6 (June), www.washingtonmonthly.com/books/1999/9906.krugman.lexus.html

Macaskill, Ewen, 2011, "US Left Finds its Voice Over Wisconsin Attack on Union Rights", *Guardian* (24 February), www.guardian.co.uk/world/2011/feb/24/wisconsin-union-rights-protest

Mason, Paul, 2011, "From Paris to Cairo, These Protests are Expanding the Power of the Individual", *Guardian* (7 February), www.guardian.co.uk/commentisfree/2011/feb/07/paul-mason-protest-twitter-revolution-egypt

Morozov, Evgeny, 2009, "The Brave New World of Slacktivism", *Foreign Policy* (19 May), http://neteffect.foreignpolicy.com/posts/2009/05/19/the_brave_new_world_of_slacktivism

Morozov, Evgeny, 2010, *The Net Delusion: How Not to Liberate the World* (Allen Lane).

Musgrove, Mike, 2009, "Twitter is a player in Iran's Drama", *Washington Post* (17 June), www.washingtonpost.com/wp-dyn/content/article/2009/06/16/AR2009061603391.html

Penny, Laurie, 2010a, "Out With the Old Politics", *Guardian* (24 December), www.guardian.co.uk/commentisfree/2010/dec/24/student-protests-young-politics-voices

Penny, Laurie, 2010b, "A Response to Alex Callinicos", *New Statesman* blog (27 december 2010), www.newstatesman.com/blogs/laurie-penny/2010/12/deregulating-resistance

Seymour, Richard, 2010, "More Than Mutual, I'd Say", Lenin's Tomb (30 December), http://leninology.blogspot.com/2010/12/more-than-mutual-i-should-say.html

Sifry, Micah L, 2009, "The Obama Disconnect: What Happens When Myth Meets Reality", techPresident (31 December), http://techpresident.com/blog-entry/the-obama-disconnect

Smith, Martin, 2007, "The Shape of the Working Class", *International Socialism 113* (winter), www.isj.org.uk/?id=293

Swartz, Jon, and Matt Krantz, 2011, "Is a New Tech bubble Starting to Grow?", *USA Today* (March 17), www.usatoday.com/money/perfi/stocks/2011-03-16-new-tech-bubble-.htm

Viner, Katherine, 2009, "Internet has changed foreign policy for ever, says Gordon Brown", *Guardian* (19 June), www.guardian.co.uk/politics/2009/jun/19/gordon-brown-Internet-foreign-policy

Walker, Tom, 2010, "Sit-in Wave Sweeps Through Colleges", *Socialist Worker* (18 December), www.socialistworker.co.uk/art.php?id=23386

White, Micah, 2010, "Clicktivism is Ruining Leftist Activism", *Guardian* (12 August), www.guardian.co.uk/commentisfree/2010/aug/12/clicktivism-ruining-leftist-activism

Žižek, Slavoj, 2006, *How to Read Lacan* (Granta), www.lacan.com/zizhowto.html

The student movement today

Dan Swain

The month-long period between 10 November and 9 December saw the birth of the largest and most militant student movement Britain had experienced for decades.[1] A wave of walkouts, demonstrations and occupations shook university managements and the government, bringing it to the brink of defeat. The demonstrations in London and Manchester on 29 January brought the movement back to the streets, and there have been occupations in Glasgow, Kent and Birmingham already this year. This movement marked a sharp break with student politics of recent years, but it didn't drop miraculously from a clear blue sky. To understand the movement it is essential to understand the transformation of higher and further education in Britain, and the changing place of students in society.

The number of students in further and higher education has grown massively over the past 30 years, meaning that students now represent a large and distinct social force within society. Students find themselves at a transitional point in society, between childhood and full incorporation into the world of work. While, as I will discuss more below, more students than ever before work to support themselves, the majority still do not. At the same time, universities and colleges are increasingly geared towards preparation of students for the workforce. This gives students an ambiguous place in capitalist society, with no direct relationship to the means of production.

1:   This article benefited greatly from discussions with Mark Bergfeld and Hannah Dee, as well as comments from Jonny Jones, Alex Callinicos and Joseph Choonara.

Students are not directly exploited in the way that workers are. On the other hand, the mass expansion of education means the days are long gone when students could be said to be a privileged section of society. Exams, debt, poor housing and many other factors mean students can be profoundly alienated. This ambiguous position affects both the consciousness of students and the rhythm of their struggles.

Growing radicalisation

The period immediately preceding the rise of the current student movement was one of fairly high levels of political radicalisation. Students played a prominent role in the anti-war movement, with Stop the War societies set up on many campuses. As well as building opposition to war and occupation these groups often played an important role in campaigning alongside Islamic Societies against the Islamophobia and attacks on civil liberties unleashed by the "war on terror". While not on the scale of recent ones, there were significant walkouts by school students on the day Iraq was invaded in March 2003. In 2005 Student Respect was launched, which at its best translated the radicalism of the anti-war movement into alliances capable of winning elections in student unions. Student Respect had some success within the NUS, as well as winning some positions in local student unions in Manchester and Essex.

The anti-capitalist movement at the beginning of the last decade also had a strong influence, seeing the growth of groups such as People and Planet, as well as more radical organisations like Globalise Resistance. People and Planet was set up as a student focused group to campaign against corporate power and environmental degradation. In 1999 People and Planet had groups at nearly 150 university campuses, and they played an important role in mobilising for campaigns against Third World debt and global poverty.[2] However, People and Planet also argued that those in Western countries needed to cut their consumption in order to solve poverty and climate change. This led to a focus on changing behaviour rather than changing the system that was sometimes counter-productive. People and Planet was also organised as a loose network, with a certain hostility to involvement by political parties, especially in local groups. In this respect it was an important precursor to some of the more autonomist minded forces in the contemporary student movement, who share this suspicion of organisation. Globalise Resistance, in contrast, did not share this suspicion, but also did not grow on the same scale.

2:    Ashman, 1999.

An important precursor to the current movement was the wave of occupations during and following the Israeli invasion of Gaza in early 2009. These were tiny when compared with the recent revolts, but nonetheless saw dozens of universities being occupied. University managements were undoubtedly rattled, and delivered a range of concessions, including sending old books and computers to Gaza. These played an important role in putting the tactic of occupations back onto the agenda, with even the *Guardian* suggesting that "students are awakening from the political apathy of which they are often accused".[3] The activists involved with the Gaza occupations often used the experiences learned in the far larger occupations over fees and cuts.

This reflects the way in which university campuses are far more politicised than wider society. Students come to university expecting to think critically about the big questions. Often these hopes are somewhat dashed by a stifling orthodoxy, especially in economics and social sciences, but there is still far more space for this at universities than in wider society. Even the caricature of Marxism taught to students is far more than they get from the mainstream media, and the gap between the expectations of new students and the reality can itself be a source of frustration and radicalisation. Furthermore, the increase in the number of international students in Britain means that international solidarity becomes far from abstract. Students are much less constrained by the weight of the past, far more likely to assert that another world is possible. Thus students can be far quicker to make connections between struggles and to generalise to big political questions. This has been on show throughout our movement, whether it is the prevalence of Palestinian flags on the anti-fees demonstrations, the activists bringing cardboard cut-outs of works of philosophy to shield themselves from the police, or the ease with which we won the argument for demonstrators to march to the Egyptian Embassy following the London demonstration in January, linking the struggle against austerity with the struggle against Mubarak.

Yet despite this high level of politicisation, the level of struggle on specific student questions had been fairly low. One of the reasons the turnout for the National Union of Students (NUS) demonstration on 10 November was so spectacular and surprising was that the last time they had called a demonstration over fees, in 2006, the turnout was derisory. This came after a long period in which the NUS had failed adequately to challenge successive Labour governments. The NUS was dominated by Labour Students throughout the 1990s. When Tony Blair was elected in 1997 Labour Students agreed with the scrapping of grants, and offered only token

---

3:    Lipsett and Benjamin, 2009. See also Ruddick, 2009.

resistance to the introduction of fees. Education secretary David Blunkett even gave a speech at the Labour Party conference thanking the NUS for their support for his policies.

Whilst the official leadership of the NUS dithered, it was left to other organisations like the Campaign for Free Education and the Stop the Fees Campaign, led by socialists and left wing independents, to build serious opposition.[4] While the NUS did organise a campaign against top-up fees (the increase of fees to £3000 a year), bringing Tony Blair to within a few votes of defeat in the House of Commons, it failed to build on the movement, focusing merely on channelling students into lobbying campaigns rather than a mass movement. The NUS's reluctance to challenge the Labour Party was a huge barrier to the movement, and it is no coincidence that its biggest mobilisation for decades came only once Labour was in opposition.

Whilst Labour Students' hold on the NUS gradually decreased, this was not replaced by a left wing pole of attraction. Instead various "independents" (invariably Labour members) gained control and the NUS continued to tail the agenda of the Labour Party. The NUS went on first to abandon its commitment to campaigning for free education and then to advocate means tested loans. Having failed to lead a fight, the NUS decided it wouldn't even fight at all. This was met with opposition from the left, but was in the end passed worryingly easily, with very little outcry from students. While the attacks on education were nothing like on the scale we see today, the picture was far from rosy. Universities were subjected to ever more neoliberal marketisation, well documented by Alex Callinicos in *Universities in a Neoliberal World*, but opposition was limited to the occasional isolated anti-privatisation campaign.[5]

An important sign that this was beginning to shift was the occupation at Middlesex University in May 2010, following the announcement of the closure of the award-winning philosophy department. The defence of Middlesex philosophy brought together an explosive cocktail of factors. The department was at the sharp end of the business driven logic of modern universities, threatened with closure not because it wasn't profitable, but because it wasn't profitable *enough*. Middlesex's attempt to further orientate towards business-led research meant there was no space for a philosophy department, even an internationally renowned one. Furthermore, Middlesex's philosophy department had a deserved reputation for teaching and research into radical and critical philosophies. It hosted the journal

---

4:   Swain, 1997, and Thompson ,1997.
5:   Callinicos, 2006.

Radical Philosophy and was home to Marxist influenced academics like Peter Hallward and Peter Osborne. This gave an important ideological dimension to the campaign, which became as much about the defence of critical thinking in universities as about one department. The Middlesex occupation lasted for 12 days and brought support from across the world. The occupation held teach-ins and discussions that brought in hundreds of activists to discuss both the big ideas of philosophy and the fight against management. It played a significant role in putting militant opposition to education cuts on the agenda, and many of the activists involved at Middlesex have been at the forefront of the recent movement.[6]

Another straw in the wind was provided, also during the 2009-10 academic year, by the strong support given by students at Leeds and Sussex universities, and at King's College London to campaigns by lecturers against redundancies. At Sussex this led to two occupations and a successful campaign against the attempted victimisation of student activists. The balance-sheet of these campaigns was mixed — the compulsory redundancies were withdrawn at Leeds and at King's, though the threat to jobs remained; at Middlesex the prestigious Centre for Research in Modern European Philosophy, with its postgraduate programmes, was saved through a move to Kingston University, but the undergraduate degree left behind at Middlesex is being run down. Nevertheless, the struggles in 2009-10 helped to revive the tradition of student militancy and to create links between activists in the universities. The formation of the Education Activists Network (EAN) in early 2010, bringing together student and trade union activists, was a product of these developments, as was the National Campaign Against Fees and Cuts (NCAFC), which developed with the aim of coordinating local anti-cuts campaigns. Both coalitions went on to play an important role in the movement as the main organisers of demonstrations at a local and national level.

These struggles showed features that have been characteristic of student activism in the past, and of the movement that has arisen since. While workers are constrained by both routine and bureaucracy, students can operate far more freely. In particular, student struggles can be led by a militant minority of students, in a way that workers' struggles rarely are. The most important forms of industrial action require the participation of the majority of the workforce, and so workers are constrained by the necessity of collective action in a way that students are not. This was clear on 10 November, when a large minority broke away from the main demonstration to lay siege to the Conservative Party headquarters on Millbank. This breakaway was led

---

6:    For more on Middlesex see http://savemdxphil.com/about/ and Bhattacharyya, 2010.

by activists from the EAN and other organisations which already had experience of occupations and direct action. Thousands of students surrounded the building, while hundreds occupied inside. This became the iconic image of the day, and the spark for the inspirational movement that followed. It showed how students' struggles can suddenly explode and move very quickly.

Yet the counterpoint to this explosive pace is how quickly such movements can dissipate. Most student activists have the experience of returning following the Easter break to find most of their contacts refuse to leave their rooms because of exams. While the nature of workplace struggles encourages solidarity and workers have to stick together to defend themselves, no such automatic tendency exists amongst students. In fact, the competitive system of exams can tend towards division. This tendency has been exacerbated by the cuts in grants and introduction of fees. Students are encouraged to see themselves as isolated consumers determined to "get their money's worth" from university, which only heightens the division and alienation between students. All of this can lead to rapid division and demoralisation. Only time will tell whether the movement of November-December 2010 can sustain itself and overcome these tendencies, but the creation of permanent campaigns and networks of solidarity like the EAN and NCAFC will play an important part.

Expansion of education

The last quarter of the 20th century saw an enormous expansion of education in the UK. In 1971 there were 1.7 million students in further education and 621,000 in higher education. In 2009 this had grown to 3.5 million and 2.5 million respectively.[7] This reflects the restructuring of the economy in this period, which required an increasingly educated workforce. Successive governments have seen the need to expand education as crucial to reproducing the labour power required by advanced capitalism. When Gordon Brown was chancellor of the exchequer, a Treasury document asserted that "for the UK economy to succeed in generating growth through productivity and employment in the coming decade, it must invest more strongly than in the past in its knowledge base, and translate this knowledge more effectively into business and public service innovation".[8] This constant rhetoric of "expanding our knowledge base" and "investing in skills" reflects the fact that the expansion of higher education has been very clearly driven by the needs of business and the state. Universities and colleges are as much

---

7:     ONS, 2009, pp31-32.
8:     Quoted in Callinicos, 2006, p2.

about preparing students for the workforce as they are about education and learning, and few make any secret of it.

The massive expansion of higher education meant a move away from it being a preserve of the elite in society. In 1969 Alexander Cockburn could argue that higher education institutions "largely exclude the sons and daughters of the working class, so that where class discrimination and sex discrimination combine a working class girl in Britain has a six hundred to one chance against receiving higher education".[9] Today, while it is still harder for them, hundreds of thousands of working class children go to university. Over 30 percent of students in higher education come from the lowest socio-economic classes and nearly 90 percent were educated at state schools.[10] While in 1971 there were twice as many men in university as women, in 2006 there were more women than men in both further and higher education.[11] A similar expansion has taken place in further education, where in 2005 even among manual working class families over 60 percent of children stay in education after the age of 16.[12]

Just as universities are no longer the playgrounds of the children of the rich, they are no longer solely the training grounds of the future ruling class. Writing in this journal in 1975 Alex Callinicos and Simon Turner noted:

> Higher education is no longer a preparation for, or an entry ticket into, the ruling class. Most students will become some form of worker. If a student takes his or her degree in science or engineering he or she can expect to become a highly skilled worker employed in industry and playing an integral part in the capitalist productive process...A student taking an arts subject is more likely to become a white collar worker of some sort, employed in the middle echelons of the state machinery or industry.[13]

The 35 years since have only accelerated this process. While you only need to look at the famous Bullingdon Club photographs of leading Tories to see that certain universities still do educate the future ruling class, most students cannot expect to step into management positions when they graduate. Having a degree may mean access to better-paid jobs, but it no longer opens doors to positions of authority in the way it used to.

Most graduates will step straight onto a treadmill of low-paid

9:   Cockburn, 1969, p17.
10:   HESA, 2010.
11:   ONS, 2009, Table 3.9.
12:   ONS, 2009, Table 3.8.
13:   Callinicos and Turner, 1975.

administration or call centre work. For example, a recent study of call centres in Scotland found that over a quarter of workers had degree level or higher qualifications.[14] These people were working in largely low-paid, inflexible and stressful jobs. The economic crisis and the subsequent austerity agenda will only deepen the tendency for students to move into low-paid jobs or no jobs at all. The anarchy of the system is such that universities are still churning out graduates to fill roles in the public sector that are being destroyed at a rapid rate. Whilst graduates could once hope for a job in some aspect of civil service or local government, it is precisely these jobs that are disappearing. It should be no surprise that graduate unemployment is at its highest for a decade, and has risen even more sharply than unemployment as a whole.[15]

A feature of the steady erosion of sources of funding for students has been a sharp increase in the number who work to support themselves. The abolition of grants, followed by the introduction of fees, followed by an increase in those fees, placed ever greater financial pressures on students. During the ten years from 1996 to 2006, which saw all of the major changes to funding take effect, the number of students in work increased by 50 percent.[16] These students are overwhelmingly concentrated in the retail, hotel and restaurant industries.[17] These are highly precarious, low-paid and exploitative jobs. A joint TUC and NUS study in 2006 found, unsurprisingly, that "there is a significant likelihood that the poorer a student's background, the more likely they are to need to work".[18] This undoubtedly contributes to a sense of stress and alienation, with 40 percent of full-time students and more than half of part-time students with jobs reporting that their employment had impacted upon their studies. The pressures of work can also be a factor which dampens down student activism, restricting its freedom and spontaneity. It is striking that it is those universities where the fewest students work that have seen some of the largest occupations and demonstrations. Oxford saw a large demonstration against the secretary of state for business, innovation and skills Vince Cable in October 2010, while Cambridge had one of the largest and longest occupations. On the other hand those universities where the most students work tend to lack traditions of militancy.

The picture in further education is even clearer. For many the true

---

14: Hyman and Marks, 2008, p201.
15: www.bbc.co.uk/news/education-12286264
16: NUS/TUC, 2006, p4.
17: NUS/TUC, 2006, p6.
18: NUS/TUC, 2006, p14.

highlight of last year was the sudden appearance of a mass movement of school and college students of the sort this country has never seen before. These were overwhelmingly the children of working class parents, hit by the double whammy of the scrapping of their Education Maintenance Allowance (EMA) and the closing off of their future educational opportunities by the fees increase. The EMA was a means-tested grant providing up to £30 a week to 16 to 18 year olds who stay in further education, and many of these students spoke eloquently of how this was the only thing keeping them from having to work to support themselves and their families. The students demonstrating outside parliament came from the poorest parts of London and took to the streets in unprecedented numbers. Drawing a direct comparison with the youth movements in France, BBC's Paul Mason called them "banlieue-style youth from Croydon, Peckham, the council estates of Islington".[19] These students gave the most visible lie to the tedious Conservative rhetoric about the student movement being a revolt of the privileged middle classes.

The expansion of education gives structural reasons to think that solidarity between workers and students, while not inevitable, should be easier than ever before. While the increased numbers of students in work can act as a brake on their militancy, it also means students are more likely be sympathetic to workers' struggle. Arguments for solidarity with workers have gained a lot of traction in the movement. Conversely, most working class families will have a child in either further or higher education. This goes some way to explaining why the attempts to witch-hunt activists following the London demonstrations fell so flat, and why there was such widespread support for the students in the labour movement. Working class people saw their own children being beaten by the police and fighting back. Almost everyone knew someone affected by the EMA cuts or the fee increases. When Susan Matthews, whose son Alfie Meadows was seriously injured by a police truncheon on 9 December, made the call in the *Guardian* for parents to march with their children, it echoed a widely felt sentiment.[20]

The official student movement

The role of the NUS and the local student unions that affiliate to it has been the source of a great deal of controversy in the movement. The NUS threw its resources into 10 November, delivering a turnout more than double what they expected. While activists on the ground played a key role, the NUS's political, financial and organisational backing was essential in delivering the

---

19: Mason, 2010. "Banlieu" is the French word for suburb.
20: Matthews, 2011.

largest student demonstration for decades. Yet the NUS went on to denounce the occupation of Millbank that inspired so many on that day, and then dizzyingly vacillate in the weeks that followed. One minute Aaron Porter was full of self-criticism, apologising to the University College London occupation for his "spineless dithering" and pledging NUS support for occupations.[21] The next he was engaging in another round of denunciations, refusing to support those demonstrating outside parliament. What explains this behaviour? In part the NUS bureaucracy are placed under the same pressures as the trade union bureaucracy to compromise and hold back. They find themselves stuck between the government and the student movement, and are scared of losing their place at the negotiating table. Indeed, Porter's behaviour is neatly mirrored by that of Sally Hunt, general secretary of the University and College Union, in the same period. However, there are also a number of factors particular to student unions that shouldn't be overlooked.

A modern day student union at a large higher education institution will look more like a medium sized business than a representative body. The "services" side of most unions—bars, shops, night clubs—tend massively to outweigh the representative side, both in the agenda of the union and in its public perception. It is now common for unions to encourage standing in sabbatical elections on the basis of the experience of being in charge of a multi-million pound budget, rather than any political engagement. While they are run as non-profit organisations, the logic of maximising revenue from services tends to dominate. The original raison d'etre of union venues as a shared, independent space for student interaction can easily be eroded. For example, (a trivial one perhaps) my student union bar now does not allow students to bring in their own food, forcing you to buy from the bar instead. The corporate aspect gives rise to a permanent apparatus of full-time unelected union employees, whose interest lies in not rocking the boat. Even if a radical student is elected to a sabbatical position they can expect to be faced with a chief executive or general manager who has been at the union longer than they have even been a student. A sabbatical officer will be in the position for a maximum of two years and will find it hard to transform an institution in that time.

In further education the situation is even harder. While further education institutions are legally required to have some form of student representation, this is extremely patchy. They often consist of little more than student representative committees, with members of staff overseeing them. They are chronically under-resourced and often entirely co-opted by college

---

21: See Kingsley, 2010.

authorities. This makes genuine democratic structures difficult or impossible to establish, so officers, however well meaning, can be unaccountable and easily ignored by college management. Less than 50 of over 400 colleges across the country have a full time elected officer. As the current NUS vice-president for further education puts it: "Many colleges have something they call a student union that bears no resemblance to the model of what a student union should look like".[22]

In this context a deeply conservative trend has developed, where student unions see themselves as mere service providers for students. This inevitably narrows the horizons of what is seen as legitimate campaigning. Many student unions tend to regard themselves as a wing of the university that provides student support, rather than as representing students *against* the university authorities. I write this after coming from a student union election hustings in which candidates argued that stopping cuts was less important than "ensuring the student experience is not adversely affected by them". The elephant in the room, of course, is that it is impossible to prevent 80 percent cuts to funding adversely affecting students. Yet these candidates saw their role as smoothing over management's attacks, rather than stopping them. An even worse consequence of this culture is the way in which a narrow construal of student interests can pit students against staff. In 2006, when lecturers undertook an examination boycott, a number of unions played a disgraceful role in attacking lecturers. For these unions "defending students" meant pitting them against staff.

This culture in student unions filters up to the NUS itself through its federal structure. Unlike national trade unions, the NUS does not have branches, and is based rather on local student unions affiliating to it. This makes it financially dependent on the affiliation of individual student unions. The disaffiliation of a large union such as Manchester could have catastrophic consequences for the NUS. This means the threat of disaffiliation can be used as blackmail to pull the leadership to the right. This was essentially the position Aaron Porter found himself in December last year, pulled from the right by those who thought the NUS had been too radical, and from the left by the growing movement, with his base in the middle ground evaporating.

Another important factor in understanding student unions today is their changing legal status. From the mid-1970s onwards a series of legal changes began to restrict the campaigning remit of student unions, and by proxy the NUS. Student unions are now registered charities, and thus restricted in what they are able to do by the Charity Commission. The

---

22: Murray, 2010.

exact restrictions are a source of great dispute, but broadly charities law restricts the capacity of student unions to campaign on issues which do not directly affect students. This gives a ready-made excuse to sabbatical officers or general managers, which is familiar to anyone who has tried to get their union to campaign over the war, or in solidarity with Palestine, or against fascism: it's illegal. However, the charitable status of student unions has to be understood as part of a long process of restricting their power and influence. The law does not come from nowhere.

The landmark cases that established that student unions are charities are striking. Two of the three cases that are generally cited involve student unions engaging in wider political campaigning. In 1972 the University of Sussex Student Union was legally blocked from making a £500 donation to War on Want, and spending £800 on a campaign against the then secretary of state Margaret Thatcher's proposal to end free school milk. In 1985 the Polytechnic of North London Student Union made donations of £5,000 to support the miners' strike and £5,000 for the relief of Ethiopian famine, which were ruled illegal.[23] In both of these cases it was ruled that since the universities they were attached to had charitable status, the unions themselves also had this status. The charitable status of student unions, though largely taken for granted now, is intimately linked to a political agenda to erode solidarity between students and workers in struggle.

Nonetheless, in this period student unions remained less regulated by the state than they are now. They still had a fairly ambiguous legal status, without uniform structures and organisation. All of this changed in 1994. Following a wave of occupations and demonstrations against cuts in student grants, John Major's Tory government moved to restrict the power of student unions further. The 1994 Education Act established in law a set of rules for student unions that remain today. Whilst these appear fairly innocuous— allowing opt outs for membership, setting rules about elections, etc—they represented another step in transforming the culture of student unions from campaigning bodies to service providers.

The 1994 act established that student unions were "unincorporated associations", while the Charity Commission considered them to be "exempt charities". This legal ambiguity gave a certain scope to argue about exactly what kind of campaigning was permitted. This changed with the Charities Act of 2006, which transformed all student unions into fully registered charities, imposing very stringent guidelines on their political campaigning. According to the Charities Commission,

23: AMSU, 2003.

union funds cannot be used to promote or support campaigns on matters which may be of general interest or concern but which do not affect members of the union as students. Examples would be industrial disputes, general campaigning on environmental matters, eg environmental policies and road building, or the treatment of political prisoners in a foreign country. A students' union cannot, for instance, pay for coaches to transport students to demonstrations on such issues.[24]

These legal restrictions have led to a climate of terror about the legal repercussions of militant action. This goes some way to explaining just how extreme Porter's "dithering" has been; he undoubtedly has the NUS's senior management filling him with panic about the law. It is important to note that there has so far been no legal action taken against unions on the basis of these changes, and it is clear that many unions have quietly continued to campaign on such matters. Nonetheless, this represents a breathtaking restriction on the political independence of student unions.

The most striking thing about the 2006 act was the response of the leadership of the NUS and of most student unions. Instead of rejecting this further restriction on their independence, they embraced it with open arms as an opportunity to go further along the corporate road. Unions became infected with a corporate language of "good governance" and suddenly unions that had been functioning perfectly well undertook "governance reviews" to "improve their structure". Despite being cloaked in the language of accessibility and participation, these tended to be the exact opposite. Most prominent was the NUS's own governance review, which paralysed the union for two years. After initially being narrowly defeated by the left of the union, the reforms were driven through two successive emergency conferences. This involved shrinking the size and representativeness of conference, and the creation of an unaccountable "trustee board" with the power of veto over the executive on certain decisions. Most controversial was the presence of "external trustees" included for their "experience". These were invariably successful business people, with interests far removed from those of students. The trustee board model has been replicated at student unions up and down the country.

Reclaiming the NUS?
The erosion of democracy in the NUS and the increasing legal restrictions on what student unions can do has led to many activists abandoning the NUS as a site of struggle altogether. This was pithily expressed by an activist

---

24: Charity Commission, 2010.

a few years ago who argued that wanting a democratic and campaigning NUS was like asking for a democratic and campaigning Commission for Racial Equality. Certainly the NUS conference is hardly a hospitable place for the left. It is dominated more than ever before by cliques of sabbatical officers. Delegate cuts mean it is ever harder for grassroots activists to get to conference. However, to abandon the NUS would be a mistake. The NUS can still be forced by pressure from below into taking action. This was evident in the call for a demonstration on 10 November, something the leadership has at times been less than enthusiastic about. Similarly, despite his dramatic about face following it, his address to UCL occupation was an indication of the pressure that a serious mass movement placed on Aaron Porter. The leadership of the NUS traditionally aspire to positions either in the Labour Party or the trade union bureaucracy, and, just like those bodies, they can be pushed into action by militancy from its grass roots.

Furthermore, history shows that when militant student movements are on the rise they can quickly shake up the official structures. In 1969 David Widgery wrote about the NUS as the student movement's "muffler". The NUS he describes then, while far smaller, is strangely reminiscent of the NUS today. Widgery describes an NUS that had "bored a generation of students to political death" in which "debate appears so infantile, organisation appears so manipulative and elections appear so deeply conditioned by hucksterism that the value of enlarging the radical enclave within the NUS is very questionable".[25] One thing this indicates is that there has never been a golden age of NUS democracy. However, the 1970s did see a genuine opening up of democratic space within the NUS, of victories for Broad Lefts and the growth of a serious revolutionary current within it.[26] This democratic space has never been perfect, and has always been contested, but when student militancy is on the rise it can break the ossified structures open.

This does not mean, however, that winning positions is enough, that we can "reclaim" our union through winning a majority on the executive. The only candidate to successfully break the stranglehold of Labour Students and right wing independents over the NUS presidency in the past decade was the Campaign for Free Education candidate Kat Fletcher. Fletcher was elected in 2004, on a high tide of disillusionment with New Labour over war and top-up fees, when Labour Students were at their lowest ebb.[27] However, Fletcher quickly distanced herself from the left, and

---

25: Widgery, pp119, 139.
26: Callinicos and Turner, 1975, describe the growth of these forces.
27: See Caldwell, 2004.

went on to impose anti-democratic reforms.[28] She is often mentioned as a "sell-out", but this alone misses the point. She could, of course, have done more to resist the pull of the bureaucracy and the right, but these pulls were enormous. In the absence of a mass movement on the ground it was far easier for her to move to the right.

This means that radical students must understand the need to build both within and outside of the NUS. Simply squirrelling ourselves away in its arcane structures may help us win the odd election, but it will not deliver the kind of movement we need. At the same time, ignoring it cuts radical students off from a body that, despite all its faults, thousands of students look to. It is important to remember that had the left in the NUS heeded the calls of some to abandon it, 10 November simply would not have happened in the same way. The same thing goes for student unions at a local level. Whether successful or not, intervening in an election on a political basis, or proposing a motion of support for a strike or demonstration can puncture through the depoliticised culture of student unions. Such interventions can also bring radical ideas to a larger audience, polarise debate round certain issues and provide a campaigning focus which unites a radical minority on campus. If a candidate wins, or a motion passes, then so much the better, but even if they do not these interventions are not a waste of time.

Conclusion
While students remain a distinct social force in a transitional place within capitalist society, I have argued above that there are factors that tend towards solidarity between students and the working class. On the other hand, a combination of legal restrictions and a service-driven culture in student unions can pull away from such solidarity. There are reasons to be optimistic, however, that the former tendency can overcome the latter. These two tendencies came into direct conflict early in 2010 as part of the industrial dispute at Leeds University. Leeds UCU were preparing for industrial action in defence of jobs (action which never had to take place due to a climbdown by management). The leadership of Leeds Student Union proposed a referendum motion condemning the action. However, despite the efforts of the leadership, a majority of those who voted (891 to 717) rejected the motion, and therefore supported the UCU in their dispute.[29] This may only be one

---

28: See Whittaker, 2004.

29: See report at http://leedsucu.wordpress.com/2010/04/28/luu-will-not-oppose-industrial-action/.

example, but it is an important one that suggests building solidarity between students and workers is easier than in the past.

A striking feature of the recent movement has been the ease with which arguments for solidarity have been won, and the acknowledgement that students cannot go it alone. While there have been debates over the organisational forms, if any, that solidarity should take, there has been widespread agreement about the need to make links with the organised working class. This is a welcome difference from the movements of 1968, when people like Cockburn argued that students could act as an "independent revolutionary force", establishing red bases at universities that directly challenged capitalist rule. In place of this there is an acceptance that, while militant student action can achieve a great deal, the organised power of workers in their workplaces can achieve far more. Precisely because students do not have a direct relationship to the means of production, a student strike is not as effective as a workers' strike. As Mark Bergfeld, a socialist on the NUS executive, is fond of pointing out, a thousand students can stop a train, but a thousand train drivers can stop a country

This doesn't mean students should be reduced to cheerleaders for workers' struggles, or that we should all abandon challenging our own university management in favour of delivering solidarity to workers. A student occupation poses questions about what education is really for, and about how universities should be run. But it is only through linking up with workers that students can begin to provide an answer to those questions. In that respect, at least, the key questions are the same as they have been since the development of capitalism. In 1970 an editorial in this journal argued the following:

> There is a good deal of life left in the present student upsurge. It can annoy the authorities a deal more, as well as bring many more of its participants to a true comprehension of the class realities of our society. The revolutionary left must participate in it attempting to give guidance and leadership, seeing its victories as our victories. But we must also be aware of its limitations, continually pointing out that the only force for carrying through a real transformation of society lies elsewhere and that students who seriously want to solve their own problems can only do so by becoming part of a revolutionary organisation that relates to the aspirations and struggles of that class.[30]

A lot has changed in the past 40 years, but this is as true today as it was then.

30: "Editorial", 1970, p1.

References

AMSU (Association of Managers in Students' Unions), "The Law Relating To Students' Unions and the Responsibilities of Elected Officers as Trustees", 2003, www.amsu.net/pageassets/resources/library/legalstatus/2.doc

Ashman, Sam, 1999, "People and Planet Conference: Students Say 'We Do Give a Damn'", *Socialist Worker* (13 November), www.socialistworker.co.uk/art.php?id=1317

Bhattacharyya, Anindya, 2010, "Middlesex Students Occupy against Cuts", *Socialist Worker* (8 May), www.socialistworker.co.uk/art.php?id=21115

Caldwell, Sam, 2004, "Labour Loses its Grip as NUS Joins Awkward Squad", *Socialist Worker* (10 April), www.socialistworker.co.uk/art.php?id=555

Callinicos, Alex, 2006, *Universities in a Neo-Liberal World* (Bookmarks).

Callinicos, Alex, and Simon Turner, 1975, "The Student Movement Today", *International Socialism* 75 (first series, February), www.marxists.org/history/etol/writers/callinicos/1975/02/students.htm

Charity Commission, 2010, *Students' Unions: A Guide*, www.charity-commission.gov.uk/About_us/OGs/g048c003.aspx

Cockburn, Alexander, 1969, "Introduction", in Alexander Cockburn and Robin Blackburn (eds), *Student Power* (Penguin).

"Editorial", 1970, *International Socialism* 43 (first series, April/May), www.marxists.org/history/etol/newspape/isj/1970/no043/editorial.htm

HESA (Higher Education Statistics Agency), 2010, www.hesa.ac.uk/index.php?option=com_content&task=view&id=1897&Itemid=239

Hyman, Jeff, and Abigail Marks, 2008, "Frustrated Ambitions: The Reality of Balancing Work and Life for Call Centre Employees", in Chris Warhurst, Doris Ruth Eikhof and Axel Haunschild (eds), *Work Less, Live More?* (Palgrave MacMillan).

Kingsley, Patrick, 2010, "NUS President Apologises Over Spineless Dithering", *Guardian* (28 November), www.guardian.co.uk/education/2010/nov/28/student-leader-apologises-over-dithering

Lipsett, Anthea, and Alison Benjamin, 2009, "Storm of Student Protest Over Gaza Gathers force", *Guardian* (23 January), http://www.guardian.co.uk/education/2009/jan/23/student-protests-gaza

Mason, Paul. 2010, "Dubstep Rebellion—the British Banlieue Comes to Millbank", *BBC News* (9 December), www.bbc.co.uk/blogs/newsnight/paulmason/2010/12/9122010_dubstep_rebellion_-_br.html

Matthews, Susan, 2011, "It's Time for Parents to Stand with their Children at the Student Protests", *Guardian*, (28 January), www.guardian.co.uk/commentisfree/2011/jan/28/students-children-kettle-police-violence/

Murray, Janet, 2010, "Why Do So Few Colleges Have Active Students Unions?", *Guardian* (23 March), www.guardian.co.uk/education/2010/mar/23/few-college-student-unions

NUS/TUC, 2006, *All Work and Low Pay*, www.tuc.org.uk/extras/allworklowpay.pdf

ONS, 2009, *Social Trends*, http://www.statistics.gov.uk/downloads/theme_social/Social_Trends39/Social_Trends_39.pdf

Ruddick, Sîan, 2009, "Student Protests for Palestine Remain Strong", *Socialist Worker* (7 February), www.socialistworker.co.uk/art.php?id=17046

Swain, Harriet, 1997, "NUS Tuition Fee Policy Under Fire", *Times Higher Education* (17 October), www.timeshighereducation.co.uk/story.asp?sectioncode=26&storycode=104148

Thompson, Alan, 1997, "NUS Torn Apart by Leadership's Response to Fees", *Times Higher Education* (29 August), www.timeshighereducation.co.uk/story.asp?sectioncode=26&storycode=102943

Whittaker, Tom, 2004, "Attack on Democracy", *Socialist Worker* (26 June), www.socialistworker.co.uk/art.php?id=485

Widgery, David, 1969, "NUS, The Students' Muffler", in Alexander Cockburn and Robin Blackburn (eds), *Student Power* (Penguin).

The origins of the
united front policy
John Riddell

The policy of the united front is among the most effective tools for working class action inherited from the era of VI Lenin and the Russian revolution. As originally formulated by the Executive Committee of the Communist International (Comintern) in December 1921, united front policy called for the "greatest possible unity of all workers' organisations in every practical action against the united capitalists", while assuring revolutionary socialists and other participating currents "absolute autonomy" and "freedom in presenting their point of view".[1]

Initiatives to build unity in action with diverse currents in the workers' movement can be traced back to the First International and its efforts to build bridges to British trade unionists and the followers of August Blanqui and Pierre-Joseph Proudhon in France, as well as to initiatives by the Bolshevik Party in Russia before 1917. The December 1921 Comintern policy statement cited Bolshevik precedent but was framed as a response to current needs, in the context of an ebb in revolutionary struggle. In the ensuing decades revolutionary socialists have utilised united front tactics in very different circumstances, including—in recent years—to oppose imperialist wars, support liberation struggles and meet threats of violence from fascist groups.

1: Translated from Comintern, 1923b, for the English edition of proceedings of the Comintern's Fourth Congress, to be published by Brill Academic Publishers, 2011. For another translation of this text, see Adler, 1980, p406.

The evolution of united front policy was marked by ambiguities, false steps and corrections. The main driving force in its formulation was the thinking and the initiatives of the working class ranks and the urgency of their struggle for immediate needs and essential human rights.

A united front struggle is a step on the road to revolution, and yet simultaneously an effective instrument to win an immediate reform. Many critics of revolutionary socialism have seized on this fact to declare united front policy inherently contradictory or even dishonest, claiming that revolutionary socialists always sacrifice the interests of united front allies for partisan purposes. In addition, some socialists scorn united fronts, refusing to join with pro-capitalist labour officials or politicians. Others put an anti-revolutionary spin on the united front, seeing its culmination in parliamentary combinations or coalition governments with bourgeois forces.

All these positions were argued when united front policy was first formulated, and the debate has continued through the decades. But to understand how revolutionary socialists of Lenin's time acted to promote unity of the working class movement, we must first review how this movement came to be divided.

The split in world socialism

The Comintern's united front policy sought to address a profound, intractable split in the world socialist movement. When the First World War broke out in August 1914, the majority leaderships of the main socialist parties—in Britain, France, Germany and Austria-Hungary—supported the war efforts of their respective capitalist ruling classes, thus bringing about the collapse of the Socialist or Second International. An anti-war current soon took shape in the working class, and its influence was reflected in mass demonstrations, strikes, mutinies and insurrections.

Pro-war "socialists" joined or supported governments that repressed worker and soldier protests. Most of these "social patriots" also opposed the October 1917 Revolution that established the Russian Soviet government, and many backed the counter-revolutionary armies in the Russian Civil War. Revolutionary socialists took their places on the opposite side of the battle lines, supporting worker and soldier resistance and anti-war protests and actively defending the Soviet republic.

In November 1918 a workers' and soldiers' uprising overturned the German government, bringing the First World War to an abrupt end. The Social Democratic Party of Germany (SPD)—now the dominant force in Germany's provisional government—helped organise the brutal repression that restabilised capitalist rule. SPD leaders were complicit in the January 1919 murder of the best-known revolutionary leaders, Rosa Luxemburg and Karl Liebknecht. In the victorious Allied countries, right wing "socialists"—now commonly called social democrats—backed the draconian "peace" terms imposed by their governments, while revolutionary socialists sought to overturn these treaties. Right wing social democrats backed continued colonial rule over subject peoples in Africa, Asia and elsewhere, while revolutionary forces actively supported the rising colonial revolution.

By the war's end, the world socialist movement, proudly united only half a decade earlier, was splitting into warring camps: on one side, the discredited pro-war forces, generally termed the Second International; on the other, a revolutionary socialist minority, which organised in March 1919 as the Communist or Third International. Caught in the middle were forces critical of both sides, often termed "centrists". They were loosely allied in the Vienna Union, which Communists derisively termed the "Two-and-a-Half International".

In late 1918 and 1919 a tide of revolution swept across Europe, inspiring Communists with hope that the workers' victory in Russia would quickly be duplicated in major countries of Western and Central Europe. Communist parties in these countries grew to embrace tens or hundreds of thousands of members. By late 1920, however, it was clear that capitalist rule had restabilised, at least for the moment. Social democratic and labour leaders committed to defence of capitalism ("reformists" or "opportunists") still enjoyed the support of a majority of workers. Their strength posed a massive obstacle not only to socialist revolution but to effective defence of wages and working conditions against the employers' onslaught.

The united front policy aimed to overcome this obstacle to united working class action.

The Hungarian Soviet Republic

The first attempt to overcome the division in workers' ranks took place, quite unexpectedly, in Hungary, only two weeks after the Comintern's formation. In a country shaken by war, economic collapse and revolution, the head of state (a pro-capitalist aristocrat) asked the Socialists, a non-revolutionary party aligned with the Second International, to form a government. Fearing Communist influence among workers in the capital, the Socialists asked the newly formed Communist Party (CP) to join in a coalition government—and, moreover, to seal the pact through an organic fusion of the two parties.

The Hungarian Communists agreed to the fusion. They played the leading role in a government based on workers' councils that ruled for the next four months, before its violent overthrow by the armed forces of the Allied or Entente powers. Subsequent Comintern analysis highlighted the unprepared top-down fusion of the Communist and Socialist forces, which eliminated the Communists as an independent force, while leaving the regime vulnerable to Socialist vacillation and betrayal.[2]

But were Communists wrong to consider a governmental alliance with the Socialists? Later Comintern discussion barely touched on this point. The most explicit comment came from Karl Radek, a leader of both the Comintern and the Russian Bolshevik Party who had long experience in the German working class movement. The Hungarian example, he wrote, showed that "the course of events could place Communists anywhere before the necessity of forming a [governmental] coalition" of this type, but they should not give up their separate organisation. In February 1922 Hungarian Communist Mátyás Rákosi referred to the 1919 alliance, without elaboration, as a "united front," but this notion remained unexplored in subsequent Comintern united front debates.[3]

Unity against a military coup

During the months following the fall of the Hungarian Soviet government the Comintern focused its attention on drawing together genuinely revolutionary forces in Communist parties, and the question of alliances received little attention. In March 1920, however, the possibility of a coalition government of workers' parties was once again posed, as Radek had predicted, and once again the initiative came from the social democratic side. It was this event that launched the Comintern's united front debate.

During the first postwar years, Germany's capitalist ("Weimar") republic was shaken by severe class battles in a ruined economy whose recovery was blocked by demands of the Entente powers for reparations payments. Despite the defeat of revolutionary workers in early 1919, their movement remained strong, while rightist and proto-fascist forces plotted to thrust aside the SPD-led government and resume direct control.

On 13 March 1920 a rightist military detachment occupied Berlin, the capital, and drove the government into flight. The putsch, led by Wolfgang Kapp and General Walther von Lüttwitz, was countered that evening by a call from the SPD-led trade unions (ADGB) for a general strike to defend the republic. By 14 March the strike was solid across

---

2:   See *Lenin Collected Works* (Hereafter *LCW*), volume 30, pp354-355; Riddell, 1991, volume I, pp162 (Rákosi), pp296-297 (Zinoviev).

3:   Radek, 1920a, p59; Rákosi in Comintern, 1922a, p94.

the country. Workers formed local strike committees, demonstrated, and formed militias and armed detachments. In Berlin there were two separate strike committees, one led by the SPD, the other by the centrist Independent Social Democratic Party (USPD)—the latter with participation of the German Communist Party (KPD). In the important Chemnitz industrial region, by contrast, Communists succeeded in uniting all workers' organisations in a structure of workers' councils, which led the struggle there. Armed resistance spread across the country, and on 17 March the putschists capitulated and fled.[4]

The general strike continued, however, as workers demanded a new government and decisive action against the rightist militarist threat. Carl Legien, chair of the union confederation, responded by proposing that the SPD's coalition with bourgeois parties be replaced by a workers' government formed by the SPD, the USPD and the trade unions. The KPD leadership expressed support for this proposal, stating that "formation of a socialist government, free of the slightest bourgeois or capitalist element, would create extremely favourable conditions for vigorous action by the proletarian masses," and promised, subject to certain conditions, to act towards such a government as a "loyal opposition".[5] The USPD, however, refused to participate in such a government, effectively killing the proposal. Legien then obtained promises of pro-worker reforms from the existing government. The strike gradually died away, and the government and army re-established control.

The KPD's "loyal opposition" statement came under strong criticism from party leaders of many viewpoints. Many viewed the purely socialist government envisaged in this statement as similar to the joint SPD-USPD government immediately after the November 1918 Revolution, which had assured the restoration of capitalist power, and which the KPD had opposed. The party central committee rejected, by a vote of 12 to eight, the notion that such a regime could play a progressive role.

MJ Braun, a supporter of the minority viewpoint, drew a parallel with the Bolsheviks' call, shortly before the October 1917 Revolution, for Mensheviks and Social Revolutionaries to break with the bourgeoisie and form a government based on the soviets. Radek, the Comintern Executive's liaison with the German party, said that the Russian example did not apply because the relationship of forces in Germany was more

---

4:   For an account of the Kapp-Lüttwitz putsch and other events in the German Revolution of 1918-23, see Broué, 2006, and Harman, 1982.
5:   Broué, 2006, p369.

unfavourable. In Radek's view, the "loyal opposition" position reflected the emergence of a "possibilist" (ie reformist) current in the KPD. Lenin, however, while criticising the KPD statement for erroneous formulations, judged it to be "quite correct both in its basic premises and in its practical conclusions" and affirmed that the Bolsheviks' approach in 1917 was indeed relevant to the German discussion. Lenin's comments had sufficient authority to end the discussion, but the disagreement remained unresolved.[6]

Early united front initiatives

The prevalence of action committees uniting all workers' parties during the Kapp struggle aroused little comment in the subsequent KPD debate. However, the Hungarian Communist Béla Kun, a leading spokesperson for an ultra-left current in the Comintern, branded the "unity' ideal" expressed in the Kapp actions as "counter-revolutionary". Communists should not try to persuade centrist parties to join in united action but act alone, Kun said.[7] Kun's viewpoint was far from isolated in the International; Lenin wrote a celebrated pamphlet that spring on the errors of "left wing" communism.[8] Lenin did not comment specifically on united fronts, but his pamphlet did recommend that British Communists give electoral support to Labour Party candidates and apply for affiliation to the party. This policy had been previously practised by the British Socialist Party, a Comintern affiliate, which secured its adoption at the International's Second Congress in July 1920. Later, in February 1922, Gregory Zinoviev, president of the Comintern, said that in these proposals by Lenin "we already find the entire united front policy, adapted to British circumstances".[9]

The as yet unformulated united front approach was tested in an international campaign against a Polish government invasion of Soviet Russia in April 1920. Polish armies, supported by the French and other Entente governments, captured Kiev, capital of Soviet Ukraine, on 7 May. In response, a wave of worker solidarity actions began halting arms shipments to Poland in Britain, Germany, Austria, Czechoslovakia and Danzig. When the British government decided in July to send war material to Poland, the Labour Party and unions threatened a general strike, forcing cancellation of the

---

6:    Braun, 1920, p167; Radek, 1920a, pp170-175. Both writers had in mind Lenin's article "On Compromises", in *LCW*, volume 25, pp309-314. For Lenin's comments, see *LCW*, volume 31, pp109 and 166.
7:    Kun, 1920, pp349, 441.
8:    See Lenin, *"Left-Wing" Communism—an Infantile Disorder*, in *LCW*, volume 31, pp17-118.
9:    See Comintern, 1922a, p37; Riddell, 1991, pp36-37, 50-51, 156-157, 760-761.

shipment. Everywhere the blockade of Poland owed its success to workers' unity in action. In Germany the social democratic and union leaderships formed joint committees to lead the actions, in which Communists were able to participate on a local level.[10]

Another arena for united action opened up after 1917 with the spread of liberation struggles among the oppressed Asian peoples within the old tsarist empire. The left wing of these movements viewed the Soviet government as their peoples' best defence against religious, national and racial oppression, and formed alliances with the Bolshevik Party. The Second Comintern congress, held in July-August 1920, proclaimed the need for such alliances across the colonial world, pledging the International's support for "the revolutionary movement among the nations that are dependent and do not have equal rights". In September the Comintern convened the First Congress of the Peoples of the East—a gathering in Baku, Azerbaijan, of almost 2,000 delegates from across Asia. The congress acclaimed the call "Workers of all lands and oppressed peoples of the whole world, unite!"—an expanded version of the *Communist Manifesto*'s historic appeal. The Baku congress manifesto proclaimed a "holy war for the liberation of the peoples of the East".[11]

Stuttgart workers take the lead

As capitalist attacks intensified in the summer of 1920, efforts began to recreate the fighting unity of the Kapp days. Two years later KPD leader Edwin Hoernle recalled events in the industrial region of Stuttgart: "We did not then have any theory of united front, comrades. But our party organisation, that of the old Spartacus League, instinctively applied this policy when there was a demonstration against inflation and a strike against a 10 per cent deduction from wages".[12]

The successful resistance to the Kapp putsch increased the confidence of working people in Germany, giving the revolutionary left new energy. A majority of the USPD voted in October to join the Comintern and fused with the KPD in December, creating a united party with more than 300,000 members. The right wing minority broke away and retained the name USPD. German capitalists had failed to stabilise the economy, and

---

10: See Hájek and Mejdrová, 1997, p251; Thalheimer in Comintern, 1922a, p71.
11: See Riddell, 1991, volume I, p286; Riddell, 1993, pp219, 231. On the origin of the "workers and oppressed peoples'" call, see *LCW*, volume 31, p453. On the alliance between Bolsheviks and Muslim revolutionaries in Soviet Asia, see Crouch, 2006, Martin, 2001, Smith, 1999.
12: Comintern, 1923b, p384.

working people faced falling living standards and desperate poverty. Still, among workers voting for socialist parties, the united KPD enjoyed the support of fewer than a fifth, and the hostility between the three workers' parties remained a formidable barrier to effective action.[13]

In November 1920 a promising initiative to break this deadlock was taken by the ranks of the KPD in Stuttgart. The role of Stuttgart workers was not unprecedented. Socialist workers of this city had been in the vanguard of the pre-1914 SPD left; it was they who convinced Karl Liebknecht, when he visited the city on 21 September 1914, to cast his historic parliamentary vote against credits for the imperialist world war.[14] Stuttgart was also the home base of Clara Zetkin, among the KPD's most influential leaders.

The KPD district committee in Stuttgart decided in November, in consultation with the Berlin party leadership, to launch a campaign for workers' unity in action. The Stuttgart Communists made a proposal in the local metal workers' union, which was chaired by KPD member Erich Melcher, to petition the union's national leadership and the ADGB unions for united action. Acting on this initiative, the leadership of the 26,000 Stuttgart metal workers adopted five demands reflecting workers' most urgent needs, demands "held in common by all workers":

- Reduce prices for necessities of life.
- Produce at full capacity and increase unemployment benefits.
- Reduce taxes paid by workers and raise taxes on the great private fortunes.
- Establish workers' control of supply and distribution of raw materials and foodstuffs.
- Disarm reactionary gangs and arm the workers.[15]

The demands were placed before a general assembly of Stuttgart metal workers, with the participation of Robert Dissmann, a leader of the rump USPD and the metal workers' national chairman. Overwhelmingly adopted, the demands then went out to metalworkers' local branches across the country. The national KPD declared its support for the initiative on

---

13: The estimate of KPD support is based on the February 1921 elections in Prussia, which included the majority of Germany's population. The SPD won 26.3 percent of the vote; the KPD, 7.4 percent; and the anti-Comintern USPD minority (which retained the name) 6.6 percent. www.wahlen-in-deutschland.de/wlPreussen.htm

14: Riddell, 1984, p173.

15: Reisberg, 1971, p50.

2 December. Radek endorsed it, remarking, tellingly: "If I had been in Moscow, the idea would not even have crossed my mind".[16]

Leading bodies of the ADGB, USPD and SPD at first ignored the Stuttgart initiative. But in the local union bodies it found a warm welcome, and soon, according to the trade union editor of the KPD's *Rote Fahne,* "resolutions of support were piling up in our office by the hundreds". [17] Forced to speak out, the SPD declared the demands to be unrealistic, while the USPD regretted that they did not include nationalisation of the mines and heavy industry.[18] Dissmann, under heavy pressure from the union ranks, tried a novel stratagem, asking locals that adopted the five points to explain how they proposed to implement them. When they responded that formulating a plan for implementation was the job not of base units but of the union's national executive, Dissmann declared triumphantly that since no one had proposals for implementation, the demands were unacceptable.[19]

The "open letter"

Impressed by the strong response to the Stuttgart initiative, the KPD central leadership (Zentrale) decided on 29 December to initiate a generalised movement for united working class action. Although supported by Radek, the decision was opposed by many members of the Zentrale, particularly those coming from the former USPD left wing. The objections, reminiscent of Béla Kun's arguments earlier in the year, focused on the need for the newly united party to take initiatives in action on its own account, without trying to rope in the social democratic leaders. But when the proposal for a united-action campaign was laid before a conference of district secretaries on 7 January 1921, it was approved almost unanimously. Delegates from the Rhineland-Westphalia region, which included the Ruhr industrial heartland, reported that they had already taken such an initiative on their own.

The result was an open letter of the KPD to the USPD, SPD, KAPD (Communist Workers Party, an ultra-left split-off from the KPD), and four trade union federations, calling on them to come together in actions to fend

16: Broué, 2006, p469.
17: Reisberg, 1971, p51.
18: The USPD focused on the nationalisation demand as the spearhead of their own united front efforts in 1921 and 1922. The KPD supported nationalisation but did not prioritise it in their action programme, which focused on immediate workers' mobilisation and "was contemptuous of attempts to squeeze socialism out of the existing capitalist order"—Morgan, 1975, p392.
19: Reisberg, 1971, p52.

off the bosses' offensive against workers, in order to demand "the minimum that the proletariat must have now in order not to perish".

The open letter's proposed demands, published 8 January in the KPD's *Rote Fahne,* were an elaborated version of the Stuttgart Five Points:

1. United wage struggles to defend all workers and employees.
2. Increased pensions.
3. Reorganisation and increases in unemployment allowances.
4. Government provision of food ration cards at reduced cost.
5. Seizure of housing space for the homeless.
6. Measures to provide food and other necessities under the control of factory councils.
7. Disarmament and dissolution of armed bourgeois detachments and formation of workers' self-defence organisations.
8. Amnesty for political prisoners.
9. Immediate establishment of trade and diplomatic relations with Soviet Russia.[20]

The open letter pointed out that the listed demands would not end workers' poverty. However, "without giving up for a moment our propaganda amongst the masses for a struggle for the dictatorship [that is, a workers' state similar to the Soviet Republic]", the party "is ready for common action with the workers' parties to win the above-mentioned demands".[21]

Drafted jointly by KPD central leader Paul Levi and Radek, the letter was the Communists' first attempt to engage with the social democratic parties not just in a given factory or locality, but on a national level. However, the response from national leaderships was negative. On the very day of the Open Letter's publication, the SPD published a reply affirming its willingness to negotiate while condemning the letter for its "absurd demands" and its "foolish and ludicrous procedure". The following day, in an overhasty response, the KPD interpreted this statement as a rejection and appealed to the SPD ranks. The SPD executive thereupon declared on 10 January 1921 that the KPD had withdrawn its offer and that the matter was closed.

The USPD's official rejection followed on 13 January, claiming that the open letter represented merely an insincere attempt by the Communists

---

20: Reisberg, 1971, p54.
21: Broué, 2006, p470.

to break out of their isolation. The ADGB accused the Communists of trying to "destroy the unions" and threatened to expel local organisations that endorsed the letter. Even the KAPD rebuffed the open letter as "opportunist, demagogic and misleading". Yet these negative responses failed to stem a wave of support from rank and file union and social democratic organisations. *Rote Fahne* provided daily reports of favourable resolutions, and at the beginning of March the KPD estimated that more than two million workers were on record as favouring the open letter demands.[22]

Soon there were signs of motion in the social democratic camp. The SPD newspaper *Vorwärts* printed appeals for struggle to aid destitute unemployed workers. This call was taken up by a Berlin assembly of factory council representatives, which called for a united action. Emil Barth, the USPD head of the councils, opened negotiations with all parties and unions. He asked the KPD if it was prepared to:

1.   Carry out unified agitation and cease incitement against fraternal organisations.
2.   Submit to the strict discipline of the united action's leadership.
3.   Cease calling for unions to affiliate to the Red International of Trade Unions, a Comintern affiliate.
4.   Not carry out actions on its own.
5.   Not demand an escalation of the slogans.

The KPD responded that it could not agree to point three, and that the response to point five would depend on the strength of the action. However, it accepted points one, two, and four—a major step towards overcoming the prejudices of social democratic workers. This particular action did not come to be, but the Berlin factory councils went for a bigger prize, opening up negotiations with the ADGB leadership for national action to counter unemployment. On 26 February 1921 the ADGB executive published ten demands "to combat unemployment", including emergency work projects, increased payments to the jobless, and the mandated rehiring of unemployed in the factories at the employers' expense. The KPD criticised the ADGB's "ten demands" as inadequate, but declared it would do everything possible to support them and help achieve their victory. For the moment, therefore, it set aside the open letter programme.[23]

22: Reisberg, 1971, pp57-65.
23: Reisberg, 1971, p66.

This discussion led to gains for the idea of united action and for the KPD itself. But no major joint actions resulted.

For the social democratic bureaucracy, united initiatives were a loser, shifting focus to the terrain of mass action where they could be rapidly bypassed. The KPD's united front initiatives resulted in a draining away of SPD support to the Communists, regardless of whether or not the SPD joined in united actions. This was particularly true in the unions, where Communist influence was now rapidly increasing.[24] The SPD leadership viewed the united front campaign as partisan, an attempt to shift the relationship of forces in the KPD's favour. There was a kernel of truth in this: only by radically increasing its influence in unions and the working class could the KPD exert the pressure needed to force the social democratic parties and ADGB into united action and, ultimately, to create the preconditions for revolutionary victory.

To work through these contradictions required time, and in March 1921 time suddenly ran out.

March 1921: a setback for unity

Even as the German Communists' campaign for workers' unity scored gains, there were increasing calls in the KPD for the party to take bolder initiatives in struggle—on its own, if necessary. The strain between these two approaches reflected divisions within the German working class as a whole. After the defeat suffered by revolutionary workers in early 1919, the class struggle remained deadlocked for four years: the objective conditions cried out for revolution, but the working class was unable to break through.

Among German workers a vanguard was frustrated and impatient to act, but the majority were pessimistic and relatively passive. In the words of Clara Zetkin, the workers were "almost desperate" yet "unwilling to struggle". A member of the left opposition within her party later commented: "Everything was bogged down. We faced a wall of passivity. We had to break through it, whatever the cost." In a discussion with Zetkin, Lenin referred to "discontented, suffering workers who feel revolutionary but are politically raw and confused... World history does not seem to hurry, but the discontented workers think that your party leaders don't want it to hurry".[25]

Calls for a bolder course were also fed by the tangible progress of the Communist movement, whose members—after the fusion with the left

---

24: Peterson, 1993, p405.
25: Zetkin, 1922, p1; an unnamed KPD member quoted by Trotsky in the Third World Congress, Comintern, 1921a, pp642-643; Zetkin, 1934, p38.

USPD in December 1920—now numbered hundreds of thousands. The unification convention adopted a manifesto, drafted by Radek, which declared that a party that "has an audience of millions must recruit mainly by what it does. The VKPD [the fused party]—is strong enough to go alone into action when events permit and demand this".[26] At the KPD's last pre-fusion convention, Radek had phrased this concept as a sharp criticism of Levi, accusing him of "wanting to do nothing but educate Communists until the party has white hairs on its super-intelligent head". There is much evidence that Radek encouraged left wing critics of the party leadership during this period.[27]

In late 1920 the decline of the postwar revolutionary upsurge was not yet apparent, and in the International an impatience for action was widespread. In the Moscow leadership, Zinoviev and Bukharin were sympathetic to this view, which was now promoted by Kun and other leftist-inclined Hungarian leaders who had been incorporated into the Comintern general staff. Radek's role was ambiguous, defending the united front initiatives in Germany even as he undercut the authority of its chief proponents. It soon proved impossible to conduct these two policies simultaneously.

During November the Comintern Executive (ECCI) voted to recognise as a sympathising party the KAPD, which had broken with the KPD in part over objections to its course during the Kapp events. This move, which the ECCI hoped would lead to the KAPD's reintegration into the official section, was strongly and unanimously protested at by the KPD Zentrale.

The KAPD's opposition to the open letter was echoed within the KPD by a new "leftist" opposition, headed by Ruth Fischer, Arkadi Maslow and Ernst Reuter Friesland, which led the Berlin-area regional organisation. They charged the Zentrale with "exaggerated centralism" for having presented the open letter policy for approval to the party's regional secretaries, without having previously laid it before the Central Committee.[28]

Their views found strong support in the Comintern Executive. A meeting of its Small Bureau in February heard assertions that the open letter showed an "alarming wavering towards opportunist tendencies and an element of passivity"; a majority seemed ready to condemn it. This view was echoed in the full ECCI meeting by Bukharin and Zinoviev, while Radek defended the open letter. Lenin sent a message terming the KPD's tactic "absolutely correct", and this prevented its condemnation. The ECCI referred the issue

---

26: Broué, 2006, p465. From the December 1920 fusion until August 1921 the German Communists took the name VKPD—United Communist Party of Germany.
27: Broué 2006, p464. Regarding Radek's ambiguous role in KPD politics, see Fayet, 2004, pp352-353, 369-370, 389-393.
28: Reisberg, 1971, pp69-70.

to the coming Third Comintern Congress, while unanimously criticising the German party for "inadequate activity on many issues".[29]

A seemingly unrelated issue brought tensions in the German party to a head. On 21 January 1921 the left wing of the Italian Socialist Party, a Comintern affiliate, split away, with strong encouragement from ECCI representatives, founding a Communist Party. The German majority leadership held that the split had been mishandled, unnecessarily leaving many Comintern supporters outside the newly formed party. The minority disagreed, and posed the issue as a question of confidence in the Comintern leadership. At a 22 February meeting of the German party's Central Committee, ECCI emissary Mátyás Rákosi forced the issue. Rákosi was a Hungarian colleague of Béla Kun who had represented the ECCI the previous month in Italy. He strongly attacked the German majority leadership, suggesting that the KPD as well would benefit from a split. A motion endorsing the Italian split, narrowly adopted, had the effect of withdrawing confidence from the Levi leadership. Levi, Zetkin, and three supporters resigned from the Zentrale.

The new leadership that took the helm was made up of those favouring what was now becoming known as the "theory of the offensive"—that is, the notion that Communists, even with only minority support among workers, should launch an all-out assault on capitalist power. In Moscow, Zinoviev and Radek both reacted favourably to the changes. The open letter was effectively overturned.

In March the policy of offensive action was put to the test in Germany. In conditions of great social tension the party geared up for a showdown. Three ECCI emissaries arrived from Moscow—Béla Kun and two others sympathetic to his ultra-left views. There is no evidence that Kun had specific instructions from the ECCI, but given his well known opinions, it came as no surprise that he threw his full authority behind the drive for a revolutionary offensive. The government offered a provocation: an order for police in the state of Saxony to occupy workers' strongholds and disarm workers' detachments. The KPD responded with what was essentially a call for an insurrectional general strike. Across Germany worker ranks were deeply divided, and only a minority followed the KPD call. In many cases Communist activists seeking to enforce a strike clashed with workers trying to enter their factories. In Berlin, where a few weeks earlier Communists had mustered 200,000 votes, a KPD-KAPD demonstration drew only 4,000 participants. The government quickly crushed

---

29: Reisberg, 1971, pp82, 84. Lenin expressed his view in two months later in a letter to Levi and Zetkin; see *LCW*, volume 45, pp124-125.

worker resistance. Thousands of workers were jailed, tens of thousands fired and blacklisted. In a few weeks the KPD lost more than half its membership, and its ties to the ranks of workers were greatly weakened.

Levi sharply attacked the party's conduct in the "March Action" as "the greatest Bakuninist putsch in history".[30] He published his views as a pamphlet, an action which resulted in his expulsion for indiscipline. When the Third Comintern Congress convened in June, Clara Zetkin led a minority of KPD delegates defending Levi's viewpoint. The KPD majority stood by its record in the March Action, and initially at least it seemed likely to have majority support in the Comintern congress.[31]

First steps to recovery

On 30 March 1921 the KPD's *Rote Fahne* blamed the individual members of the social democratic parties for bloodshed during the March Action: "Shame and disgrace on those workers".[32] The open letter seemed truly dead and buried. Yet only two weeks later, on 15 April 1921, a circular from the KPD Zentrale, while proclaiming the need to continue March Action policies, also stated that the demands of the open letter—that is, immediate demands—provided a platform for common struggle against the capitalist offensive. The KPD's May Day appeal went further, calling for support for the ADGB's ten demands. The appeal had been drafted by the party's trade union commission, most of whom had been opponents of the March Action. The ADGB leaders rebuffed this overture, but the Communists swung into action on a local level and achieved many united actions. In Rhineland-Westphalia party leaders continued formally to endorse the theory of the offensive while implementing a diametrically opposed policy. By mid-June, as the Third Congress convened, the KPD had rebuilt some of its mass influence and was once again able to initiate mass demonstrations. While the World Congress debated the March Action, the party ranks had begun to implement the opposite course—the policy charted by Levi leadership before its ousting.[33]

Early in 1921 the KPD also initiated a broadly based committee for defence of working class political prisoners, which joined in June to form the Red Aid of Germany, chaired by Zetkin.[34] It was the forerunner of

---

30: Levi, 2009, p. 132. MA Bakunin was a 19th century anarchist theorist and opponent of Marxism.

31: For fuller accounts of the overturn in the KPD leadership and the March Action, see Broué, 2006, pp475-525; Hallas, 1985, pp61-64; and Harman, 1982, pp191-220.

32: Levi, 2009, p133.

33: Reisberg, 1971, pp138-140; Peterson 1993, pp82-84.

34: Sommer, 2008, p107.

International Red Aid (Russian acronym MOPR), founded during the Fourth Comintern Congress in November 1922, which achieved impressive scope and reputation, notably in its defence of the framed US anarchists Nicola Sacco and Bartolomeo Vanzetti.

"To the masses"

The Comintern's Third World Congress (23 June-12 July 1921) was dominated by debate on issues arising from the March Action. Bolshevik leader Leon Trotsky later wrote that at the start of the congress the prevailing mood was to generalise the KPD's March policy, an "attempt to create a revolutionary situation artificially—to 'galvanise the proletariat', as one of the German comrades put it".[35] This view was argued by the German leadership majority, with initial support from Zinoviev, Bukharin and Radek. The opposition to this course was led by Lenin and Trotsky in the Russian delegation, and Zetkin in that of the KPD. The congress decision, which sought to quell ultra-left impulses, was summarised in a sentence of its *Theses on Tactics*: "At the present moment the most important task of the Communist International is to win a dominant influence over the majority of the working class and involve the more active workers in direct struggle"—a strategy summed up in the slogan, "To the masses".[36]

With regard to the March Action dispute, the congress adopted a compromise decision, which noted errors by the KPD leadership but termed the experience "a step forward" and passed over the ECCI's role in silence. Levi's expulsion was endorsed. The majority of Levi's associates in the KPD leadership subsequently followed him out of the party, while most of the March Action leaders resumed the open letter policies Levi had helped initiate. Fischer and Maslow stayed in opposition, at the helm of an ultra-left faction based in the Berlin region.[37]

Two aspects of the Third Congress decisions prefigured the united front policy adopted by the International six months later. First, a passage in the *Theses on Tactics* concerning the need for Communists to lead the masses into struggle endorsed the KPD's open letter as an "excellent example" of this policy.[38]

35: Trotsky, 1971, p33. See also Trotsky, 1936, pp87-91.
36: Adler, 1980, p277.
37: For more on the Third Congress, see Broué, 2006, pp527-552, Harman, 1982, pp210-216, and Carr, 1966, pp381-393. For its verdict on the March Action, see Adler, 1980, pp290-91
38: Adler, 1980, p289. In February 1922 Radek claimed, with some exaggeration, that the entirety of the united front policy was contained in this passage—Comintern, 1922a, pp66-67.

Second, the Theses articulated a new conception of the type of programme that Communists should advance in a period of preparation for a struggle for power. The heart of this approach was summarised in a single sentence:

> In place of the minimum programme of the reformists and centrists, the Communist International proposes a struggle for the concrete needs of the proletariat, for a system of demands that, in their totality, undermine the power of the bourgeoisie, organise the proletariat, and mark out stages in the struggle for its dictatorship; each of these demands gives expression to the needs of the broadest masses, even if they do not yet consciously set the goal of proletarian dictatorship.[39]

This strategic vision, although prefigured in Bolshevik experience, was most likely articulated on the basis of German experience. Pierre Broué tells us that the notion of transitional slogans was "a favourite idea of [KPD leader Heinrich] Brandler".[40]

Summarising the congress's outcome, Zinoviev wrote that the Comintern had "adapted its policies to new conditions". The Communist parties were much stronger than in 1919, he stated, but "the factor of spontaneity in mass struggles...has grown weaker; the enemy has become strong". The Comintern was traversing a "period of preparation" leading towards decisive struggles, in which Communists must "take part in all the proletariat's minor daily struggles". The world working class was traversing an epoch between two revolutionary waves. "The revolution is not over; the opening of new struggles is not distant".[41]

The KPD embraces the united front
The compromise decisions of the Third Congress did not end the conflict within the German party. A strengthened ultra-left opposition launched a campaign against those who had shared Levi's criticisms of the party's conduct, and they secured Zetkin's exclusion from the Zentrale. The ECCI too remained divided: an article by Radek echoing some of the German ultra-lefts' charges was publicly rebuked by Lenin.[42]

The KPD's 22-26 August congress in Jena accepted the Third

39: Comintern, 1921b, p47. For a different translation based on a Russian text, see Adler, 1980, p286.
40: Broué, 2006, p649.
41: Zinoviev, 1921, pp3-4, 7-8, 16-17.
42: Reisberg, 1971, p210; *LCW*, volume 32, pp515-516.

Congress *Theses on Tactics* and its criticisms of the March Action, but voted to criticise Trotsky's Third Congress report on the world situation, which had envisaged the possibility of temporary periods of capitalist expansion. Echoes of the "theory of the offensive" were heard in the ultra-left's concept of an absolute limit to capitalist accumulation. Yet the congress also adopted a 12-point programme for a "struggle against hunger and poverty" as a basis for efforts towards united action both nationally and locally. It restored Zetkin to the Zentrale, now made up entirely of supporters of the Third Congress decisions.[43]

Hours after the Jena congress closed, an ultra-right organisation assassinated a leading German bourgeois politician, Matthias Erzberger, who rightists reviled as a signatory to the armistice ending the First World War. The KPD's *Rote Fahne* immediately called for united action, including with the Christian trade unions linked with Erzberger's pro-Catholic Centre Party. In Berlin all three workers' parties called for a united demonstration, although the SPD later withdrew from the joint committee. The murder, one of a series by right wing extremists, was widely seen as part of a concerted attempt to undo the work of the November 1918 Revolution and install a reactionary dictatorship.

On 31 August half a million marched in the Berlin demonstration. Marches and strikes across Germany embraced about five million protesters, and many workers used the occasion to press their wage demands. The KPD was unable to achieve a united national committee to lead this movement, but almost everywhere it was able to take its place in united protest actions.

During the Erzberger protests *Rote Fahne* declared that "only the working class can defend the republic from reaction... The working class has the right and duty to undertake [this task]." Objections to this statement were raised in the KPD and also the ECCI; the party's task, critics argued, was not to defend the bourgeois republic but to overthrow it. The issue, which had implications for the struggle against fascism, was left unresolved.[44]

During the months that followed, the KPD resumed fully the course of the open letter, and its initiatives for united action made encouraging headway. Among the most successful initiatives was the launching of an international campaign for aid to Soviet Russia, launched by the ECCI on

---

43: Trotsky, 1972, volume I, pp238-261; Reisberg, 1971, pp220, 225, 227; Hájek, 1969, pp26-28.
44: See Reisberg, 1971, p. 234, and Radek's remarks in the Fourth World Congress, Comintern 1923b, p99.

27 July 1921 in response to a widespread and severe famine in war-torn Soviet Russia. When a united campaign with social democratic parties proved impossible, the Comintern founded the International Workers' Aid Society, which enlisted the support of many non-Communist intellectuals and workers. Soon its aid was directly supporting 200,000 Soviet citizens.

Workers' government: three variants

What kind of government should Communists advocate for the achievement of the demands in their united-action programme? Debate on this question raged in the KPD during the final months of 1921. The party was pledged to establish a proletarian republic based on workers' councils similar to the Russian soviets. But in 1921 such councils did not exist in Germany or elsewhere in Europe west of the Soviet border. The KPD's majority leadership, in collaboration with Radek and the ECCI, sought to formulate a governmental demand that related to Germany's existing political institutions, while pointing towards the goal of workers' power. Reaching back to the concept that emerged during the Kapp struggle, they called for a "workers' government". According to Radek, the workers' government demand was "the only practical and real means of winning the majority of the working class to the idea of a dictatorship of the proletariat".[45]

But what was a workers' government? Three different conceptions emerged in the Comintern discussions:

1. *A pro-capitalist "workers' government"*. Labour Party governments in Australia, while carrying out some reforms, had functioned as pliant instruments of capitalist rule. The Comintern anticipated that a future Labour Party regime in Britain would have this character, at least initially. Zinoviev used the adjective "liberal" to describe such a pro-capitalist government by workers' parties; the Comintern's Fourth Congress, held in 1922, called this a "fictitious workers' government". In his 1920 pamphlet, *"Left-Wing" Communism*, Lenin had advocated that Communists give critical support to British workers' efforts to put Labour in office, so that workers could learn from their own experience the need to take a revolutionary course. In Germany this approach implied calling on the SPD to break its alliance with bourgeois parties and seek to form a government of workers' parties.[46]

45: Radek's letter of 7 November 1921, quoted in Broué, 1997, p262.
46: Comintern, 1923b, pp1015-1017; *LCW*, volume 31, pp84-85.

2. *"Workers' government" as a synonym for the dictatorship of the proletariat.*
The minority led by Fischer and Maslow in the KPD held that the term
"workers' government" could be used only as a popular way to present the
concept of workers' rule—that is, as a synonym for the dictatorship of the
proletariat. Zinoviev advanced this view in 1922 and again in 1924, stating
that "the workers' government is a pseudonym for the dictatorship of the
proletariat". Supporters of this view maintained that there could not be any
transitional stage between bourgeois and workers' rule.

3. *"Workers' government" as a component of a transitional programme.* This interpretation, advocated by the KPD majority leadership and Radek, placed the
workers' government in the framework of the Third Congress call, already
discussed, for a set of demands that "undermine the power of the bourgeoisie,
organise the proletariat, and mark out stages in the struggle for its dictatorship". Such a government, while possibly constituted by parliamentary means,
would rest on the workers' mass movement and take measures to dismantle
the bourgeois state. In the German context it was linked with demands that
included workers' control of production, confiscatory taxation of capitalist
property, disarming of right wing militias and arming of the proletariat.

The Comintern's position on a workers' government emerged from
the experiences of the German working class and can be traced through a
series of decisions by the KPD.

• In November 1920 elections in the German state of Saxony produced a
narrow majority for the three workers' parties, with KPD deputies holding
the balance. The KPD refused to join a social democratic led government.
Instead the Communists supported an SPD–USPD regime, subject to conditions, and continued this support even when its conditions were not met.
• In July 1921, at the height of controversy over the "theory of the offensive", the SPD–USPD government of Saxony proposed taxation changes that
would raise workers' rents. The KPD opposed the measure, but nonetheless
voted with the Social Democrats in parliament, in order to prevent the government's overthrow by rightist parties.
• Subsequently the KPD supported SPD–USPD governments in the states
of Thuringia and Brunswick. During these experiences the KPD refused to
bloc with rightist parties to oust the government, seeking instead to counter
reactionary government measures through independent working class action.
• On 9 October, after extensive discussions with KPD leaders, the ECCI
recommended that the German party pledge support for a workers'

government on condition that it act decisively for arming the proletariat and confiscatory taxation of capitalist property ("confiscation of real values"). The KPD applied this position in the German governmental crisis that broke out in Germany on 22 December, but stopped short of declaring its readiness to join such a government.

• After consultation by German leaders and Radek with Lenin, the KPD leadership declared on 8 December that "the drive for a united front must find political expression in a socialist workers' government, which should be counterposed to a coalition regime [with bourgeois parties]". The KPD undertook to use every means to promote the formation of such a government, "and also join such a government, if a guarantee exists that it will act to defend against the bourgeoisie workers' interests and demands, such as confiscation of real values, prosecution of the Kapp criminals, liberation of jailed revolutionary workers, and so on".[47]

Discussion in Bolshevik leadership

Recalling two years later the 1921 united front discussions in the Comintern leadership, Zinoviev said: "Actually, I too had misgivings then. Much was not yet entirely clear... It was a difficult transition, and we went through an intense inner struggle".[48]

No record is available of how the Bolshevik leaders came to agreement. However, at the end of November 1921 Zinoviev, Radek and Bukharin proposed to the Bolshevik Party's Political Bureau that the Russian party support extension of the German united-action policy to the Comintern as a whole. The Bureau's motion, drafted by Lenin, approved this course and also directed Bukharin to write up the Bolsheviks' pre-1917 experience of blocs with the Menshevik Party. A page-long passage on this topic appears in the ECCI united front resolution adopted later that month. This passage evoked little discussion, and Bolshevik experience in the revolutionary year of 1917 remained mostly unexamined.[49]

Bolshevik leaders continued their discussion at a party conference that opened on 19 December. According to Russian historian Alexander Watlin, a difference in emphasis was evident. Zinoviev and Bukharin presented united front policy as short term and stressed its role in exposing social democratic parties. Trotsky, however, warned against "fatalistic conceptions" that Europe

---

47: Reisberg, 1971, pp296-297.
48: Comintern, 1923b, pp12-13.
49: See *LCW*, volume 42, p367 (politburo decision); *LCW*, volume 36, pp552-554 (letter to Bukharin); Adler, 1980, pp406-407 (ECCI on Bolshevik history).

was experiencing the final run-up to the establishment of workers' rule. Notably absent from Watlin's summary of the discussion is any hint that the specific diplomatic or political needs of the Soviet state were a factor motivating the Bolsheviks to support united front policy. Instead Bolshevik leaders' attention was focused on the prospects for workers' struggle outside Russia.[50]

The Comintern adopts the united front policy

On 4 December 1921 a report to the ECCI by Zinoviev recommended adoption of the united front as Comintern policy, referring both to the positive experience of Communist parties that had taken united action initiatives and the widespread longing for unity among workers. The discussion was notable chiefly for a debate on whether transitional demands should be included in the Comintern programme between Radek ("yes") and Bukharin ("no"). The Committee voted for the preparation of united front theses along these lines, which were presented to a subsequent meeting on 18 December.[51]

The theses bore the mark of Zinoviev's thinking, motivating the united front on the basis of the current conjuncture—"an unusual transitional period"—marked by worsening capitalist economic crisis, a shift to the left among the masses and "a spontaneous striving for unity" among workers. The theses proposed that the Communist parties "strive everywhere to achieve unity…in practical action" and "take the initiative on this question". The workers' government slogan was endorsed, although only for Germany. The KPD's experiences in pressing for united action were not mentioned. "Communists should accept the discipline required for [united] action," the theses stated, but must not "relinquish the right and the capacity to express…their opinion regarding the policies of all working class organisations", including while an action is under way.[52]

The challenge of fascism

Hardly a mention was made during the united front discussion of the rising fascist movement then terrorising and destroying workers' organisations across Italy. The question did come up, however, at the 4 December ECCI meeting. In response to the Italian delegate Egidio Gennari, who had argued that there was no objective basis for united front policy in his country, Bukharin said:

50: Watlin, 1993, p48.
51: Comintern, 1922b, pp301-319. Debate on transitional demands continued in November 1922 at the Fourth World Congress, which resolved to incorporate them into a future Comintern programme.
52: Comintern, 1923b, pp1019-1028; compare Adler, 1980, pp400-409.

In a country where fascists are shooting down the workers, where the entire land is burning, the mere existence of the fascist organisation is enough for us to say to workers: "Let us unite to strike down this riffraff".[53]

Bukharin's suggestion did not fall on fertile soil. The Italian Communists, then led by Amadeo Bordiga, held to their view that Communists should conduct anti-fascist resistance on their own, without any alliance with workers outside their ranks. When workers spontaneously formed anti-fascist combat groups, the Communists opposed them. The passage on Italy in the ECCI's united front resolution of 18 December did not mention fascism and praised the Italian CP for their implementation of a policy to which they were in fact opposed.

Bukharin raised his point again in an ECCI discussion on 24 January 1922, and he subsequently wrote a letter along these lines to the Italian party.[54] But there was no follow-up from the ECCI, and the Italian CP's failure to carry out united anti-fascist resistance contributed to Mussolini's triumph in November 1922. At the Fourth World Congress that convened later that month, the need for an anti-fascist united front was raised not by the Italian CP, not by the ECCI, but by Communists from Germany, Czechoslovakia, Austria and Switzerland, who secured adoption of their position as the congress ended.

Anti-imperialist unity

The ECCI's united front discussion focused on Europe and the US and did not take up tasks in the colonial world. However, a parallel process, building on the work of the Second and Baku Congresses on colonial liberation as well as practical experience especially in what is now Indonesia, led to the convening in Moscow, on 21 January 1922, of the First Congress of the Toilers of the Far East, with 136 delegates from ten countries. Included in the congress were guest delegates from the Kuomintang, a bourgeois-led national-revolutionary movement in China. GI Safarov, a Russian Communist representing the ECCI, expressed to the Kuomintang delegates the essence of the Comintern's policy for unity in national revolutionary struggles:

We are supporting and will continue to support your struggle in so far as it is a matter of a nationalistic and democratic uprising for national emancipation.

53: Comintern, 1922b, pp317-318.
54: Comintern, 1922b, pp393-394; Behan, 2003, pp107-108.

But at the same time we shall independently carry on our Communist work of organising the proletarian and semi-proletarian masses of China.[55]

The anti-imperialist united front was integrated into overall Comintern policy at its Fourth Congress in November-December 1922.

International debate and ratification

The Comintern's new united front policy encountered far more opposition in the member parties than it had in the initial ECCI discussion. One of the most frequently voiced objections was that the united front should be built "from below" rather than "from above"—that is, social democratic workers should be recruited directly to Communist campaigns, without reference to their organisations. ECCI leaders responded that it was precisely the impossibility of forging effective unity in this way that made a formal approach to the social democratic leaderships necessary. In a 10 January 1922 letter to the KPD the ECCI stressed the need to make clear to the masses "that we are prepared to sit down together with the Social Democrats, despite all their disgraceful deeds", in order to help clear away the obstacles these leaders were erecting to workers' unity.[56]

When an expanded plenum of the ECCI met in Moscow, from 24 February to 4 March 1922, the united front was the main agenda item. One hundred and five delegates attended, from 36 countries. Among the five most influential Comintern sections outside Russia, the French and Italian parties opposed the united front policy and the Norwegian majority believed it did not apply to their country. In Czechoslovakia and Germany significant minorities resisted the policy. Opinion was similarly divided in smaller parties.

Since the adoption of the united front policy in December two developments had altered the context for this discussion. First, the centrist Vienna Union issued an appeal in January to the Second and Third Internationals to join it in an international conference to consider the economic situation in Europe and workers' defensive struggle against reaction. Second, on 6 January, the Entente powers invited Soviet Russia to participate in a broad international conference, which was to convene on 8 March in Genoa, Italy, to consider economic conditions in Europe and, specifically, relations between Russia and the capitalist states.

55: Comintern, 1970, pp193-194. For a 1922 report on the Indonesian experience, which served to some extent as a model for the Comintern's intervention in China, see www.marxists.org/archive/malaka/1922-Panislamism.htm.
56: Trotsky, 1972, volume 2, pp93-95; Comintern, 1922b, p384.

For the Comintern, the proposed world workers' conference had the potential to establish a united alternative to the capitalist attacks on workers and the Soviet Republic that the Entente powers intended to promote at the Genoa Conference. United front policy now had an overriding urgent goal. It was at this moment—not, as some claim, at the time of the Kronstadt uprising and the onset of famine in Russia in 1921—that the immediate diplomatic interests of the Soviet state became interlocked, for several months, with a Comintern policy.

Opponents of the united front outside the Comintern seized on this fact, claiming that the new policy was being imposed on workers in the West in order to serve the narrow needs of Soviet diplomacy. This charge also echoed through the debates at the ECCI conference. Bolshevik leaders indignantly protested that the interests of the Soviet state were identical to those of workers in the West. No "sacrifice" was involved. "Often comrades say sincerely, 'We must save the Soviet Republic!'" said Zinoviev. "Comrades, don't save us, save yourselves. Save the working class of your country."

At the close of the conference, the united front policy was adopted by a vote of 46 to ten.[57] The ECCI made no attempt to force member parties to apply this policy. However, through a succession of discussions and experiences in the national sections, acceptance of the united front policy widened. At the Fourth World Congress, in November-December 1922, debate focused on how, not whether, to apply it.

With the onset of Stalinism in the middle 1920s the Comintern entered a period of decline, in which the policies for united workers' action developed during its first years were distorted and eventually abandoned. Nonetheless, the ideas and experiences of the Communist movement of Lenin's time in forging workers' unity in action have lived on to form part of the heritage of socialist movements today.

A window into Lenin's Comintern

The story of how united front policy evolved provides insight into how the Communist International functioned in Lenin's time, one that refutes assertions that the world movement was run from the top down or manipulated by the Russian party. This story also shows that the united front was conceived not only as a defensive mechanism against capitalist attack but as a tool that could help forge the unity needed to achieve workers' power.

Several characteristics of this process stand out:

• United front policy originated in massive working class struggles in

---

57: For conference proceedings, see Comintern, 1922a.

capitalist Europe and in the longing of rank and file workers for unity in action.

● Ultra-left resistance to the policy arose from the very same struggles, reflecting the impatience and inexperience of many advanced revolutionary fighters.

● These two policies were codified and developed primarily by the parties immediately engaged in the main anti-capitalist struggles: for united front policy—the German party; for the ultra-left alternative—the Hungarian emigrants, the German left opposition and the Italian party.

● Members of the Comintern's central leadership, including the Bolsheviks assigned to it, diverged in their responses, some more sympathetic to united front initiatives, some more critical.

● The Comintern Executive responded inconsistently, sometimes destructively (during the run-up to the 1921 March Action) and sometimes playing a far-sighted and indispensable role (run-up to the December 1921 united front decision).

● Despite all these contradictions, the International's mechanism of world discussion and world gatherings served as a constructive arena for the exchange of experiences. Notwithstanding shortcomings and errors of judgement, the Communist movement as a whole was able to advance beyond the level of understanding that any of its components could have achieved on their own.

The potential of internationalism

Fifty years ago a US Communist leader of the early days, Jim Cannon, wrote that during the decades following the First World War "revolutionary national parties in every country have had to look to the Russian Revolution and its authentic leaders. That's where the ideas are".[58]

There is a great truth in this statement, if rightly understood. The experience of the Russian Revolution was in itself an inadequate basis for a world movement. The lessons of struggle around the world in postwar conditions had to be absorbed and understood. The leading Bolsheviks headed that process, but they acquired that knowledge not by introspection but by listening and by absorbing new ideas. In the process they shared in the insights, uncertainties, follies and divisions of the world movement's components. Strategy and tactics emerged from the interplay between living forces inside and outside the Soviet republics.

Comintern activity in the united front field was marked by many ambiguities and missteps; the leadership in Moscow was often indecisive,

---

58: Cannon, 1962, p333.

divided or simply wrong. Yet the influence of rank and file activists was strong enough, and the democratic structures functioned sufficiently well, that the International found its way forward. The Comintern managed to develop an understanding that integrated the experiences of its different national sections, including their minority currents. Its leadership succeeded in setting aside previous strategy, overcoming its own divisions, and responding to the initiatives and needs of its working class base. To be sure, the process through which the Comintern developed policy was flawed. But without the Comintern there would have been no process at all. It was the International that brought together experience and innovation; leadership and base; geographical breadth—the factors needed for policy development.

The position on united fronts hammered out during the Comintern's first three years remains one of the essential foundations for action by social and political movements for revolutionary change in the very different circumstances of our time. Moreover, the process through which united front policy emerged testifies to the potential of an international workers' International, both then and now, to contribute to the liberation struggle of humankind.

References

Adler, Alan (ed), 1980, *Theses, Resolutions and Manifestos of the First Four Congresses of the Third International* (Ink Links).

Behan, Tom, 2003, *The Resistible Rise of Benito Mussolini* (Bookmarks).

Braun, MJ ("Spartakus"), 1920, "Der Kapp-Lüttwitz-Putsch," *Kommunistische Internationale*, number 10.

Broué, Pierre, 1997, *Histoire de l'Internationale Communiste 1919-1943* (Fayard).

Broué, Pierre, 2006, *The German Revolution 1917-1923* (Brill).

Cannon, Jamas P, 1962, *The First Ten Years of American Communism: Report of a Participant* (Lyle Stuart).

Carr, EH, 1966, *The Bolshevik Revolution*, volume 3 (Harmondsworth: Pelican Books).

Comintern, 1921a, *Protokoll des III Kongresses der Kommunistischen Internationale* (Verlag der Kommunistischen International).

Comintern, 1921b, *Thesen und Resolutionen des III. Weltkongresses der Kommunistischen Internationale* (Verlag der Kommunistischen Internationale).

Comintern, 1922a, *Die Taktik der Kommunistischen Internationale gegen die Offensive des Kapitals: Bericht über die Konferenz der erweiterten Executive der Kommunistischen Internationale, Moscau, vom 24. Februar bis 4. März 1922* (Carl Hoym Nachf).

Comintern, 1922b, *Die Tätigkeit der Exekutive und des Präsidiums des E.K. der Kommunistischen Internationale vom 13. Juli 1921 bis 1. Februar 1922* (Verlag der Kommunistischen Internationale).

Comintern, 1923a, *Protokoll der Konferenz der erweiterten Exekutive der Kommunistischen Internationale, Moskau 12-23. Juni 1923* (Carl Hoym/Cahnbley).

Comintern, 1923b, *Protokoll des Vierten Kongresses der Kommunistischen Internationale* (Verlag der Kommunistischen Internationale).

Comintern, 1970, *The First Congress of the Toilers of the Far East* (Hammersmith Books).

Crouch, Dave, 2006, "The Bolsheviks and Islam", *International Socialism* 110 (spring), www.isj.org.uk/?id=181

Fayet, Jean-François, 2004, *Karl Radek, 1885-1939* (Peter Lang).

Hallas, Duncan, 1985, *The Comintern* (Bookmarks).

Harman, Chris, 1982, *The Lost Revolution: Germany 1918-23* (Bookmarks).

Hájek, Miloš, 1969, *Storia dell' Internazionale Comunista (1921-1935): La Politica del Fronte Unico* (Riuniti).

Hájek, Miloš, and Hana Mejdrová, 1997, *Die Entstehung der III. Internationale* (Temmen).

Kun, Béla, 1920, "Die Ereignisse in Deutschland", *Kommunismus*, numbers 11-15 (March–April).

Lenin, VI, 1960-71, *Collected Works*, 45 volumes (Progress).

Levi, Paul, 2009, "Our Path: Against Putschism", *Historical Materialism*, volume 17, number 3.

Martin, Terry, 2001, *The Affirmative Action Empire* (Cornell University Press).

Morgan, David W, 1975, *The Socialist Left and the German Revolution* (Cornell University Press).

Peterson, Larry, 1993, *German Communism, Workers' Protest, and Labor Unions* (Kluwer).

Radek, Karl, 1920a, "Die Kommunistische Partei Deutschlands während der Kapptage", *Die Kommunistische Internationale*, number 12.

Radek, Karl, 1920b, "Die Lehren der ungarischen Revolution", *Die Internationale*, 2:21 (25 February).

Reisberg, Arnold, 1971, *An den Quellen der Einheitsfrontpolitik* (Dietz Verlag).

Riddell, John (ed), 1984, *Lenin's Struggle for a Revolutionary International: Documents 1907-1916* (Pathfinder).

Riddell, John (ed), 1991, *Workers of the World and Oppressed Peoples, Unite! Proceedings and Documents of the Second Congress, 1920*, 2 volumes (Pathfinder).

Riddell, John (ed), 1993, *To See the Dawn: Baku, 1920—First Congress of the Peoples of the East* (Pathfinder).

Smith, Jeremy, 1999, *The Bolsheviks and the National Question*, (St. Martin's Press).

Sommer, Heinz 2008, "Clara Zetkin und die Rote Hilfe", in *Clara Zetkin in ihrer Zeit: Neue Fakten, Erkenntnisse, Wertungen*, edited by Ulla Plener (Dietz Verlag).

Trotsky, Leon, 1936, *The Third International After Lenin* (Pioneer Publishers).

Trotsky, Leon, 1971 [1937], *The Stalin School of Falsification* (Pathfinder).

Trotsky, Leon, 1972 [1924], *The First Five Years of the Communist International*, 2 volumes (Monad Press).

Watlin, Alexander, 1993, "Die Geburt der Einheitsfronttaktik: Die Russische Dimension," in *Die Komintern 1919-1929: Historische Studien* (Decaton).

Zetkin, Clara 1922, "Die Lehren des deutschen Eisenbahnerstreiks", in *Kommunistische Internationale*, number 20.

Zetkin, Clara, 1934, *Reminiscences of Lenin* (International Publishers).

Zinoviev, Gregory, 1921, "Die Taktik der Kommunistischen Internationale", in *Die Kommunistische Internationale*, number 18.

The Tories, Eton and private schools
David Renton

One of the most striking features of the new government is the dominance within its ranks of individuals showing every sign of class privilege. The *Sunday Times* reports that 18 of the 23 full-time members of the cabinet are millionaires, having between them a capital wealth of about £50 million.[1] David Cameron is an Old Etonian descended from three generations of stockbrokers.[2] George Osborne was educated at St Paul's and endowed by his parents with a £15 million stake in his family wallpaper business,[3] while Boris Johnson, Cameron's contemporary at Eton, is a son of a Tory MEP. An image much reproduced in the general election showed Cameron, Osborne and Johnson together in evening dress as members of Oxford's Bullingdon Club. Appearing in the same image are the less familiar faces of the future Baron Altrincham, Earl Wemyss and Lord Northbourne.

The willingness of the Conservatives to be led by a cohort of millionaires and the privately educated is a dramatic change from the past four decades of Tory practice. Part of Edward Heath's appeal to Conservative electors was that he was the son of a mere builder, while Margaret Thatcher was a grocer's daughter and John Major had famously run away from the circus to join the Conservative Party.

1: Milland and Warren, 2010. Thanks to Anne Alexander and Lawrence Black for comments on earlier drafts of this piece.
2: Levy and Gysin, 2009.
3: Reade, 2010.

Now, the purpose of electing leaders from "ordinary" backgrounds was always to mask the deeper reliance of the Tories on a narrow layer of society. In 1979, 73 percent of Tory MPs had been to private schools.[4] Even today the equivalent figure is still 54 percent. By comparison, just 7 percent of the school population is privately educated, a proportion which has remained steady for four decades. And the increasing number of Conservatives in parliament following the 2010 election has meant that the number of privately educated MPs has also risen. There are now 20 Old Etonian MPs in parliament. Two more private schools, Highgate and Millfield, come second with five MPs each.[5] But the best sign of changing times is to compare the relative ease of David Cameron in getting elected leader of the Conservative Party and now prime minister with the difficulties of Douglas Hurd, whose bid to follow Margaret Thatcher to the same position was defeated when John Major complained precisely of Hurd's past as an Etonian: "I thought I was running for leader of the Tory party," Major complained, "not some demented Marxist sect".[6]

Gordon Brown attempted to play the same trick on David Cameron at a by-election in Crewe and Nantwich in 2008.[7] In the run-up to the 2010 general election, Brown described Cameron as a PR man (this was the reference to the sole brief period of employment in Cameron's CV between leaving school and becoming a full-time worker for the Tories) who had drawn up his tax policies "on the playing fields of Eton". Cameron then complained of Brown's "pettiness and spite".[8] If Brown's attempts failed, this was because of the exhaustion of New Labour after 13 years of government, plus Labour's own well-known record of toadying to the rich.[9]

Private schools exist to hoard power among those who already have it. In 1954, 65 percent of those earning £1,000 or more had been to private school, and of those earning £1,000 or more with sons of school age,

---

4: I refer to private schools rather than the more common term "public schools", for the simple reason that whatever else they may be, these institutions are in no sense "public".

5: Sutton Trust, 2010, pp2-5; Baker and Fountain, 1996, pp86-97.

6: Taylor, 2008.

7: Labour distributed photographs of Tory candidate Edward Timpson in a top hat and images of what was described as his "big mansion house" outside the constituency. Labour campaign materials also included a fake "Tory candidate application form" asking: "Do you oppose making foreign nationals carry an ID card?"

8: Prince, 2009.

9: There is no better illustration of the narrowness of the British political elite than the fact that both Cameron and Tony Blair were educated at Eton and Fettes by Eric Anderson, Blair's housemaster and Cameron's headmaster.

95 percent were sending them to private schools.[10] In 1991 John Scott estimated that around 35 of the 200 richest families in England were headed by Old Etonians.[11] In March 2009 the Sutton Trust estimated that 70 percent of the top judges in Britain had been educated at private schools, along with 62 percent of the House of Lords, 55 percent of the senior solicitors, 54 percent of company chief executives and 54 percent of the best-paid journalists.[12]

Eton: citadel of privilege

In any account of the private schools, special attention has to be given to Eton College, not merely because it is the school at which the present prime minister was educated, but more importantly because it is the best known of the private schools, the one most associated with the process of passing on privilege.

Eton College was founded in 1440 by Henry VI as a community of ten fellows, four clerks, six choristers, one schoolmaster, twenty-five poor scholars, and 25 poor and infirm men. The scholars were to learn grammar and be prepared for entry to King's College in Cambridge. Within 12 years of its foundation Eton's Statutes had been amended twice, the third version extending the number of scholars to 70 and reducing the number of almsmen to 13. By the later years of the 15th century rich non-scholars were allowed to attend Eton, but not bastards, villeins, the diseased or those showing any physical imperfection.[13]

In 1861 a Royal Commission was established to "enquire into the Revenues and Management of certain Colleges and Schools, and the studies pursued and instruction given therein". Eton was one of the nine schools chosen by the commissioners. On the first day of their enquiries, the college had to admit that over the preceding years its provost and fellows had pocketed an extraordinary £127,700 which should have gone to the school.[14] Published in 1864, the Commission's report bemoaned the narrowness of the curriculum, the over-emphasis on Latin and Greek, and the poor knowledge of many departing pupils:

> For the ordinary boy Latin and Greek could scarcely have been less stimulating subjects to learn. The books had been in use for centuries and were hopelessly out of date... A boy might well have to do the same books over and over

10: McKibbin, 2010, p238.
11: Scott, 1991, pp 112-117.
12: Sutton Trust, 2009, p5.
13: Card, 2001, p12.
14: Royal Commission, 1864, pp57-64.

again during a period of three years—not only the same authors, but also the same amount of these authors and in the same compositions... Subjects other than the classics were practically ignored.[15]

In recent years the picture has been utterly reversed, and Etonians presently benefit from every conceivable resource. Facilities include a student to teacher ratio of ten to one; a library of equal size to many university libraries; 24 science laboratories; three language laboratories; a natural history museum; several theatres; music lessons in any instrument of a pupil's choice; two dozen rugby and football pitches; 20 tennis hard courts, ten clay courts and five acrylic courts; an Olympic standard rowing lake; a golf course; and indoor and outdoor swimming pools. These are shared by a school population of just 1,300 pupils.

One of the reasons why the school is able to afford lavish expenditure on its pupils is that the school benefits from a public subsidy of £39 million per year. Parents who send their children to Eton as to any private school with "charitable status" may claim back the fees from their personal taxes.[16] This was an abuse repeatedly acknowledged but uncorrected by Labour.[17] Oddly enough, for all the talk of austerity and common sacrifice, the coalition government has no plans to remove the subsidy of private education in the present round of cuts.

The whole purpose of Eton College is expressed by the statistic that 19 of its former pupils have gone on to become prime ministers. It is a school which encourages the young into an acquisitive attitude towards wealth and power; its pupils are taught to believe that they are entitled to good things and that the only way to get good things is to struggle hard to grab them. A few well-known examples of Old Etonians' venality range from the former Tory MP William Waldegrave, named in the 1996 Scott Report as a key figure in the conspiracy to supply arms to Saddam Hussein,[18] to Simon Mann, the British mercenary sentenced to a 34-year prison term for his role in a failed coup d'état in Equatorial Guinea in 2004 (but

---

15: Hill, 1948, p74.

16: Canovan, 2002. Eton is also subsidised by the Gift Aid scheme, under which any private donation of £75,000 to the school is matched by a further tax subsidy to the school of £28,205 and a tax rebate to the donor of £25,000.

17: Belatedly, the Charities Commission has since modified its rules so that private schools are no longer entitled to this grant as of right but must prove they provide a genuine public benefit. The private schools lobbyists of the Independent Schools Council responded to this modest tightening of the rules by threatening to sue the Commission—BBC, 2010.

18: Scott, 1996.

subsequently pardoned), and David Hart who financed the efforts to try to bribe miners back to work in 1984-5.[19]

One principal lesson taught at Eton is the unshakeable inequality of people. People who work for a living are perceived by Etonians as "primitive, people holding up their trousers with bits of twine and that sort of thing".[20] This message is reinforced constantly. The school is separated from the world. Only the children of those able to afford fees higher than the average annual wage are able to be admitted.[21] There are no female pupils.

The school is characterised by continuous internal selection. Older pupils are physically marked off from their juniors. All of the youngest pupils are forced to wear plain school uniforms; while most of the older pupils are entitled to wear different clothes for lessons (either stick-up instead of plain collars, or silver buttons on waistcoats, or coloured waistcoats and grey trousers in place of plain waistcoats and black trousers).[22] Pupils are assessed academically each term, and placed in a strict hierarchy by their performance. Every boy knows where they came in their year in each subject, whether first out of 242 in their year, or 242nd.

Alongside the sanctioned formal hierarchies are innumerable hierarchies which are discreetly encouraged by the school. One of the most vivid witnesses to this process is Dillibye Onyeama who left Eton in December 1968, having being tormented by boys calling him "wog" or "nig-nog". Onyeama ended up hallucinating that there were pupils teasing him, even when he was in his room alone:

My mind became a mass of confusion. Heavy anger filled me; and at the apex of my anger, my tormentors stood there, jeering and laughing uncontrollably. Suddenly I could stand it no longer. "Wog" and all their other names scraped along my nerves until I longed to scream hysterically and break the tension

---

19: Simons, 2011.
20: Rory Stewart MP, quoted in Martin, 2010. Compare the account of the bellicose, illiterate and ignorant ordinary inhabitants of Afghanistan that appears in Stewart, 2004.
21: In 2009-10 school fees were £29,862 per year—www.etoncollege.com/currentfees.aspx In addition, parents were expected to pay registration and entrance fees, as well as the costs of maintaining the pupil in the school (uniforms, furniture, books, etc). For a typical pupil, the total bill is very roughly twice the school fee. By comparison, in April 2009 the median gross wage in the UK was £25,428—Office for National Statistics, 2009.
22: In Lindsay Anderson's film If... there are the same multi-coloured waistcoats. Anderson himself, however, based his film on his experiences at Cheltenham College, where the film was also shot. The writer David Sherwin provided a fake script to obtain the school's permission to film. Afterwards Anderson was forbidden to set foot on the school's premises again—Cottrell, 2010, p20.

coiled like a spring within me. My eyes screaming murder, my blood at boiling point, I suddenly leapt to my feet like a madman. With black rage I started mercilessly slogging thin air, imagining I had charged at my tormentors and was beating the hell out of a particular one. The whole thing seemed as it if it was really happening, though I knew of course that it was not.[23]

In his narrative Onyeama describes being teased repeatedly for being black and intermittently for being gay: he seems to have responded to the latter taunt, with some success, by groping his accusers whenever the accusation was made. Racism, by contrast, was unshakeable throughout his five years at the school.

Corporal punishment was in use at Eton long after its decline in state schools:

Flogging by the Head Master, or in the case of Lower Boys by the Lower Master, is, apart from expulsion, the severest form of punishment inflicted... The right to inflict corporal punishment is retained by certain boys, principally by the Captain of the School, the Captain of the Oppidans, and the Captains of Houses. The offences with which they deal are usually minor breaches of school rules or house rules, and matters of internal discipline.[24]

The right to beat, on this account, was restricted to around 40 or so persons. Yet this is to underestimate both the freedom allowed to many other senior boys to beat, and the frequent arbitrariness of the beatings.

Another of the distinctive ways in which junior boys have been kept in their place is through the "fagging" system, as described by one outsider in 1948:

The right to fag belongs to the Library and to a few other boys at the top of the house. Only the Library have the privilege of shouting for a boy; others have to search the highways and byways of the house for a peculiarly elusive prey. The call for a fag is a long, rolling, cacophonous shout of "Boy", emitted usually from the doorway of the Library. It is followed by a thunder of footsteps as every fag within earshot rushes to answer the summons... Fagging varies from casual calls, which involve errands up town or to other

23: Onyeama, 1976, p200. Also Maudgil, 1989, in which the author complains—without rancour—of being on the receiving end of repeated racist remarks.
24: Hill, 1948, p138.

houses, to the regular task of preparing tea for the fagmaster to whom one is allotted.[25]

Since this was written, some of the most authoritarian practices have been abolished. The school has repeatedly banned fagging, although it was still pervasive in the 1980s. But one essential part of the school's DNA has been retained. The most senior pupils have powers to fine junior pupils for a breach of any one of the myriad school rules. Older boys start off as the bullied; they end their days as the bullies. They are taught on the miniature scale of a school community the experience of controlling other people's lives, in preparation for doing the same for real outside.

Two big processes of socialisation are at work. The first lesson taught is that it is natural for some people to have more rights than others; the second is that those at the top are there by merit and must be allowed to stay there. Both of these lessons are made to appear so obvious that any person who has been institutionalised in this way should have no reason to question them again through all their adult life.

Eton and politics

When fascism was a creed that had the ear of the English upper classes, there were Etonian fascists, such as James Strachey Barnes, whose account of fascism was published with a foreword by Mussolini and approved in the *Eton College Chronicle* in February 1928.[26] More typical though was the story appearing in the same newspaper following the Conservative triumph in the 1931 election: that the Etonian presence in parliament had increased to 104. All were Tories.[27]

The politics of Eton in particular can be compared to a rowing race which used to be run at the school in the 1940s between the light and dark blues. Any shade of politics is allowed as long as they are Tory.[28]

25: Hill, 1948, p104. "The Library" is archaic Eton slang for the boys in their final year in any house at the school.

26: Barnes, 1928.

27: Ollard, 1982, p182.

28: Just occasionally more interesting voices have been found just outside the school. For example, "Eton had never seen anything like it. Right to Work marchers met Rock Against Racism punks weaving through the streets of Eton behind Crisis, a band pounding out driving rock music from the back of a lorry. Two movements coming together outside Eton public school, heart of privilege and pomp. The chants, 'Annihilate the National Front', fake upper class accents, 'What does one want—the right to work', 'Eton boys rather naughty, Liverpool boys rather good'."—*Socialist Worker*, 17 June 1978. The episode presumably was the inspiration for The Jam's "Eton Rifles", released the following year.

David Cameron left Eton in 1984, and some idea of the range of opinion among his immediate contemporaries is provided by stories appearing in the school newspaper during his final year. In February 1984 a front page article in the *Eton College Chronicle* attacked Thatcherism as politics gone too far to the right: "The once-lauded idea that there should be as little government intervention as possible is now a public danger: Mrs Thatcher has surrounded herself with men who think it a cardinal sin to subsidise anything".[29] Articles printed in the following month reported speeches to Eton's Political Society by Francis Pym and William Waldegrave. Pym, it was complained, had been "reptilian", failing to acknowledge criticisms of the government that he as a former minister could easily have accepted. As for Waldegrave, it was suggested that he was one to watch in the future.[30]

The organising concept at Eton, as it was in much of the press commentary at the time, was Tory "wets" versus Tory "dries", the former being represented in the upper reaches of the Tory party by Old Etonians including Pym and Lords Hailsham, Carrington and Soames. Anyone who thought that Eton was only a preserve of Tory wets would however have been reassured by an article in the *Eton College Chronicle* in October 1984 comparing the striking miners of the NUM to the Brighton bombers: "Those who condone violence at the collieries admit the legitimacy of any attempt to reduce a government by violent means: effectively, then, they condone the IRA".[31]

Education at Eton (or indeed any private school) is intended to develop habits of Conservative voting. The Labour Party policy document *Towards Equality*, published in 1956, observed that: "Children who attend these schools develop a sense of being different, and, unmistakeably, a separate class outlook and behaviour. The broad effect is to heighten social barriers, to stimulate class consciousness, and to foster social snobbery".[32] A similar view is taken by the historian Ross McKibbin who names the private schools, along with the monarchy, the aristocracy, the armed forces and the structure of industrial management, as one of the chief "ideological supports" of Conservatism over the past six decades.[33]

29: Wood, 1984.

30: Howard-Sneyd, 1984. Waldegrave is now Eton's provost, although this may not be quite the promotion that the author had in mind.

31: Anonymous, 1984.

32: Labour Party, 1956; Montague, 1958, pp333-335.

33: McKibbin, 2010, p164. Attlee's Labour, McKibbin laments, had a once in a generation opportunity to reform or abolish these obstacles to democratic socialism. Its failure, he explains by references to Labour's ideas, and in particular, "a peculiar form of socialism; the

Given the long preponderance of the privately educated among Tory MPs, it is worth asking whether there are any characteristics of British Conservatism that have been shaped by this common educational history. Various matters come to mind.

The Conservatives have long recruited individuals, even MPs, on an ostensibly anti-ideological basis. Long before it was possible to join the Conservatives as an individual, the only way that a person could affiliate to the Tories was by joining the Carlton Club and dining with fellow Conservatives. A century later the Carlton still manifested the same combination of social and political headquarters. Again one part of the Conservative success in the 1950s, at a time when the Young Conservatives alone claimed 200,000 members and the parent party could rely on a total membership of nearly three million,[34] was the ability of the party to appear almost above politics, as a popular institution with a vibrant social life representing almost the entirety of the UK's middle classes, irrespective of their gender, age, religion or political belief.[35] Private schools were a recruiting ground for Conservatism, one of several institutions (the City, the Church of England, the army, the legal professions) within which the party enjoyed a near unanimity of support.

Although the model of Tory recruiting through social ties persists, the links of class and patronage which underlay this structure have over time atrophied. Individual membership of the Conservative Party has fallen by roughly 95 percent in 60 years. Party membership is no longer defined by their "social life" (a phrase looking back to the model of the 1950s and before),[36] but in negative terms by an ideological hostility to unions and "socialism". Paul Whiteley's, Patrick Seyd's and Jeremy Richardson's research into Conservative Party membership in the early 1990s suggested that only 23 percent of the party's membership had been educated at a private school.[37]

---

socialism of a particular generation, one which drew a clear distinction between the economy and social policy on the one hand [which was deemed to be capable of reform], and Britain's status and class system on the other [which was not]".

34: The peak membership of the Conservative Party was 2,900,000 in 1951—Marshall, 2009. By way of contrast, the last public figure for the total membership of the Conservative Party is 200,000 (2007), and informed observers put the true figure at around 150,000 to 170,000—Lee, 2010.

35: Lawrence Black gives the example of a 1965 recruit to the Young Conservatives, who on joining described his interests as jazz, drama and banning arms sales to South Africa, and was told: "Don't worry, we talk about everything here except politics"—Black, 2010, p94.

36: Black cites a 1956 survey of South Kensington Tories which found that 83 percent had joined for social reasons—Black, 2010, p82.

37: This was based on a sample of 2,429 Conservatives surveyed in 1992 for Whiteley, Seyd and Richardson, 1994, p7.

This is admittedly a disproportionate presence, yet a far more typical figure in the Conservative grassroots is a retired businessman or woman, having an above average household income, and owning shares, born into a lower middle class or working class home, proud of their perceived advancement, and opposed to left wing politics out of a fear of being pulled back into a lower social class.[38] Private education represents to this group not something that they experienced themselves, and possibly not that they could afford for their own children, but a principle that *somebody, somewhere* should be safe from absorption into the unloved masses.[39]

Almost all private schools have a competitive "house" structure in which pupils live and eat with and are expected to learn habits of sociability among strangers, the selection of whom is done not by them but arbitrarily by the school. This is part of a pattern under which certain shallow competing allegiances (Oxford v Cambridge, Eton v Harrow, Liberal v Conservative) are deemed to be entirely compatible with the deep hegemony of class rule. Pupils internalise this culture of horizontal competition and express it in later life. Its influence can be witnessed weekly in the scenes of MPs braying at Prime Minister's Question Time.

For many years it was part of the self-image of the Tories that they were the loyal party. The corollary of horizontal competition, in other words, is vertical loyalty. Devotion to their leaders was said to be the genius that had sustained such unpopular figures as Neville Chamberlain, Winston Churchill or Anthony Eden in the twilight periods of their premierships, enabling a transition—at the most effective time—from one leader to another, with minimum public controversy and therefore minimum damage to the party. Thus between 1951 and 1957, for example, the Tories were able to win three successive general elections under three different leaders (contrast the evident difficulties of Labour in 2008-2010, wanting to but unable to ditch as leader the now tired and unpopular figure of Gordon Brown). There is a very strong correlation between the Tories' self-image as the loyal party and the private school ethos of playing the game, determined as it is not merely by constant ideological repetition, but also by the lengthy prison-like intimidation of junior pupils. The effect is to teach the younger members of the middle classes that in

38: Seyd and Richardson, pp42-71.
39: A comparison could be drawn with Swinton College, the stately home located in rural Yorkshire, which provided Conservative political training between 1948 and 1975. After its demise a series of Swinton's former pupils mourned the "deep Englishness" that the building provided. "Englishness" in this sense is best understood as meaning a large house in a rural setting with a teeming entourage of servants—Black, 2011.

order to survive they simply have to keep their heads down and do always only what they are told.

At key moments in the Conservatives' history the party has been able to enter or remain in government, or has been forced out of office, not as a result of electoral success, but from the defection of MPs into or out of the party (Peelite Conservatives out from 1846 onwards, Liberal Unionists in after 1886, Coalition and National Liberals in from 1916 and 1931 onwards). This kind of party opportunism has been made much easier by the fact that for much of the last 200 years many of the leaders of both of the main parties in a usually two-party House of Commons have been educated at the same or similar schools and have been trained to approach politics in a similar way. On this model, the close coopera- tion that we have seen since the general election between Eton-educated David Cameron's Tories and Westminster-educated Nick Clegg's Liberal Democrats is just an episode in a much longer story of class employing privilege to hold power.

In an account published in 1972 Nigel Harris suggested that there were only two figures of stature in the Conservative intellectual pantheon, Edmund Burke and Benjamin Disraeli. Burke established the Tories as a party of aristocratic reaction against industrial society. Disraeli retained the notion of aristocracy, while denuding it of some of its specific content. Conservatism after Disraeli was a doctrine to conserve a ruling class, that class being defined nebulously (often as an aristocracy "of spirit"). The ideo- logical gap between the Conservatives and the Liberals (the latter being the historic party of British business) was dramatically narrowed, a process that later enabled the wholesale absorption of the Liberals into the Tory party during the period of Labour's advance. "In the inter-war period", Harris wrote, "some [Conservatives] wanted to strengthen the monarchy, some the state, some businessmen. But all prescriptions tended to circle the basic concern: the survival of a ruling class".[40]

Under post-Disraelian Conservatism, Eton and the private schools played a key part as a seeding ground of the ruling class. Since that time Thatcherism has redefined Conservatism as a politics not so much for the defence of any one class of people, but as an ideology of general defer- ence to property. "Cameronism", writes Richard Seymour, is a "pragmatic adaptation to the needs of neoliberal statecraft"—ostensibly centrist, heavily dependent on techniques of media management borrowed from New Labour, it distances itself from Thatcherism while maintaining fidelity to

---

40: Harris, 1972, p276.

Thatcherism's policy orientations.[41] The visible return of the Etonians under Cameron actually conceals a longer shift in Conservatism, and in neoliberal politics generally, in which the private schools, like other historical institutions of privilege (for example, the monarchy), are becoming less important.

The preponderance of private education among Tory MPs is a sign of a sort of division of labour in which the private schools in general and Eton in particular are expected to train future generations of Conservative MPs. The schools maintain relationships with the Tories. MPs frequently speak at school assemblies and meetings of the school's various political societies. It is relative easy for children to get fast tracked from the private schools to Oxford or Cambridge, and then immediately into junior roles working for the Tories, from which they can be picked for greater things. But the Conservative Party is not the ruling class, merely its political representative in parliament. The super-rich, in general, are an increasingly integrated international class, whose members might have a house in London and business interests throughout Europe, Asia or America. Private education in England is but one option for the children of the rich, and by no means the most advantageous.

Precisely because of their baggage of ostentatious privilege, the Bullingdon generation are actually *un*representative of the class whose interests they articulate. The populist Conservatism of Heath, Thatcher and Major and the bland universalism of "regular guy" Tony Blair represent a more viable long-term strategy to achieve sustained capitalist rule. These models are more akin to the ways that capitalists ordinarily do their ideological business. They work better as strategies to maintain the distinction between economic and political power on which bourgeois democracy ordinarily rests. The weakness of having Cameron *et al* at the top of the political system is that their presence invites ordinary voters—once their popularity wanes, as it must—to look beyond the inevitability of class rule altogether.

41: Seymour, 2010, p83.

References

Anonymous, 1984, "Brighton: Unity and Resolve", *Eton College Chronicle* (22 October).

Baker, David, and Imogen Fountain, 1996, "Eton Gent or Essex Man? The Conservative Parliamentary Elite", in Steve Ludlam and Martin Smith, *Contemporary British Conservatism* (Macmillan).

Barnes, JS, 1928, *The Universal Aspects of Fascism* (Williams and Norgate).

BBC News, 2010, "Private schools want legal ruling on charity status" (8 July), www.bbc.co.uk/news/10541553

Black, Lawrence, 2010, *Redefining British Politics Culture, Consumerism and Participation* (Palgrave).

Black, Lawrence, 2011, "Tories and Hunters: Swinton College and the Landscape of Modern Conservatism", unpublished paper.

Canovan, Cherry, 2002, "Does Eton need our charity?", *Times Education Supplement* (27 September), www.tes.co.uk/article.aspx?storycode=369194

Card, Tim, 2001, *Eton Established: A History from the 1440s to 1860* (John Murray).

Cottrell, Roger, 2010, "George Orwell and Lindsay Anderson: the Convergence of Perspectives Between *Such, Such Were the Joys* and *If...*", *New Interventions* 13/2.

Harris, Nigel (1972), *Competition and the Corporate Society: British Conservatives, the State and Industry 1945-1964* (Methuen and Co).

Hill, BJW, 1948, *Eton Medley* (Winchester Publications).

Howard-Sneyd, J, 1984, "Political Society", *Eton College Chronicle* (23 March).

Labour Party, 1956, *Towards Equality* (Labour Party).

Lee, Adrian, 2010, "A Big Chief, but Not Many Indians", *Critical Reaction* (6 October), http://critical-reaction.co.uk/2768/06-10-2010-a-big-chief-but-not-many-indians

Levy, Geoffrey, and Christian Gysin, 2009, "Claims that David Cameron has a £30m fortune sit uneasily with taxpayers. So what is the truth about his money?", *Daily Mail* (6 June), www.dailymail.co.uk/news/article-1191155/Claims-David-Cameron-30m-fortune-sit-uneasily-taxpayers-So-truth-money.html

Marshall, J, 2009, "Membership of UK Political Parties", House of Commons Library (17 August).

Martin, Stephen, 2010, "New Tory MP Rory Stewart describes parts of his Cumbria constituency as 'primitive' and that some residents 'hold up their trousers with bits of twine'", *Daily Mirror* (26 July), http://bit.ly/cmTzp0

Maudgil, S, 1989, "Racism in Eton", *Eton College Chronicle* (20 March).

McKibbin, R, 2010, *Parties and People: England 1914-1951* (Oxford University Press).

Milland, Gabriel, and Georgia Warren, 2010, "Austerity cabinet has 18 millionaires", *Sunday Times* (23 May), www.timesonline.co.uk/tol/news/politics/article7133943.ece

Montague, JB Jr, 1958, "Are Eton and Rugby Doomed by Socialism?", *The Clearing House* 32/6.

Office for National Statistics, 2009, "Annual Survey of Hours and Earnings" (12 November), www.statistics.gov.uk/StatBase/Product.asp?vlnk=15313

Ollard, R, 1982, *An English Education: A Perspective of Eton* (Collins).

Onyeama, Dillibye, 1976, *Nigger at Eton* (Satellite Books).

Prince, Rosa, 2009, "David Cameron: Labour class war attacks are 'petty and spiteful'", *Daily Telegraph* (6 December), www.telegraph.co.uk/news/politics/6743486/David-Cameron-Labour-class-war-attacks-are-petty-and-spiteful.html

Reade, Brian, 2010, "George Osborne—the Tories' little rich boy with an identity crisis", *Daily Mirror* (5 February), www.mirror.co.uk/news/top-stories/2010/02/05/cabin-boy-george-115875-22019856/

Royal commission, 1864, *Report of Her Majesty's Commissioners Appointed to Inquire into the Revenues and Management of Certain Colleges and Schools, and the Studies Pursued and Instruction Given Therein; With an Appendix and Evidence,* volume I (HMSO).

Scott, John, 1991, *Who Rules Britain?* (Polity Press).

Scott, Richard, 1996, *The Report of the Inquiry into the Export of Defence Equipment and Dual-Use Goods to Iraq and Related Prosecutions* (HMSO).

Seymour, Richard, 2010, *The Meaning of David Cameron* (Zero Books).

Simons, Mike, 2011, "David Hart: the Scum's Scum", *Socialist Worker* (11 January), www.socialistworker.co.uk/art.php?id=23570

Stewart, Rory, 2004, *The Places In Between* (Picador).

Sutton Trust, 2009, *The Educational Backgrounds of Leading Lawyers, Journalists, Vice Chancellors, Politicians, Medics and Chief Executives* (Sutton Trust), www.suttontrust.com/research/educational-backgrounds-for-submission/

Sutton Trust, 2010, *The Educational Backgrounds of Members of Parliament in 2010* (Sutton Trust), www.suttontrust.com/research/the-educational-backgrounds-of-mps/

Taylor, Matthew, 2008, "Under the Green Oak, an old elite takes root in Tories", *Guardian* (12 August), www.guardian.co.uk/politics/2006/aug/12/uk.conservatives

Whiteley, Paul, Patrick Seyd, and Jeremy Richardson, 1994, *True Blues: The Politics of Conservative Party Membership* (Oxford University Press).

Wood, J, 1984, "Softening Up", *Eton College Chronicle* (10 February).

I love the sound of breaking glass: the London crowd, 1760-2010

Keith Flett

On the BBC's *Weekly Politics* programme on 9 December 2010 the historian David Starkey commented on the tuition fees protests in London that day that the capital had seen nothing like it since the Chartist period of the 1840s. Starkey is a historian of the 16th not the 19th century so he is hardly best placed to make an informed comment. However, the broader point was well made.

According to some media coverage—for example the London *Evening Standard*—the student protests of late 2010 constituted mob violence and on occasion riot. While the fevered imagination of right wing journalists seeking easy headlines may not be the best historical benchmark, for much of the time since the mid-18th century—when the London "mob" makes its first real historical appearance—it has been a factor in shaping what took place.

The definition of what consitutes a riot and rioters according to the law has changed over time. The reading of the Riot Act was clear enough and has modern day parallels, when police warn crowds, albeit with much less legal backing. But the state's definition of what was or was not a riot and who were or were not rioters was quite clear. John Stevenson, in a useful survey of the historical incidence of riot in the UK and secondary literature about it, notes that historically speaking the definition of a riot was that three or more people gathered together and, crucially, had a mutual intent in doing so.[1] In other words the law argued that it was not just the act of riot that was the issue but whether there was a planned intent behind it or not.

A further criterion was whether what took place was sufficient to concern someone of robust physical condition. It may be argued that the London mob goes much further back than the 1750s. What, for example, about Wat Tyler and the Peasants' Revolt? What of London during the 1640s and 1650s? The London Apprentices' riot of this period was certainly very much an urban proto working class affair. The point here is that the crowds involved were mostly pre-proletarian but in the earlier cases pre-plebeian as well and that may have given them a rather different character from the gatherings considered here.

Eric Hobsbawm's *Primitive Rebels* looks at some historical examples. He refers, for example, to the Palermo riot of 1773 and the Bolognese riots of 1790 but his emphasis is more on the mob as a reactionary pre-capitalist formation rather than a progressive element.[2]

Whether the events in central London on 9 December 2010 really constituted a riot by either protesters or police is arguable, but there were certainly scenes reminiscent of the poll tax demonstration at the end of March 1990. That protest helped to spark a wider movement that saw the poll tax axed and is thought to have contributed to Margaret Thatcher's departure from office.

Trying to understand these events is a problem for right wing media commentators who believe that the era of street protest is long gone. Grasping what happens when ordinary people decide to protest has been an issue for as long as the inequalities and divisions of market capitalist society have sparked the protests themselves. This is really, at least in part, where the term "the mob" comes from. It is used to describe a group of protesters where those in authority have little idea about who, if anyone, might be leading them, and what they plan to do.

This disturbs those in authority but it is a function of large cities like London. It is possible in crowded urban areas for people to get up to all kinds of things without it being officially noticed. Well-off Victorians had a fear of the working class living in areas adjacent to them. They worried that the inhabitants might attack them or their property and then disappear back into the mysterious neighbourhoods from whence they came. So, for example, in 1848 the cry of "The Chartists are coming" was sometimes heard in well-off London neighbourhoods, heralding an imminent

---

1: Stevenson, 1992, introduction.
2: Hobsbawm, 1959.

invasion of protesters supposedly intent on creating havoc. In the main, Chartist demonstrations were orderly affairs. But there were occasions, for example in early 1848, when Chartist influence was less, where less predictable protests took place.

Much the same fear underwrites current talk of "the mob". It is not an anonymous group in reality. It is a mixture of the more and less committed, of all kinds of ideas and strategies and on occasion none. That is, as we show below, why the left has sometimes preferred not to use the term "mob" and has tended to refer to "the crowd".

The pioneering work is "The London 'Mob' of the Eighteenth Century" by the late Marxist historian George Rudé who also wrote the classic text *The Crowd in History*. Rudé has referred to the sense of the "crowd", "rather than a stratum of society or hired strong arm gang".[3]

It could be said that the difference between "the mob" and "the crowd" is that the former has sometimes been reactionary while the latter is generally progressive. Not all London riots have been of the left and some attacked left wing causes, for example during the period of the French Revolution in the 1790s. But there is a tradition of left wing crowds, from those who stood up for "Wilkes and Liberty" in the 1760s, to the unemployed who marched and rioted in London in the 1880s and who formed an audience for the Marxist Social Democratic Federation, right up to the modern day with the poll tax.

It could be said that the street protests and their often chaotic nature represent an absence of the orderly traditions of the labour movement. Or we might argue that they are a force that can be organised to achieve real change, a great start pointing to better things.

In the last significant review of the historical literature on riots published in a 1978 issue of *Social History*, RJ Holton identifies four strands of thinking on the left about the nature of riots.[4] For Richard Cobb, who wrote about the French Revolution, the focus is on popular mentalities. For Eric Hobsbawm, who worked on pre-industrial societies, there was a framework of banditry and primitive rebels, which he continues occasionally to revisit. Charles Tilly looked at collective violence while for George Rudé the emphasis was on the crowd and the social process that led people to protest rather than on concepts of the mob or the masses.[5]

Holton makes several critical points that still hold true: firstly that the "treatment of the patriotic and jingo crowds is...incomplete"; secondly he

3: Rudé, 1959, pp1-2.
4: Holton, 1978.
5: Tilly. 1995.

draws attention to the potential difference between the pre-industrial and the industrial crowd.

The London riot—some historical examples

Here we look at a number of historical examples of London riots: the Wilkes and Liberty riots of the 1760s, the Chartist riots in the 1840s, the riots on the Irish question in 1887 that led to Bloody Sunday, and, a century on, the poll tax riot of March 1990.

A narrative of the events themselves is not provided in detail—these can easily be established elsewhere. Charles Dickens's novel *Barnaby Rudge,* about the Gordon Riots of 1780, is possibly the first fictional account of them. But these days, prudent allowance for errors (deliberate or otherwise) and lack of rigour being made, Wikipedia entries provide reasonable ways in for those who wish to know more about a particular episode.

Rather our interest in these four well known periods of London rioting is their characteristics. Rudé sees the historical treatment of "the mob" as falling under three headings: first, as an "omnibus term for the lower orders", second, as a "hired gang acting in the interests of a particular political group", and third, what interests him, as a crowd engaged "in riots, strikes or political demonstrations".[6] In the last case, the rioters would tend to be mostly in employment, as opposed to unemployed, and often skilled tradespeople. It should also be the case that there were some underlying economic factors that motivated the need to protest beyond the ostensible reason for doing so.

The focus here is very specifically on the urban, indeed on the crowd or mob that from time to time appeared in central London, the location of the central apparatus of the British state, the symbolic centre of power.

Looking at historical episodes of riot from the 1760s to the 1990s, similarities are striking. Riots invariably and always involve the smashing of a large number of windows, with subsequent glaziers' bills. The authorities inevitably condemn the action and state their intention to track down and bring to justice those responsible. Later, where the results are clear in official papers, they frequently admit that the attempt to do so was not particularly successful.

The London mob was certainly in existence by the end of the first quarter of the 18th century. In fact Rudé suggests that "popular rioting" was "endemic" throughout the period.[7] He notes, for example, that in 1733 a

---

6:    Rudé, 1959, pp1-2.
7:    Rudé, 1962, p13.

riot took place as a crowd besieged Parliament with a cry of "No slavery, no excise, no wooden shoes". The impact was dramatic as the prime minister Robert Walpole withdrew his Excise Bill.

However, the London mob really enters the stage of history as a regular fixture from the 1760s, and it is this point that is captured in Rudé's book, *Wilkes and Liberty*. John Wilkes was a radical bourgeois politician—he referred to his supporters as "the inferior sort of people", was an early example arguably of the gentleman leader and was an MP and mayor of London in the final decades of the 18th century. He had battles with the establishment and spent time in jail for seditious libel, but he was also a successful political figure, perhaps one of the first of the modern era.

For example, Wilkes published a paper, the *North Briton*, for which he was prosecuted. Parliament met to consider the nature of the paper and ordered it to be burnt by the common hangman at Cornhill in the City of London. Unfortunately for the authorities a mob of 500 people gathered and the burning could not go ahead. In March 1768 Wilkes stood as an MP for Brentford in West London. Under the pre-1832 and pre-1867 unreformed parliament there was no secret ballot and polling went on for several days. Wilkes and his supporters ran an energetic and high profile campaign and easily won the seat ten miles west of central London.

Many of those responsible for trying to keep order in the capital, decades before the first regular police force appeared, decamped to Brentford to keep an eye on Wilkes and his campaign. Unfortunately for them this left rather few forces in central London, where on 29 and 30 March 1768 the election of Wilkes was greeted with a two-day celebratory riot aimed at those in authority who had been trying to persecute him.

Rudé reports: "A mob of 100 men and boys setting out from Charing Cross about 9pm in the evening...smashing windows in Leicester Fields, Covent Garden, Russell Street, the Strand, Long Acre, Oxford Street and Piccadilly...drank two gallons of beer to Wilkes and Liberty in the Six Cans Tavern Turnstile Holborn".[8]

What followed set a pattern for riots to come. Rudé indicates that the Guildhall advertised in the press—the official *London Gazette*—"to prosecute with utmost rigour such persons who have been active in the said riots" on 30 March, the day after the riot. It appears that the success rate in apprehending and bringing rioters to court was rather poor as it was agreed that "the results proved decidedly meagre".[9]

8:   Rudé, 1962, p43.
9:   Rudé, 1962, p45.

Who were those who participated in and organised the London riots of the 18th century? Historical research on who organised the processions in support of Wilkes is slim, but someone was responsible, as the authorities understood. Those who suggest that events happen spontaneously are really just saying that they don't know who organised them. It may well be that the same elements of the radical bourgeoisie that supported Wilkes's election in Brentford were responsible, but again detail is mostly lacking.

But it is known who the rioters were, in so far as they were arrested. The striking thing here is that while distinction is frequently made between the pre-industrial and industrial London crowd—for example by David Goodway in his excellent work on London Chartism in the 1840s, which is considered below—the composition of the rioters in the period Goodway covers appears similar to that of the crowd that supported Wilkes.[10]

The latter were invariably not what might be termed the "lumpenproletariat", casual labourers or, mostly, the unemployed. In fact skilled workers predominated. Commenting on the Wilkesite crowd Sir John Fielding refers to "the infinite number of chairmen, porters, labourers and drunken mechanics".[11] Rudé himself notes that those involved were "wage earners…rarely criminals".[12] Finally, the reasons for arrest follow a well-worn pattern and usually focus on being involved with a mob or leading it, breaking windows or rioting.

As we've seen in 18th century London the forces of "order" that the state could mobilise to control and prevent riot were relatively limited. In that sense a riot was relatively easy to organise and an effective method of political protest. The organised labour movement and political parties as membership organisations did not exist in a significant way.

Chartist riots

As industrial capitalism developed and London became the centre of the world's first capitalist power, so the forces of order developed. Indeed Goodway has described the London of the 1840s as a "fully policed" city and certainly the only one that was. The decade of the 1840s—which saw peak Chartist activity in the metropolis—saw the first significant riots in London since the Gordon Riots.

The protests around the 1832 Reform Act had certainly been robust but no riots took place. Similarly the events of 1839, for example the

---

10: Goodway, 1982.
11: Rudé, 1962, p6.
12: Rudé, 1962, p15.

attempt at a rising in Newport, took place some distance from London. Indeed when the riot returned to London it had a focus on events that were happening elsewhere.

August 1842 saw the "plug plot", a general strike in northern mill towns, and troops were despatched by train from Euston station to keep order. The departure of the troops was the occasion for what Goodway suggests was a "week and a half of daily meetings, processions and fighting with the police".[13]

From 13 to 15 August crowds gathered near Euston station and in Regent Street. The crowd groaned and hissed at the troops and by 15 August the Chartist paper the *Northern Star* reported that troops were compelled to charge the people at the point of the bayonet before they could gain entry to the railway station. After the first few days Chartist meetings and gatherings were called to consider the general strike in the north and the role of the army.

The first meeting was at Stepney Green on 16 August 1842, followed by a gathering at Islington Green two days later. It was this event that provided probably the first recorded instance of a familiar occasion to modern day protesters in London: questions were asked about what the police had been doing as the mob traversed central London unimpeded.

The meeting on Islington Green dissolved peacefully and the police, assuming that this was it for the evening, stood down. In reality the Chartists re-grouped and marched to Clerkenwell Green—around 15 minutes away. Meanwhile another group of Chartists appeared at Lincoln's Inn.

The police, however, had been expressly instructed to stop the Chartists from gathering in central London and the police commissioner Sir Richard Mayne was required to account for events to the prime minister Sir Robert Peel and his home secretary Sir James Graham. Graham had been forced to interrupt his dinner and go to the Home Office to take charge of matters. Mayne's excuse was that for much of the time the Chartists had not been in the Metropolitan Police area but that of the City of London Police, and so this was nothing to do with him.

On 19 August 1842 the temperature in London reached 92°F and further Chartist gatherings and encounters with the police took place at Clerkenwell and Lincoln's Inn, despite the fact that on that very morning the government and Lord Mayor of London had banned all meetings. The authorities were simply ignored.

After these tumultuous few days a further characteristic of such occasions

---

13: Goodway, 1982, p106.

may be noted. For several days absolutely nothing at all happened. Then on Monday 22 August events reasserted themselves in a slightly different register.

In Victorian London the tradition of the working week running from Tuesday until late Saturday, with Sunday as a day off and "Saint Monday" as an unofficial holiday, remained strong. So a large day time demonstration on an August Monday—Bank Holidays were not introduced until 1871—was not in itself a surprise. By the afternoon of 22 August Goodway estimates 40,000 Chartists were gathered on Kennington Common. It was a day of cultural activities—a phrenologist lectured, games of cricket were played—until at 6.30pm the meeting started.

The police were determined to prevent the assembly and, as a cry from the crowd of "The peelers, the peelers" went up, police on horseback rode into the crowd. It has become a familiar tactic in the 170 years since. The press reaction likewise set a tone that was to continue. The *Times* praised the police for a "masterly style" and avoidance of "unnecessary violence". The Chartist *Northern Star* by contrast noted that 300 to 400 people had been injured.

Finally, as in more recent times, the police tactic did not work effectively. The crowd were driven into surrounding streets where they were able to re-gather and spend the evening throwing missiles at the police. Similar scenes took place with a crowd of 10,000 at Paddington station, where a fight with the police lasted for three hours starting at 6.30pm, before the area round the station was cleared.

Who took part in these August 1842 protests in central London that led to confrontation with the police and the army and some episodes of rioting? Goodway estimates that at least 80 people, "and probably considerably more" were arrested but details are available for only 22.[14] However, they echo precisely Rudé's earlier point about who the rioters were. Goodway's account indicates that there were three shoemakers, three carpenters, two tailors, a surgical instrument maker, several people employed in the building trades, a printer and a paper-stainer. In short, from this sample most were skilled craftsmen. Official records indicate that three people arrested were drunk and three were known to be Chartists. Finally, not all were young by any means. A shoemaker was 40, a tailor 32, a plasterer 39, and a carpenter was described as a "very respectable looking elderly man".

The next period of significant riot in London was in 1848, the year of revolutions. The obvious influences here—and ones that were to feature

---

14: Goodway, 1982, p111.

again in episodes of riot, were revolutionary events abroad, initially in France, and economic depression at home over the winter of 1847.

On 6 March Charles Cochrane called a rally in Trafalgar Square against income tax. The square was not yet completed but Cochrane's call elicited the first ever police ban of a demonstration at the venue. The first ever traditional response followed on as Cochrane withdrew but maverick Chartist, journalist and best selling novelist GWM Reynolds stepped in to chair it.

A sketch from 6 March shows the square packed with protesters and in the foreground police officers grappling with them. A Chartist rally of around 10,000 was about to dissolve peacefully when, the *Northern Star* reported, some provocative remarks by an anti-Chartist bystander caused a scuffle.

Matters would probably have gone no further than that were it not for the fact that the police made an ill timed intervention into what was after all a banned protest. By 6pm police reinforcements had gained control of the square and withdrew. At that point the crowd that had been dispersed into surrounding streets returned. Again, in what was probably a first, the crowd took down wooden hoardings from around Nelson's Column and proceeded to use them to defend themselves.

During the evening of 6 March a group broke away from the crowd at the square and, raising the cry "To the palace", headed towards Buckingham Palace, smashing windows and gas lamps as they went.

There was a second day of rioting on 7 March from as early as 9am, and disturbances in the Trafalgar Square area and the West End of London continued for a week. Goodway reports that by 8 March well over 2,000 police officers were deployed to contain the rioters. That day there were further marches and window smashing in central London including plate glass windows in Swan and Edgar's shop in Regent Street and other establishments.

After this the disturbances melted away as suddenly as they had arisen. They were clearly partly politically influenced by Chartist and other radical demands, but the fact that on occasion bakers were forced to hand out bread suggests other more immediately material demands were also at work. Goodway's summary of the 127 arrested during the week of riots shows that 61 were less than 20 years old.

Events then moved after a lull of a week to Camberwell, south of the Thames, on 13 March. This time GWM Reynolds was joined by other Chartist leaders in organising a meeting. There were 3,881 police on duty and a crowd of protesters numbering 500 maximum. However, it did no good. The crowd was local and, departing at noon, took back-ways where the police could not follow. Window smashing and some minor looting took place.

The whole thing took an hour and later arrests saw 18 men sentenced to seven to 14 years' transportation. In other words, the state was now determined to crack down hard on rioters. Many were young but again Goodway's research notes that most had trades including baker, shoemaker, ropemaker, printer and glass-blower.

The events of 13 March and the reaction to them set the tone for the massive government presence on the Chartist demonstration of 10 April. In fact, although the protest for the Charter and the vote at Kennington Common on Monday 10 April was one of the world's first mass demonstrations, it did have an element of riot to it that has remained largely unresearched by historians.

Frustrated that, having gathered at a location south of the Thames, the bridges allowing a march back to parliament were then blocked by police and troops, a significant number of Chartists marched to the south side of Blackfriars Bridge once the Kennington rally had finished on the Monday afternoon. Here took place a serious confrontation and significant fighting that was only dispersed because it started to rain heavily.

There were outbreaks of riot associated with London Chartism in late May and June 1848 and these followed the pattern we have outlined above in the main. However, elements of the focus of the London crowd since the 1840s also made an appearance. For example, on 29 May 1848 a crowd of 3,000 to 4,000 heard Chartist speakers and marched down Fleet Street, halting to hoot and groan at the offices of the *Weekly Dispatch*. Cries were also heard to march to the offices of the *Times*.

Goodway identifies the final London riot associated with Chartism in the London of the 1840s as taking place at Bethnal Green on 4 June 1848.

As David Starkey was aware commenting on the recent student protests, the Chartist riots provide the historical template for such events in London, which is why they are considered in some detail here.

Before looking at two more recent examples of London riots, Bloody Sunday and its aftermath in 1887 and the poll tax protest a century later in 1990, it is worth reviewing some of the issues that can be drawn out from the Chartist period that have a wider application to the London mob.

The issue of the weather remains an interesting one. It may be argued that the very hot weather in August 1842 facilitated crowd activity and riot, as much as the rain prevented a more serious outbreak of rioting on 10 April 1848. Certainly the day of the London poll tax riot, 31 March 1990, was itself a very warm and sunny day for late spring in the capital. It would be wrong to argue that the weather is a key factor in such matters but it may from time to time be a contributory matter.

The other point raised by the events on the afternoon of Monday 10 April 1848 is why the day is characterised historically as a mass demonstration rather than a riot. Here it may be argued—and the historical criteria have remained implicit rather than explicit—that the intent was an organised demonstration. The riot was a subsidiary affair, and also in practice less significant than the demonstration. The same point might well apply to the anti-Suez protests in central London in 1956 and the anti-Vietnam War demonstrations at Grosvenor Square in 1968. Both contained elements of riot, as considered here. What they all lacked was the sense of a crowd or a mob in procession through the streets and damage to property, in particular, the smashing of windows.

The other side of the equation is how the state, primarily the police, handled the Chartist riots. Goodway argues that "one of the most striking aspects of the next two or three decades was the virtual elimination of riot".[15] That may be a historically accurate statement but the policing tactics of the 1840s are unlikely to have been the decisive factor. The reality that the Chartist challenge to the state was ultimately defeated was probably the key issue. However, the tactics of the police in the "Chartist decade" are strikingly similar to those used since.

The range available has not changed much even if some of the technology has. In 1842 the police occupied some meeting places such as Clerkenwell Green to prevent crowds doing so, though this clearly depended on the weight of numbers on either side. On occasion speakers were arrested or their identity noted by officers for arrest after the event. Goodway notes that on the whole the "mistake" of not allowing "adequate exits for dispersal" which invariably led to riots, then and now, was not made. The method of dispersing a crowd has also stood the test of time. A favourite method was for a line of police to advance and push the crowd away from its location using force such as the truncheon where needed. If fighting ensued, as Goodway again notes, bystanders caught up in the melee were as likely to get injured as rioters.

The result of all this was that even as early as the 1840s the policeman "had displaced all other objects as the symbol of oppression...and the Londoner's hatred of him helps to explain the single-minded concentration on battling with the force that typified the Chartist riot", and, it might be added, on numbers of other occasions since too.[16]

The difference between the riot of the pre-industrial era of the 1700s

15: Goodway, 1982, p123.
16: Goodway, 1982, p125.

and the industrial one of the 1800s is a fine one but an important one. In the former period the riot was the main form of political expression. In the latter it was not. It was a by-product of attempts to hold meetings, address crowds or march that were in various degrees frustrated by authority—usually the police. Yet the actual form of a riot once it started was very similar, if not identical, in both periods.

Bloody Sunday

While Goodway argues that London was quiet in the decades after the 1840s, it is always possible to find examples of demonstrations that had elements of riot about them. For example the protest on 6 May 1867, led by the Reform League campaigning for manhood suffrage, which defied a government ban on demonstrations in Hyde Park, tore down the railings and held a rally anyway, certainly had elements of a riot about it. The result was the resignation of the home secretary and the passage of the Second Reform Act, a salutary historical note to those who argue that robust protests never achieve anything.

However, it was in the 1880s, with the beginnings of the modern general trade unions and the birth of Britain's first Marxist grouping, the Social Democratic Federation (SDF), that regular protests returned to the streets of central London. The most well known—well covered by socialist historian John Charlton—is termed "Bloody Sunday", and took place on Sunday 13 November 1887 in Trafalgar Square.[17]

The preceding years had seen a series of large demonstrations in central London, sometimes over the impact of slumps in the economy, sometimes over overtly political issues such as government coercion in Ireland and on occasion a mixture of both. The SDF had played a role but window smashing had also been a feature.

The demonstration on the November Sunday had been banned by the Metropolitan Police Commissioner, Sir Charles Warren. The police, armed with cutlasses and guns, were very heavy handed indeed with protesters. The radical MP for Lanark, Cunningham Grahame, was brutally arrested and injuries were numerous.

The movement gained momentum and a further protest was held the following Sunday, 20 November 1887, when a young clerk Alfred Linnell was killed by police action. This led to further protests and a mass political funeral for the unfortunate man.

Events such as Bloody Sunday remain contentious even though they took place well over a century ago. The Metropolitan Police website is still

---

17: Charlton, 1998.

today keen to cover up and spin the violent role that the police played in these events, despite the fact that any officer serving at the time is long dead.

Charlton argues, following Frederick Engels, that the events of Bloody Sunday taught a new generation of protesters a good deal about the brutality of the state when push came to shove. That is clearly right and is an issue in all the episodes we look at here. An aim of the police is invariably to use tactics that remind people that there are penalties for daring to protest. The impact of this is much harder to judge. Some no doubt are dissuaded. Others may draw political lessons and become more determined.

The century between Bloody Sunday and the poll tax riot of 1990 did not, of course, see London protest and riot free. We mention anti-Suez and anti-Vietnam War confrontations above. The Great Unrest of 1911 and the General Strike of 1926 certainly saw tumultuous events in London, as elsewhere, but these were centrally related to industrial disputes that provided the broader political framework.

The great poll tax riot

The poll tax riot of Saturday 31 March 1990 certainly, however, takes its place in history as a key moment of rebellion in the capital's history. The poll tax, which replaced the old household rating system as a way of funding local council services, had been introduced a year earlier in Scotland and was due to be implemented in England on 1 April 1990.

A mass campaign of opposition to it had grown up, organised by a range of left wing and community based groups. The Trade Union Congress had stayed clear of the campaign and did not back the 31 March demonstration, while Labour local authorities implemented the charge and prosecuted non-payers.

There was real anger about the poll tax. First, it was a new tax and often a quite substantial cost for people who had not previously had to pay it—it applied to everyone. Secondly, it was a regressive tax since everyone in the same area was charged the same, however rich or poor they were. Finally, the poll tax was a product of the hated Thatcher Tory government and had been designed in such a way that Tory councils such as Westminster had to charge very little.

The 100,000-strong protest gathered at Kennington Common, the scene of some of the most robust Chartist protests, and marched to Trafalgar Square for a rally. It was here that a riot broke out and it contained all the classic elements described above. Over-zealous and thuggish policing provoked sections of the crowd into retaliation. Temporary portakabins being used for building work around Trafalgar Square were set alight and as the evening wore on groups of protesters made their way round parts of central London, and windows were smashed.

In the following days there was a media furore—the riot was every bit as embarrassing to the authorities in modern terms as the central London riots in March 1768 by supporters of Wilkes—and just as that time demands were made for those involved to be brought to justice.

Rough music to revolution

The focus here has been on a slice of the London crowd and the riots that have sometimes led on from its activities in the last 250 years or so. The aim has been to try and understand some of the core elements of the crowd and some well known riots in London history to see how they have related to the political agenda of the left.

Certainly in the industrial era from the 1820s on it would be reasonable to argue that the left has not sought out riots as a deliberate strategy but has understood that tensions and crisis in society and the actions of the authorities around that can sometimes spark riots.

The work of Charles Tilly has attempted to provide some kind of historical/sociological indices of riots and assess their numbers and types.[18] But what differentiates the riot from the political demonstration or simply the crowd that may gather in central London on significant political occasions?

The most prominent elements that identify a riot as distinct from any other form of political gathering are the announced procession of a mob through some of the wealthier parts of the West End, the frightening of well to do people, and the breaking of glass.

This suggests that once formed, or often more accurately provoked, the London crowd feels antagonism towards the rich and the symbols of the rich, but this does not mean it is likely to be acting on a revolutionary programme. It is a sign of wider discontent to be harnessed or suppressed.

Some perspectives are also needed. Taking the broad sweep of several London centuries, perhaps the interesting thing is how relatively peaceful and riot free the capital has been for much of the time, not how often riots have taken place. This does not suggest that Londoners are on the whole a placid lot but rather, as David Goodway has argued, with the capital being the first fully policed metropolis in the world, when a riot does occur in London it is a sign of very serious political issues indeed.

We must also recognise that not all the crowds that have gathered in London have been politically progressive although that has been what

---

18: Tilly, 1995.

we have considered here. The Church and King riots of the 1780s were certainly not in themselves in any way "on the left". However, curiously, it may well be that by demonstrating about often quite reactionary demands the crowd gained a sense of its own power and could become a threat to the establishment.

As the crowd, or probably more accurately the mob, that gathered to embarrass transgressors against social mores in pre-industrial and early industrial Britain in EP Thompson's "Rough Magic" suggests, very often the demands were reactionary.[19] There was nothing automatically progressive or left wing about a crowd. But the possibility that it could come from the left was not denied. The Rough Music gathering, so called because of the cacophony it made outside the house of the apparently guilty party late at night, was as likely to be condemning a wife beater as it was a gay man, but both were possibilities.

The point here is that it is important to understand the politics and the possibilities of the crowd and its behaviour and not to lump all instances of disorder and discontent in the same framework.

A recent book by Clive Bloom, *Violent London*, is guilty of just this trend.[20] Even if we accept that London is a particularly violent capital, which is historically doubtful, the fact that fascists and other reactionaries sometimes cause disturbances in it does not tell us anything much at all about the nature of the London crowd or mob.[21]

The one thing we can say about London mobs and London riots is that they have defied over several centuries all attempts by the authorities to make their reappearance impossible and every effort by academics to argue that they are definitively a thing of the past. That seems set to continue to be the case.

19: Thompson, 1991.
20: Clive Bloom, 2010.
21: *Guardian,* 18 November 2010.

References

Bloom, Clive, 2010, *Violent London* (Palgrave Macmillan).

Charlton, John, 1998, "London, 13 November 1887", *Socialist Review* 224 (November), http://pubs.socialistreviewindex.org.uk/sr224/charlton.htm

Goodway, David, 1982, *London Chartism* (Cambridge University Press).

Hobsbawm, EJ, 1959, *Primitive Rebels* (Manchester University Press).

Holton, RJ, 1978, "The Crowd in History: Some Problems of Theory and Method", *Social History*, 3:2.

Rudé, George, 1959, "The London 'Mob' of the Eighteenth Century", *Historical Journal*, 2:1.

Rudé, George, 1962, *Wilkes and Liberty, A Social Study of 1763-1774* (Oxford University Press).

Rudé, George, 1964, *The Crowd in History: A Study of Popular Disturbances in France and England 1730 – 1848* (John Wiley & Sons).

Stevenson, John,1992, *Popular Disturbances in England 1700-1870* (Longman).

Thompson, EP, 1991, "Rough Music", in *Customs in Common* (Merlin).

Tilly, Charles, 1995, *Popular Contention in Great Britain, 1758-1834* (Harvard University Press).

Facing the crisis:
the strategic perplexity of the left
Stathis Kouvelakis

Everyone knows the joke that, of the last three crises, Marxists have predicted at least five. What the joke doesn't say is that they failed to predicted a sixth, their own crisis, to which I will devote these remarks. To put it differently I will focus on the political aspect of the crisis, because, it seems to me, it is at this level that the contradictions of the economy are concentrated and that their ultimate resolution is decided. Actually my topic is much more restricted than this, since I will restrict myself to the European left and its strategic perplexity facing the current crisis. And given that the general title of this seminar is "Marxism and the alternatives", I thought it would be useful to try to reflect on the reasons that have so far prevented such alternatives from emerging on the left, or indeed elsewhere. [1]

Reinventing Marxism
My starting point is nevertheless more general. I think that moments of crisis such as the current one have an all-encompassing dimension: the crisis is, at its core, economic but we have reasons to think that it is not an ordinary one, the passage from one economic cycle of growth or capital accumulation to another, but a deeper, systemic crisis. This is why it becomes also a social, a

1:    Paper given at the "Marxism and the Alternatives to the Crisis" seminar organised by *International Socialism* on 7 December 2010 at the School of Oriental and African Studies in London. Many thanks to Sebastian Budgen for his help.

political and an ideological crisis, never forgetting its environmental dimension. But this also means, or rather it means first and foremost, that the crisis creates a new situation, which provokes a crisis in the ways we interpret and understand reality, and that seems to be valid for Marxists as well. Of course, it's legitimate to say that Marxism has the immense advantage over other theories of providing an understanding of the properly immanent character of the crisis, through which the system encounters its own limits but constantly displaces and transforms them, thereby reinventing itself at a certain cost, of course. However, I think a properly historical and materialist, that is to say a Marxist, understanding of Marxism itself shows that each major crisis of capitalism destabilises Marxism, both in its cognitive coordinates and in its practical, political dimension, forcing it to reinvent itself as it does with capitalism.

To give a concrete example, I don't think that it makes much sense to understand the crisis of the 1930s as a confirmation of a kind of general prognosis Marxists had about capitalism. Quite the contrary Marxists were extremely disoriented by what was happening, and the first political effects of the crisis, starting with the destruction of the German workers' movement, amounted to total disasters, defeats on an unprecedented scale. It's hardly necessary to emphasise the enormous and almost desperate energy with which Trotsky or Gramsci tried in that situation to provide an analysis of the situation and a strategic reorientation for the workers' movement. On the economic side of the analysis, things proved perhaps even more arduous since it's only after the Second World War that we started having a specific analysis of the crisis of the 1930s, actually when Marxists started reading and reflecting on Keynes and the importance of Keynesianism.[2]

In other words, this process of reinventing Marxism is anything but a painless exercise. Furthermore not only is it a process that can take time, which is in itself problematic since it indicates a possible disconnection with the specific temporality of politics which is the "here and now", but also a process that is quite open in its outcome, which means that it is a process without any guarantee of success, unless we hold to a religious and dogmatic conception of Marxism as a set of stable and secure truths, that is to a very un-Marxist conception of Marxism itself.

The social democratic left
I'll move now to my point, which is the left, and more particularly the radical left, which is, I think, the reference point of most of us in this room

---

2:   We can here mention, in a purely indicative way, among the pioneering works, those of Paul Baran and Paul Sweezy, Paul Mattick, or, in the 1970s, the French "regulation school".

and certainly the only one that may be connected, even loosely, with Marxism. What I will do here is to propose a kind of typology of its reaction to the crisis in order to understand better the reasons and of the characteristics of what I've referred to as its strategic perplexity.

I'll start with some brief remarks concerning the systemic left, the social democratic left, which has actively participated in the recent period in the management of the system and the neoliberal turn. I'll just say two things about what remains, it has to be said, the main force of the European left.

The first is that, being deeply embedded in the management of the system and having actively promoted the neoliberal policies that are at the root of the current crisis, this left simply cannot understand, even on a purely intellectual level, the reasons for and the mechanisms of the crisis. This is why it puts forward superficial explanations usually structured around the idea that there have been some unfortunate excesses of something that is basically sound—excesses of deregulated markets, of financial speculation, etc—and therefore that some corrections are necessary. It has to be said that even right wing politicians expressed similar views in the first period after the start of the crisis, for instance the French president Nicolas Sarkozy.

Actually, and this is the second point, even this kind of minimal critical distance can be considered now as outdated, following the displacement of the centre of gravity of the crisis from the financial sphere to the level of public debt and expenditure. From that moment on, we can say that in every country where it is in government (Greece, Portugal, Britain up to May 2010), social democracy has embraced the austerity politics put forward to satisfy the immediate demands of the dominant classes, and more particularly of banking and financial capital. And it has done so overall with remarkably little internal differentiation and dissent, at least so far. Even in the countries where it is no longer in power, there are virtually no indications of social democracy distancing itself from the dominant agenda. The most telling example is probably that of France, where the Socialist Party has been in opposition for nearly a decade now. But the candidate who seems the most likely to win the primaries as candidate for next year's presidential elections is the current managing director of the International Monetary Fund, Dominique Strauss-Kahn, appointed to that position with Sarkozy's support.

There are a few counter-tendencies to this predominant trend, such as the recent defeat of the Blairite candidate in the race for the Labour Party leadership and the subsequent at least symbolic break with the Blair legacy, but this change is too recent and too fragile to alter the overall image, which is one of social democracy entering an even more advanced stage of its neoliberal mutation, which also means of its crisis and possible future disintegration.

The left of the social democratic left

Let's turn now to the forces to the left of social democracy, which constitute the bulk of this space I've called the "radical", or to phrase it in a more neutral and topological way, the "left of the social democratic left". This field is quite diverse, and not necessarily very radical, but it offers at least some line of demarcation with neoliberalism and a level of active involvement in the social resistance against it.

I will start by examining those forces of the anti-neoliberal left that are represented in national parliaments, essentially constituted by former Communist parties, or forces coming from splits on the left of social democracy or even from a process of convergence of far-left forces like the Portuguese Left Bloc. It is also in that part of the left that we still find some traces at least of references to Marxism, and in some cases some more substantial forms of relating to the Marxist analysis. Of course, things are more interesting here, since there is at least some level of understanding of and of debate on the deeper causes of the crisis and an awareness of the necessity to present some kind of alternative proposals to the forces fighting against the consequences of the austerity politics. However, we have to say that so far these forces have delivered remarkably little, both in terms of analysis and in terms of alternative proposals with any kind of substance and credibility. A quick look at the document approved by the most recent conference in Paris in December 2010 of the Party of the European Left is eloquent in this respect.[3]

This remarkably poor performance is probably not unrelated to the fact that, without being worse than previously, the electoral results of these forces since the start of the crisis are tending rather towards stagnation. As such these parties do not seem to be in a particularly favourable position to benefit from the crisis of social democracy. Indeed, the absence of a clearly discernable turn to the left is a remarkable pattern of the current crisis so far, with the partial exception of Greece, about which I'll say more in a moment.

The interesting question is actually why this is so. As a hypothesis, rather than a full answer, I'll suggest the following: the first is that in terms of understanding, the analysis of the crisis remains quite general, denouncing the most obvious aspects of neoliberal policies such as financial speculation, fiscal exemptions benefiting capital, austerity as a cause for deepening the recession, etc. What are missing from the picture are two things. The first is the understanding of the geopolitics of crisis, the specific way the crisis unfolds within the European Union and more particularly within the eurozone. What

---

3:    The document can be downloaded at www.european-left.org/english/3rd_el_congress/ 3rd_el_congress/

is missing more precisely is the understanding of the fact that the way these political configurations operate create or accentuate all kinds of polarisations, which give to the dominant classes of the core European countries the possibility of transferring at least part of the costs to the countries of the periphery.

But, in order to grasp this, these left forces should understand the extent to which neoliberal policies and a core/periphery division are embedded within the structure of the EU and the mechanism of "European integration". They should display a will to break with the existing framework of the EU and its institutional pillars, including the eurozone. But this is precisely what these parties refuse to do, putting forward instead illusory proposals to reform the core European institutions (see the programme of the European Left) that seem now even less credible than ever before. This is especially true in countries experiencing the extreme brutality of the so-called "rescue mechanism", such as Greece and Ireland.

This lack of workable intermediate objectives, even of a reformist but at least concrete and credible kind, also explains the weakness of the rest of the proposals, which are intended to respond to immediate social demands, and which I would characterise as of a syndicalist or trade unionist type. In principle, there is, of course, nothing wrong with this. Every concrete struggle starts with these types of demands. But, deprived of a political perspective, they lack credibility, especially in a situation of crisis. Because such a situation, even in less dramatic cases than Greece or Ireland, means entering a non-standard period, a period during which what could be considered as legitimate at a previous moment now becomes a luxury we can't afford any more due to the urgency, the extraordinary character, of the situation.

To put it more simply, the problem with the slogan "We won't pay for their crisis" is that its performative dimension ("We won't pay") presupposes that our objective has already been achieved, which means that a sufficient number of people are convinced that there are other ways to deal with the crisis than those currently on offer, and that they are convinced about this alternative possibility in a situation where action is needed immediately, otherwise it wouldn't be a situation of crisis.

We need to think seriously about the insufficiency of this approach in the light of the recent cycle of social mobilisations in Europe, starting with last spring's strikes in Greece, continuing in autumn 2010 with the impressive and protracted French movement against the pension reforms and now with the mobilisations in universities in Italy and in the UK. It is now clear that a new cycle of struggles is emerging and certainly more is to come. But we also have to say that all these recent mobilisations, if we put aside the still ongoing ones in the universities, have failed. Resistances and movements are indispensable, without them nothing will be achieved, but they are not as such the solution. Daniel Bensaïd warned us repeatedly about the consequences of the "social illusion", of the widespread belief among various currents of the anti- or alter-globalisation constellation that, in order to deliver (but what exactly?), social movements should remain disconnected from politics.[4] So we are back to the question of the alternative, or rather of its absence.

Thinking the alternative

My conclusion will therefore take the form of a question: is there an alternative on the left to this lack of alternative of the main forces of the anti-neoliberal left? I'll leave this question open, not however before confessing a certain feeling of pessimism when looking at the current picture. Alex Callinicos's remarkable article "Austerity Politics", and its effort to grasp the mechanisms of the crisis and the necessity to elaborate transitional demands, seems to me an exception rather than the rule.[5] The same thing could be said about the Greek far-left regroupment Antarsya, which defended a platform including defaulting on the debt, exiting from the eurozone and nationalising the banks, and was rewarded with a significant electoral success in the last local and regional elections.

Despite signs of hope, the dominant tendencies within the far left are a kind of radicalised version of what I said before about the broad anti-neoliberal, or left of the social democratic left—that is to say a combination of general denunciations of the system, in this case named "capitalism" rather than simply "neoliberalism", with a lack of understanding of the mediations through which the dominant classes are responding to the crisis and, finally, an absolutisation of struggles and movements as delivering a solution to our problems—to put it briefly, a combination of propagandistic attitudes and syndicalist agitation. It is exactly with this that we must break if we are to think seriously about alternatives and a new political perspective for the anticapitalist forces.

And we need to start doing that immediately.

References

Bensaïd, Daniel, 2007, "The Return of Strategy", *International Socialism* 113 (winter), www.isj.org.uk/?id=287

Callinicos, Alex, 2010, "Austerity Politics", *International Socialism* 128 (autumn), www.isj.org.uk/?id=678

4:    For example, Bensaïd, 2007.

5:    Callinicos, 2010.

Sexuality, alienation and capitalism

Sheila McGregor

The last few issues of this journal have seen a debate develop over the Marxist attitude to sex work.[1] Jane Pritchard's original article, "The Sex Work Debate",[2] elicited a critical response from Gareth Dale and Xanthe Whittaker.[3] Jess Edwards replied to these criticisms in her article "Sexism and Sex Work",[4] which Dale and Whittaker responded to in turn.[5]

Pritchard's original article addressed two opposing positions on sex work, "abolitionism" and "decriminalisation". It also criticised the view that selling sex is "a job like any other".[6] Pritchard, Edwards, Dale and Whittaker all agreed that sex work cannot be "abolished" under capitalism. All agreed that the activities of both sex workers and their clients should be decriminalised. All agreed that sex work is a consequence of women's oppression, alienation and capitalist society.

The disagreement is over the nature of human sexuality and identity.[7] Dale and Whittaker believe that Pritchard's arguments "rely upon an

---

1:    I have decided to use the term "sex work" for the same reasons as Jane Pritchard—to avoid any hint of moral condemnation, but without implying that "sex work" is "a job like any other"—Pritchard, 2010, p161.

2:    Pritchard, 2010.

3:    Dale and Whittaker, 2010a.

4:    Edwards, 2010.

5:    Dale and Whittaker, 2010b.

6:    Pritchard, 2010, p161.

7:    Dale and Whittaker, 2010a, pp2-3.

idealised view of sexual activity as inextricable from our essential, inner selves".[8] Pritchard says that sex "is part of our human nature, an experience that can be fulfilling and a central part of an individual's identity",[9] while Dale and Whittaker argue that "an individual's core identity—whatever it is—may well include their sexuality but surely cannot be capacious enough to include all sexual acts in which they engage".[10]

If Dale and Whittaker are right that sexuality is not fundamental to human nature, then not only has Pritchard got it wrong, but so did I in 1989, Chris Harman in 1994 and Judith Orr in 2010—not to mention key Marxist writers such as Frederick Engels, August Bebel and Aleksandra Kollontai. This is not a case of saying that "the tradition must be right", but of indicating that there is a fundamental issue at stake here—one that accounts, I believe, for the anger in Edwards' reply to Dale and Whittaker and their equally angry response.[11]

So there is a need to establish a clearer understanding of human sexuality and its interplay with alienation and women's oppression.[12] We also need to understand how the neoliberal economic conditions prevailing since the 1990s have shaped human sexual relations, including the rise of sex work. This analysis has profound implications for developing the Marxist response to the "normalisation" of the sex industry. It also, I would argue, directly affects our vision of a future socialist society.

Sexuality and human prehistory
In the 1980s revolutionary socialists opposed radical feminist arguments that presumed men were by nature aggressive and violent, and that rape was a

---

8:     Dale and Whittaker, 2010a, p3.

9:     Pritchard, 2010, p171.

10:    Dale and Whittaker, 2010, p186. This formulation is hedged with so many qualifications it reveals the authors' own uncertainties. A few questions are in order. If sexuality is not part of our human nature, how does it emerge and why? How has the human race evolved and continued to reproduce if it isn't part of our human nature? Or are Dale and Whittaker in fact positing some sort of dualism, with a "sex instinct" to ensure reproduction and an additional dimension we can call "sexuality"?

11:    Perhaps a word of caution is in order—all of us are committed to fighting women's oppression and for a world without oppressive relationships, including sex work.

12:    I believe Pritchard did present a clear and correct analysis so in many ways I will be restating much of what she has already argued. However, Pritchard could not have anticipated that disagreement would emerge round the issue of sexuality and human nature. Hence the need to develop this argument further, as well as address the fundamental shift in the place of sex in capitalist society over the last 20 years.

weapon used by men to oppress women.[13] The arguments today are very different, but we still put forward an analysis of human sexuality rooted in a materialist understanding of the development of human society and therefore of human nature.[14] I take the fact of sexual behaviour as a given, since the evolution of humanity would not have been possible without it. The evolutionary process that gave rise to modern humans also shaped and gave rise to human sexuality.

Marx's and Engels's approach to understanding human society was based on analysing the organisation of the production and reproduction of human life. The means by which men and women secure their existence shapes the development of human behaviour, including sexual behaviour. Engels further argued that labour was the crucial motor for the transition from ape to man.[15] Human beings developed over several million years as "cultural toolmakers", as social beings who cooperated and communicated with each other to ensure their survival.[16]

Harman pointed out that patterns of sexual behaviour were changing among pygmy apes (our nearest cousins) up to four million years ago. Female pygmy apes use gestures to indicate how they want sex. They are able to initiate sexual activity.[17] He went on to argue that the greater social organisation required of our species "probably explains the change in the pattern of female sexuality, encouraging permanent ties between the sexes rather than the frenetic coupling concentrated around a couple of days a month found in the common chimp".[18] If labour, culture and tool making drove the transition from ape to human, this entailed a change in sexuality and sexual relations along the way.

Engels argued that prehistoric human beings lived in societies without class division, state oppression or inequality between men and women.[19] There was a sexual division of labour between men and women, but no oppression of women by men. This view has subsequently been backed up by a number of Marxist and feminist anthropologists. They concur that human beings evolved as small bands of hunter-gatherers in

13: See my article, McGregor, 1989.
14: For a longer analysis of this and references, see McGregor, 1989, and also Kollontai, 1977.
15: Engels, 1975.
16: A definition popularised in Duncan Hallas at meetings throughout the 1980s.
17: Harman, 1994.
18: Harman, 1994, p100.
19: Engels, 1978.

which men and women cooperated to secure the existence of the band.[20] Such bands were observed right up to the mid-20th century and exhibit traits such as cooperation, lack of hierarchy, and egalitarian relations between men and women. This sexual egalitarianism was rooted in the fact that both gathering (usually done by women) and hunting (usually done by men) contributed to the successful existence of the band.[21] Certain North American hunter gatherer tribes accept a fluidity about gender roles, in that a child could adopt a gender role different from their biological sex.[22]

So human sexual behaviour developed in an egalitarian and cooperative environment. It would have most likely been consensual in nature. Since human beings are not restricted to "mating" at only certain times of year, human sexuality appears to have evolved with a pleasurable aspect to it, unconnected to the direct needs of reproduction of the band. Early human societies were not subordinated to the discipline of the clock. Men and women would have had a degree of leisure time that would permit more relaxed relationships to develop between all members of the group.[23] If labour was the motor for our emergence as a distinctive species, we also evolved with a capacity for sexual pleasure.

This is not an "idealised view of human sexuality as inextricable from our essential, inner selves" as Dale and Whittaker suggest.[24] On the contrary, it is a materialist view that starts from the fact of evolution and embeds our development within the production and reproduction of human life through interaction with nature. We are born with the ability to see, hear, smell, touch and taste. But how we do these things depends upon the society we grow up in. We are born with the ability to speak, but which languages we learn depends on which ones are used where we grow up. And so it is with human sexuality.

Women's oppression and class society

The egalitarian relations between the sexes that characterised human pre-history came to an end with the development of agriculture. Engels argues that the oppression of women was linked to the rise of class society and the

---

20: For a full review of Engels and an updating of his analysis see Harman, 1994. For the purposes of the discussion here, whether Engels was right in all his arguments is not pertinent.

21: Hunting was usually a collective affair, sometimes involving women.

22: See McGregor, 1989, p7.

23: Marshall Sahlins makes this point in Sahlins, 2003.

24: Dale and Whittaker, 2010, p187.

family.[25] Women were subordinated to men, just as the majority of men and women were subordinated to a ruling class. This historic shift destroyed bonds based on equality and solidarity. It reshaped our personal relations according to the needs of successive class societies.

Hannah Dee provides an overview of the varieties of personal relations prior to the rise of capitalism in order to show that homosexual relationships had an important status in earlier times.[26] Kollontai has some interesting reflections on the different kinds of love in feudal society.[27] But there is a common thread running through successive class societies: the family, the oppression of women and the subordination of women's sexuality to the reproductive needs of society.

The rise of capitalist society set in train a further series of dramatic if contradictory changes to human sexual relations. In its early stages, capitalism destroyed the feudal family as a productive unit as thousands, then millions, were drawn into the new mines and factories. Such was the impact on the old society that Marx and Engels foretold the end of the family for the new working class. They were proved wrong initially as the new bourgeois class campaigned for the reconstruction of the family. This new working class family was required to ensure the reproduction of the working class. It would be the place where the next generation of workers would be born and reared until they in turn entered the production process. This reconstituted family was partly welcomed by working class people as a defence against the ravages of industrialisation.[28] But the family's re-establishment came with a raft of legislation to lay down the parameters of sexual relations:

The Poor Law Amendment Act in 1834, by outlawing outdoor relief for unmarried women, helped break earlier patterns of premarital sex. Other laws in the 1880s raised the age of consent for girls, regulated obscenity, prostitution and homosexuality and were a part of a drive to establish the marriage bed as the sole legitimate place for sexual relations at least for women.[29]

The working class family once more subordinated women to men, ensuring that women's oppression continued. It enshrined segregated gender roles with the burden of reproduction in the home falling on women's shoulders. This in turn led to discrimination both inside and outside the

25: Engels, 1978.
26: Dee, 2010.
27: Kollontai, 1977.
28: McGregor, 1989, pp10-11.
29: McGregor, 1989, p10.

home: in terms of legal rights, unequal pay and sex discrimination. Women were also expected to serve men's sexual needs.

Nevertheless, the basis of the family had changed decisively, from a unit of production under feudalism to a unit of consumption under capitalism. This also changed the basis of the partnership between men and women into what Engels called "individual sex love". "In modern capitalist society, marriage and its equivalent common law relationships are entered into freely by men and women on the basis of mutual attraction," he wrote.[30]

Mass production of household goods accompanied by mass advertising soon focused on women as consumers of household goods. Women were also encouraged to see sex and their physical appearance as a means of maintaining their husbands' interest: "Women were increasingly pushed into becoming self-conscious about their bodies and appearance. Beauty and sensuality became subordinated to consumption and the cash nexus".[31] We should not underestimate the huge change this meant for the majority of women. Their decisions over what to buy suddenly became important. And they were encouraged to look and to be sexually attractive. Women as consumers were being written into society's script—and their bodies were too.

But there were other long-term trends in capitalist society that undermined the continued existence of the working class family as a unit with a father, mother and children. These changes have fuelled a mass of contradictions in women's position in society. They have had profound repercussions for the sexuality of both men and women.

The most important change has been the way in which working class women—never entirely absent from the production process—have been systematically drawn into paid work outside the home. As Orr points out: "Today, the majority of adult women in Britain (71 percent) work outside the home... Women are almost 50 percent of the workforce in Britain".[32] This economic independence of women from men underpins the rise in divorce, the decline of marriage and the increasing number of single parent households.

Another key change has been the advent of safe contraception and legal abortion. This has given women the ability to plan the timing and the number of children they choose to have, leading to smaller families started later in life. Contraception and abortion further separated sex from reproduction and opened up the possibility of sexual relationships based

---

30: See McGregor, 1989, p10.
31: McGregor, 1989, p11.
32: Orr, 2010, p55.

on pleasure without fear of pregnancy. One other change is the advent of mass education, which partially shifts tasks of socialising and training young people from the family onto the state. Meanwhile the market has almost entirely taken over the task of producing goods to be used by the family.

The rise and fall of the Women's Liberation Movement

The years following the Second World War saw the mass entry of women into paid work outside the home and the mass education of young women alongside men at university. The conservative morality that dominated the 1950s soon began to clash with the aspirations of working class women and women students.[33] These clashes that ultimately gave rise to the Women's Liberation Movement, emerged in the late 1960s alongside other liberation movements.[34]

The Women's Liberation Movement's key demands were for equal pay, 24-hour nurseries, an end to sex discrimination and the right to abortion and contraception.[35] In addition, the Women's Liberation Movement challenged gender stereotypes around intellectual capacity, jobs and sexuality. The grounds for this challenge had been well prepared in a myriad of ways: sex and sexuality became more openly discussed in the public domain; young women won the right to wear shorter skirts if they so chose, and cut their hair shorter. Young men established their right to wear their hair longer and both sexes established a trend of wearing blue jeans. They wanted to be in control over the appearance of their own bodies, their sexuality and their reproductive capacity as well.

Young women not only wanted to open up jobs reserved for men but to be able to have sexual relationships outside marriage on an equal basis with men without being seen as "sluts".[36] A space was created in which women's sexuality could be seriously discussed by both women and men,

---

33: The Second World War saw a massive disruption in "normal" relationships as fiancés and husbands went off to war, perhaps never to return. This gave women drawn into productive work a margin of independence and freedom in personal relationships they would not otherwise have encountered. This caused difficulties for many when "normal" family life was re-established after 1945.

34: This period of revolt has been amply documented elsewhere. See Harman, 1988, and Orr, 2010.

35: I prefer to use the term Women's Liberation Movement rather than "second wave feminism" because it is a more accurate term for the development of the movement in the 1960s. The latter term seems to me to be associated with burying the idea that fundamental social change is needed to get rid of women's oppression. In any case, "second wave feminism" reminds me of advertisements for hair styling.

36: Students had to campaign to be allowed to use one another's bedrooms at night.

including how women achieved orgasm. Young women began to demand the right to sexual pleasure, backed up by the work of Masters and Johnson, even though it took Shere Hite to establish that: "the majority of women did not achieve orgasm through sexual intercourse but through clitoral stimulation".[37] Gender stereotypes began to diminish, opening up possibilities for both women and men to realise their potential more in tune with their individuality than according to their sex. For if women's oppression seriously constrained women's development, it also constrained that of men.

At around the same time in Britain an increasingly confident working class was winning key battles against the employers and the government of the day. Working class solidarity expressed itself through respect for picket lines, collections and solidarity strike action. And that experience of working class solidarity also enabled socialists and feminists to convince wide layers of the male dominated trade union movement that women had a right to control their sexuality through access to abortion and contraception.[38]

While many of these changes in women's role have proved lasting, many other ideas about women's liberation were lost as the optimism of the movements around 1968 receded. The reaction against women's liberation came from a number of directions and was underpinned by wider developments in society as a whole. Working class challenges to pay controls and trade union laws were undermined in the late 1970s, leading eventually to Margaret Thatcher's Tory government.

As the working class solidarity weakened, a layer of feminists began to argue that the roots of women's oppression lay in the biology of men, with rape as the chosen weapon for maintaining women's submission. More mainstream voices put forward the view that the demands of the women's movement had generated a "crisis" in masculinity. There was also a resurgence in the notion that human behaviour could be explained by reference to our genes or our brains, which fuelled the "boys will be boys" view that gender stereotypes are innate.

At the end of the 1980s the resurgence of male sexism occurred after the threads that connected feminism to ideas about socialism and women's

---

37:   McGregor, 1989, p13.

38:   The link between working class solidarity and combating sexism was illustrated during the Great Miners' Strike of 1984-5. A common chant by miners at the first major demonstration in Mansfield was "Get your tits out for the miners" (addressed to women police officers). At the time I commented to those around me that, with attitudes like that, the miners would never win. Yet by the end of the strike those same miners had been transformed. Miners' wives became central to organising solidarity. The Gay Liberation Demonstration in 1985 was led by a miners' banner.

liberation had been cut. The backlash against "political correctness" pursued by right wing politicians and the right wing media did not succeed in "driving women back into the home" but contributed to rehabilitating male sexism and the idea of fundamental differences in gender.

Neoliberalism and sexuality

However, this background does not account for the more recent normalisation of the sex industry, which involves the participation of and acceptance by millions of women. As Orr argues, part of the explanation lies in how "raunch culture" has been sold as being somehow empowering: "It reflects and has absorbed the history and language of women's struggles to have the right to assert their sexual needs and desires, to be more than mere objects for the enjoyment of others, all the better to continue that process".[39]

The way in which "sex" has become a commodity is equally central to this process of normalisation. An aspect of our human nature—our sexuality—has been alienated from us, dehumanised, repackaged and sold back to us.[40] And this alienated sexuality is one shaped by women's oppression. That is why the sex industry overwhelmingly involves selling images of women's bodies and sexual services provided by women.[41]

This industry is hugely profitable, bringing in an estimated $57 billion a year in revenue worldwide, with $20 billion a year coming from adult videos and $11 billion a year from escort services. Revenue from pornography is greater than that from all professional football, baseball and basketball franchises put together.[42] This has been accompanied by a "relentless seepage of values, images, behaviour and dress from the world of selling sex for money into mainstream culture and society". This in turn feeds directly into the argument that selling sex and women's bodies is "just another job".[43]

Why has this happened? The key lies in the impact of neoliberalism upon sexuality in a context of rapid changes to the working class

---

39: Orr, 2010, p36.

40: These points were amply expressed by Pritchard, 2010, pp169-170.

41: A proportion of the sex industry is devoted to servicing women clients through escort agencies and male street prostitutes. There are also transvestites involved in sex work. Pornography is heavily used by women and children. But although many of the users of pornography may therefore be girls and women, its content is about the use of women as sex objects to satisfy men.

42: See http://crossculturalconnections.org/documents/sex_stats.pdf, though note that all such statistics are hard to verify as so much of the sex industry is illegal.

43: Orr, 2010, p21.

family and a weakened working class movement where class solidarity is no longer the norm.[44]

Orr and Pritchard rightly point to the continued resilience of the working class family both as the means for reproducing the working class and as an ideal for working class women. Privatised reproduction, ie the family, is after all the source of women's oppression. But that is not the whole story. Neoliberalism has undermined the working class family—and this helps explain the ease with which sexuality has become more profoundly alienated and commodified.

The changes in sexual relationships over the last 40 years have been enormous. Sex is no longer confined to marriage. Boys and girls mature earlier and start sexual relations earlier. Women are choosing to have babies later. Increasingly women choose to remain childless. Divorce is much easier. More people are choosing to live with a partner or a series of partners. Same sex relationships are accepted in a way that was unthinkable a few decades ago. Some people change their sexual orientation in the course of their lifetime, while others are bisexual.

One consequence of these changes is that women and men have a far greater range of choice in their relationships. Another is that in longer term relationships, whether couples are married or not, individuals can at least look for sexual love and companionship (what Engels called "individual sex love") even if such relationships prove not to be viable in the longer run. All of this means that people's sexual experience is much more varied than it used to be.

But this also has to be seen against a backdrop of the stresses of working class life. Sex education is sadly wanting for both boys and girls. People are working longer hours under greater pressures from targets and managerial supervision. We live in a world where "all our human needs have been transformed into commodities" that can seemingly be satisfied as easily as buying a McDonald's.[45] Weekends are times when alcohol and other drugs promise to ease the unbearable pressures of working lives.[46]

But our sexual needs cannot be satisfied like that. The most intimate of relationships requires an acknowledgement of the other as a person, as an equal, as someone who also has needs. Human sexuality requires a human setting and human relationship, time and patience as well as a human spark.

44: An absence of working class struggle and solidarity can, of course, change very quickly.

45: Pritchard, 2010, p170.

46: I would also argue that the growth of obesity is another consequence of the commodification of the human need to eat and drink.

The very lives we lead make satisfying sexual relationships difficult. Small wonder that the sex industry plugs the gap with porn videos, sex toys, lap dancing clubs, escort agencies and old fashioned street prostitution.

And in so doing the industry reinforces the gender division of women as sexual objects and men as buyers of the product. This division traps women in a denial of their own sexual needs and men in the belief that women are bodies to be ogled at or bought. One of the beauties of contraception was that it opened up the possibility of men and women developing sexual relationships without having "to stop off at Malton".[47] Lap dancing and other forms of sexual display substitute "looking" for real sexual relations. Perhaps it is fitting that Paris Hilton, who is bored by real sexual intercourse, has become an icon recently. Compare this with Jane Birkin in Serge Gainsbourg's song "Je t'aime...moi non plus" of 1967, where Birkin seemed to be having an orgasm.[48]

A Marxist approach to sex work

What are the implications of all of this for Marxists and our attitudes to the family and sex work? First, we need to restate that one aspect of liberation for both men and women is about developing our full potential as individuals, regardless of gender. Second, we have a vision of human sexual relationships that are freely entered into and based on mutual attraction, consent and satisfaction. Whether such relationships are short or long lived, with the same or the opposite sex, between couples of the same age or with big age differences, will be a matter for the couples themselves to decide. And in a world which encourages the development of every aspect of the human personality, the utter dependence on one "love" relationship will give way to more varied relationships based on solidarity.[49]

Such a vision will only be realised through a complete transformation of society. It will only be achieved when we organise production to answer human needs rather than to maximise profits. The role of advertising to get us to buy things will disappear when we can discuss and decide what our needs are. In particular, however, it means the socialisation of all aspects of the family, in order to open the door to different kinds of loving and supportive relationships, both between adults and between adults and children. In addition, it will also require the disappearance of the sex industry so that

47: The place for stopping varied from one part of the country to the other. In any case, contraception meant that women were no longer afraid that penetrative sex would lead to conception.
48: Levy, 2005, p30.
49: Kollontai, 1977, pp288-289.

women no longer sell their bodies for sex and men no longer look to pornography, lap dancing or buying sexual services.

But where does that leave the question of organising sex workers today? We have to start from opposition to any kind of condemnation of the women and men who get caught up in the sex industry. We need to unequivocally oppose all forms of criminalisation of sex workers, and of their clients. This includes campaigning for the free movement of people around the world and their legal rights to become part of the society of their choice.[50]

We also need to be unequivocal in our support for the right of sex workers to unionise and to campaign for demands that improve their conditions. In particular we should recognise how revolutionary upheavals can enable some of the most vulnerable workers in society to transform their lives. The role played by some prostitutes in the defence of the 1871 Paris Commune is one such example.[51]

But does that mean Marxists should see the organisation of sex workers as a priority? A degree of caution is in order here. Sanders, O'Neill and Pitcher estimate that "of the seven countries where unionisation [of sex workers] exists, membership can be estimated at approximately 5,000 people".[52] These numbers are small. Dale and Whittaker themselves point to some of the difficulties involved in this field:

> It is self-evidently the case that sex workers' collective organisation, in the West as elsewhere, faces structural and social barriers. Much sex work is individualised or takes place in small workplaces... Many are independent contractors and/or have small business aspirations and, as such, are pitted in direct economic rivalry.[53]

They go on to rightly note that the same arguments can be made about "plumbers or freelance journalists or domestic workers".[54] But it is worth considering the last example more closely. There were a million, mainly female, domestic servants in Britain at the end of the 19th century. But it was the strikes by match girls alongside dockers and others in east

---

50: Pritchard, 2010, pp166-168.
51: Cliff, 1984, p42. The was not true of the majority of prostitutes, however.
52: Sanders, O'Neill and Pitcher, 2009, p108. Their figures are for 2007 and taken from Gall.
53: Dale and Whittaker, 2010a, p191. See also Sanders, O'Neill and Pitcher, 2009, chapter 6.
54: Dale and Whittaker, 2010a, p191.

London that built the first major general unions in Britain and thus transformed the prospects for working class women and men.

We have always argued that the revolutionary party has to fight for the working class to be the tribune of the oppressed. But that does not mean starting from the most oppressed. Our approach to the organisation of sex workers should run along these lines. As a rough guide, this means that individual revolutionaries organise where they find themselves. But in party branches and caucuses, the focus should be on large concentrations of workers, students and others engaged in struggle. We need to avoid the two moralisms: that of rejecting sex workers as enemies, and that of elevating them to be the focus for combating oppression.[55]

But if we positively support the right of sex workers to organise, does that mean we simply equate sex work with other work? Here it is worth looking at how Kollontai describes prostitution:

> Prostitution is above all a social phenomenon; it is closely connected to the needy position of woman and her economic dependence on man in marriage and the family. The roots of prostitution are in economics. Woman is on the one hand placed in an economically vulnerable position, and on the other hand has been conditioned by centuries of education to expect material favours from a man in return for sexual favours whether these are given within or outside the marriage tie.[56]

Kollontai is fundamentally right to pinpoint economic vulnerability as the primary reason why some women see the selling of sex or sexual services as an option: "For men as well as for women, the motivating factor for entry into the sex industry is economic need and for many this is a conscious choice, as it offers them more money than they could earn in mainstream employment".[57]

What has changed, however, is the way in which the commodification of sex has created a market for the sex industry. What effect does this have on sex workers? Dale and Whittaker claim that the stigma attached to sex work creates "greater psychological difficulties for sex workers than the work itself".[58] But there is evidence that this stigma is decreasing. A whole range of

---

55: Marxists developed similar arguments in the 1960s and 1970s against focusing on the organisation of housewives, in opposition to arguments for "wages for housework".
56: Kollontai, 1977, p264.
57: Sanders, O'Neill and Pitcher, 2009, p40. See also Carré and Agostini, 2010, p24-50, Mathieu, 2007, pp23, 105-117.
58: Dale and Whittaker, 2010a, p188.

practices associated with the sex industry are becoming more acceptable: the sexualisation of girls' bodies, girls providing fellatio for boys at a young age, the use of porn videos and so on.[59] To cite Sanders, O'Neil and Pitcher:

> Bernstein (2001) has argued that the prolific and unabridged use of sex, in particular the female body form, in advertising and other mechanisms of cultural production has produced a greater acceptability of the erotic, a normalisation of the desire for the erotic and an increasing acceptance for men (and increasingly women) to pursue these desires.[60]

So more and more people are being drawn into the sex industry, while the reactions to this range from positively welcoming the development through ambivalence to downright hostility. Orr has documented the recent growth of both raunch culture and opposition to its intrusion into society, particularly on university campuses.[61]

A Marxist understanding of sexuality

Marxists need to maintain a clear view about a number of things. First and foremost, there is a difference between the consensual sexual relationships people aspire to (whether short or long term) and anything which involves the buying and selling of sexual acts.

The difference between these two is real, which is why those involved in selling sex talk about "splitting" themselves in order to do their work. In the case of a personal relationship, individuals hope to "be themselves" without having to put up a mask or play a role. Sex work necessitates the opposite: playing a role in order to separate their sex work from their personal relationships. That is why a future society in which all human beings can experience fulfilling relationships would be one in which sex work would disappear.

Second, there is a difference between the erotic and the pornographic reduction of women's bodies to sex objects.[62] In fact I would argue that the latter leads to a de-eroticisation, which perhaps partly explains why so many young women can strive to present themselves as sexually attractive while having no real concept of, never mind experience of, stimulating

---

59: This point is made by Dale and Whittaker themselves—2010b, p203.
60: Sanders, O'Neil and Pitcher, 2009, p30.
61: Orr, 2010.
62: I am aware that this is a rather bald statement but I hope that it will suffice to just state it here.

and satisfying sexual relationships.[63] The surgical restructuring of women's sexual organs illustrates this triumph of "presentation" over sexual desire and satisfaction.

Third, there is the question of working class solidarity. Workers, through their unique position in the production process, have the power to overthrow capitalism and create a different society. But there are crucial concrete aspects to actualising this potential economic power. Unity has to be forged in the face of a common enemy. Divisions inside the working class must be overcome through a democratic process of debate and discussion. Solidarity is essential for a working class intent on transforming society. Male workers have to accept women as their equals. And all workers should accept that a person's sexuality can be varied but is always human, and that religious beliefs are strictly a private matter. As Kollontai argues, solidarity is about listening and responding to the needs of the other.[64]

How can this process occur if men think that women's bodies are sexual objects to be ogled at and occasionally bought for a quick fellatio or other sexual act? How can women feel confident about solidarity if they feel obliged to present themselves as sexual objects to men? Or that their purpose is to sexually stimulate men without experiencing the satisfaction of their own needs?

The sex industry cuts across and undermines this need for working class solidarity. Hence Marxists need to challenge its claims to be erotic, to provide a useful service or to be in any way empowering for women. Without being moralistic, we need to explain that the sex industry is part of the deformation and destruction of human sexual desire, both male and female. It objectifies those who work in it and those who use it.

As mass movements contest and challenge social structures, they inevitably throw up issues about personal relations and sexuality. Marxists should hardly be surprised that millions of people involved in fighting and transforming oppressive societies should turn their thoughts to breaking the bonds of unsatisfactory personal relationships and reshaping them. This process was visible in Cairo's Tahrir Square recently as we saw Christians alongside Muslims, men alongside women, young alongside old, all fighting together for social change. It is an intrinsic part of the revolutionary liberation process to begin to breathe, to dare, to feel and to experience in a different way. Provided we place the question of working class solidarity at the heart of what we do, we might make mistakes but we won't go far wrong.

63: See Levy, 2005, chapter 1.
64: Kollontai, 1977, p290.

References

Banyard, Kat, 2010, *The Equality Illusion* (Faber and Faber).

Carré, Jean-Michel, and Patricia Agostini, 2010, *Travailleu(r)ses du sexe: Et fières de l'etre* (Seuil).

Cliff, Tony, 1984, *Class struggle and Women's Liberation* (Bookmarks), www.marxists.org/archive/cliff/works/1984/women/index.htm

Dale, Gareth, and Xanthe Whittaker, 2010a, "A Response to the Sex Work Debate", *International Socialism 127* (summer), www.isj.org.uk/?id=664

Dale, Gareth, and Xanthe Whittaker, 2011b, "Sex Work: a Rejoinder", *International Socialism 129* (winter), www.isj.org.uk/?id=707

Dee, Hannah, 2010, *The Red in the Rainbow: Sexuality, Socialism and LGBT Liberation* (Bookmarks).

Edwards, Jess, 2010, "Sexism and Sex Work: A Response to Dale and Whittaker", *International Socialism 128* (autumn), www.isj.org.uk/?id=688

Engels, Frederick, 1978, *The Origin of the Family, Private Property and the State* (Foreign Languages Press), www.marxists.org/archive/marx/works/1884/origin-family/index.htm

Engels, Frederick, 1975, *The Role Played by Labour in the Transition from Ape to Man* (Foreign Languages Press), www.marxists.org/archive/marx/works/1876/part-played-labour/index.htm

Harman, Chris, 1988, *The Fire Last Time: 1968 and After* (Bookmarks).

Harman, Chris, 1994, "Engels and the Origins of Human Society", *International Socialism 65* (winter), http://pubs.socialistreviewindex.org.uk/isj65/harman.htm

Kollontai, Alexandra, 1977, *Selected Writings* (Alison and Busby).

Leacock, Eleanor Burke, 1981, *Myths of Male Dominance* (Monthly Review Press).

Levy, Ariel, 2005, *Female Chauvinist Pigs* (Pocket Books).

Marx, Karl, 1975, *Early Writings* (Penguin).

Mathieu, Lilian, 2007, *La Condition Prostituée* (Textuel).

McGregor, Sheila, 1989, "Rape, Pornography and Capitalism", *International Socialism 45* (winter), www.marxists.de/gender/mcgregor/rapeporn.htm

Orr, Judith, 2010, "Marxism and Feminism Today", *International Socialism 127* (summer), www.isj.org.uk/?id=656

Pritchard, Jane, 2010, "The Sex Work Debate", *International Socialism 125* (winter), www.isj.org.uk/?id=618

Sahlins, Marshall, 2003, *Stone Age Economics* (Routledge).

Sanders, Teela, Maggie O'Neill and Jane Pitcher, 2009, *Prostitution: Sex work, Policy and Politics* (Sage).

Walter, Natasha, 2010, *Living Dolls* (Virago).

Debating Black Flame, revolutionary anarchism and historical Marxism

Lucien van der Walt

This article responds to criticisms of the broad anarchist tradition in *International Socialism*, an International Socialist Tendency (IST) journal.[1] I will discuss topics such as the use of sources, defending revolutions and freedom, the Spanish anarchists, anarchism and democracy, the historical role of Marxism, and the Russian Revolution.

The articles I am engaging with are marked by commendable goodwill; I strive for the same. Paul Blackledge's article rejects "caricatured non-debate".[2] Ian Birchall stresses that "lines between anarchism and Marxism are often blurred".[3] Leo Zeilig praises Michael Schmidt's and my book, *Black Flame: the Revolutionary Class Politics of Anarchism and Syndicalism*, as "a fascinating account".[4]

1: I develop these arguments more in a paper at http://lucienvanderwalt.blogspot. com/2011/02/anarchism-black-flame-marxism-and-ist.html. Thanks to Shawn Hattingh, Ian Bekker, Iain McKay and Wayne Price for feedback.

2: Blackledge, 2010, p132.

3: Birchall, 2010, p177.

4: Zeilig, 2009 , pp221-2. I use the term "syndicalism" to refer to revolutionary trade unionism that combines daily struggles with the goal of seizing the means of production. It emerged from the anarchist wing of the First International; it is an anarchist strategy and all its forms are part of the "broad anarchist tradition".

It is important to note where we converge. The IST states it is for socialism from below through revolution. If Marx, Lenin and Trotsky are invoked here, it is because the "essence" of their works is taken to be "working class self-emancipation".[5] The term "dictatorship of the proletariat", Leo insists, means merely "the democratic defence of working class power" through "organs of self-organisation; councils, trade unions, communes etc".[6]

By any measure, anarchists favour working class self-emancipation. For Mikhail Bakunin and Pyotr Kropotkin, social revolution required a movement by *the workers and the peasants*", "the only two classes capable of so mighty an insurrection".[7] The "new social order" would be constructed "from the bottom up" by the "organisation and power of the working masses".[8] The popular classes would "take upon themselves the task of rebuilding society",[9] through revolutionary *counter-power* and *counter-culture*, outside and against the ruling class, state and capital.

We have real differences too: these require comradely yet frank discussion. The first step in avoiding "caricatured non-debate" is to engage seriously with what Leo calls the "often obscured" history of the broad anarchist tradition. It is a pity, then, that Leo's review concentrates on refuting (as I will show, not convincingly) what *Black Flame* said about mainstream Marxism. The point of *Black Flame* is not to study Marxism, but the 150 year tradition of anarchism and syndicalism—a mass movement with a sophisticated theory, usually caricatured by Marxists.

Benedict Anderson notes that the broad anarchist tradition was long the "dominant element in the self-consciously internationalist radical left", "the main vehicle of global opposition to industrial capitalism, autocracy, latifundism, and imperialism".[10] Into the 1950s its movements were often larger than their Marxist rivals. In its dark years, into the 1980s, the tradition remained important in unions and armed struggles in Asia, Latin America and southern Europe, and in the Cuban and Soviet undergrounds.[11]

Today anarchists are central to the "most determined and combative of the movements" fighting capitalist globalisation.[12] A 2007 syndicalist

---

5: Blackledge, 2010, p132.
6: Zeilig, 2009 , pp221-222.
7: Bakunin [1870], pp185,189, emphasis in original.
8: Bakunin, 1953, pp300,319,378.
9: Kropotkin [1912], p188.
10: Anderson, 2006, pp2,54.
11: See the online article for full citations.
12: Meyer, 2003, p218; Epstein, 2001.

union summit in Paris drew 250 delegates worldwide, Africans the biggest continental grouping.[13] There is a global spread of anarchist values: bottom-up organising and direct action outside the official political system.[14]

I agree with Paul and Leo that anarchists have caricatured Marxists, but the reverse is true too—often because Marxists use unreliable or hostile sources, dismissing other accounts as "liberal", etc. Ian commendably distances himself from Hal Draper's bizarre charges that Bakunin favoured dictatorship, etc.[15] Draper distorted anarchist views through manipulation and fabrication.[16] Ian instead cites former anarchist Victor Serge's recollections.[17] Serge, however, is not reliable. He claimed, Ian notes, that the anarcho-syndicalist *Golos Truda* group "made common cause" with the Bolsheviks; in fact, it charged Bolshevism with state capitalism and dictatorship, and was repressed.[18] The materials of the anarchist movement *itself*—particularly its mainstream—deserve more thorough, open-minded engagement.

Anarchism and revolutionary force

Do anarchists really deny the need for the popular classes to be "organised ideologically, politically and militarily" to defend revolution, as Paul claims?[19] Leo's *own* review of *Black Flame* admits the book shows that most anarchist currents insisted on the need to "coordinate the defence of the revolution against internal and external enemies".[20] A few syndicalists hoped for a "bloodless revolution", but not the mainstream.[21]

Bakunin wanted the existing "army...judicial system...police" replaced by "permanent barricades," coordinated through delegates with "always revocable mandates", and the "extension of the revolutionary force" between "rebel countries".[22] This is "revolutionary force", used for *emancipation,* not oppression,[23] based on the peasants and workers "federating" their "fighting battalions, district by district, assuring a common coordinated defence against internal and external enemies".[24] To be

---

13: "Conférences Internationale Syndicales—107," www.anarkismo.net/article/5434
14: Goaman, 2004, pp173-174.
15: Birchall, 2010 , pp179-180, referring to Draper, 1966, chapter 4.
16: Keffer, 2005.
17: Birchall, 2010, p178, notably Serge's *Revolution in Danger*.
18: Thorpe, 1989, pp96,98,100,164,179,197,200.
19: Blackledge, 2010, pp136,139,142.
20: Zeilig, 2010, p222. See van der Walt and Schmidt, 2009, ch4, 6.
21: For example, Chaplin [1933].
22: Bakunin [1869], pp152-154; also Bakunin [1870], p190.
23: Bakunin [1865], p137.
24: Bakunin, [1870], p190.

anti-authoritarian *requires* forceful struggle against oppressors; this is no contradiction, as Engels asserted.[25]

The need for "revolutionary force" was recognised by most key figures, Kropotkin, Pyotr Arshinov, Alexander Berkman, Camillo Berneri, Buenaventura Durruti, Emma Goldman, Praxedis Guerrero, Li Pei Kan ("Ba Jin"), Liu Sifu ("Shifu"), Ricardo Flores Magón, Errico Malatesta, Nestor Ivanovich Makhno, José Oiticica, Albert Parsons, Domingos Passos, Rudolph Rocker, Shin Ch'aeho and Kim Jao-jin. It spurred anarchist/syndicalist militias in China, Cuba, Ireland, Korea/Manchuria, Mexico, Spain, Russia, the Ukraine and United States.[26] It was the official stance of, for instance, the anarchist majority of the post-1872 First International, the syndicalist International Workers' Association (1922), the Eastern Anarchist League (1927), the Korean People's Association in Manchuria and Spain's National Confederation of Labour (CNT).

Paul says: "Once social movements are strong enough to point towards a real alternative to the *status quo*, states will intervene with the aim of suppressing them".[27] What anarchist would deny this? To suggest anarchists and syndicalists ignore the state is equivalent to insisting Marxism ignores capitalism. The anarchist mainstream does not agree with the self-proclaimed Marxist John Holloway's *Change the World Without Taking Power*.[28]

Paul claims the CNT joined the Spanish Popular Front in 1936 because anarchists lacked a plan for "coordinating the military opposition to Franco's fascists".[29] In fact, joining *violated* CNT policy, and was driven by fear of isolation and fighting on two fronts. Since the 1870s Spanish anarchists aimed to "annihilate the power of the state" through "superior firing power".[30] From 1932 the CNT and the Anarchist Federation of Iberia (FAI) organised insurrections, stressing armed defence and coordination through a National Revolutionary Council.[31] This was reiterated at the 1936 FAI and CNT congresses,[32] was still official policy in August 1936, and was partially implemented through the Council of Aragon.[33] In 1937

25: Engels [1873], 1972. See McKay, *The Anarchist FAQ*, section H 4.7.
26: See online paper for references, and "Declaration of the Principles of Revolutionary Syndicalism": Thorpe, 1989, p324.
27: Blackledge, 2010, p139.
28: Holloway, 2005.
29: Blackledge, 2010, p139.
30: Maura, 1971, pp66,68, 72, 80-83.
31: Gómez Casas, 1986, pp137, 144, 154-157.
32: Gómez Casas, 1986, pp171, 173-175; CNT [1 May 1936], pp10-11.
33: Paz, 1987, p247.

the dissident Friends of Durruti *reiterated* it, calling for a National Defence Council, not a Popular Front.[34]

Anarchism, democracy and armed defence of revolution

What is the place of participatory democracy, debate and freedom in this scenario? First, the FAI / CNT / Friends of Durruti insisted, coordinated military defence was *subject* to the basic aims of the revolution—self-management, collectivisation and emancipation—and to the popular classes' organs of counterpower. Repeating Bakunin's arguments, the National Defence Council would be "elected by democratic vote", under revocable mandate.[35] Handing power to officers or a revolutionary clique would destroy revolution *from within* as surely as external defeat.

Secondly, the revolution is for *libertarian communism,* ie *for* freedom, *against* capitalism, state and oppression. In place of the late Tony Cliff's notion that it is acceptable that "tactics contradict principles",[36] anarchists insist means must match ends, because they shape them.

Defence of revolution *necessarily* includes defence of participatory democratic processes and structures, and of political and civil rights. The democratic heart of counterpower cannot be cut out to "save" the revolution: it is *both its means and its end.*

The basic system would be popular self-government through worker/community assemblies and councils made up of mandated and recallable delegates, with basic rights protected at all times. As Diego Abad de Santillan wrote, anarchists "oppose with force those who try to subjugate us on behalf of their interests or concepts", but do not "resort to force against those who do not share our points of view".[37]

Legitimate coercion is applied to external threats, including the counter-revolutionary ruling class, and to internal anti-social crime; the majority within the system is prevented from oppressing internal dissenters and minorities; internal dissidents are prevented from forcible disruption. Anarchism will be the guiding revolutionary programme because it is *freely accepted* by the *popular classes* through *debate and participatory democracy*, in multi-tendency structures of counterpower.

The mainstream anarchist/syndicalist movement's rejection of the Marxist "dictatorship of the proletariat" was *never* based on rejecting the

34: Friends of Durruti [1938, 1978], p25.
35: Friends of Durruti [1938, 1978], p25.
36: Birchall, 2010, p175.
37: Abad de Santillan [1937], p47.

need to defend *revolution*. It arose from the view that the Marxist "dictatorship of the proletariat" was really "dictatorship *over* the proletariat".

"Real democracy", anarchism and the Paris Commune

Given this, it is odd that Paul claims (echoing Draper) that anarchists reject the "possibility of real democracy".[38] If "democracy" means the rule of the people, anarchism is radically democratic. Bakunin and Kropotkin viewed the state as a centralised, hierarchical system of territorial power, run by and for the ruling class. Here "all the real aspirations, all the living forces of a country enter generously and happily", only to be "slain and buried".[39]

The class system is defined both by *relations of production* expressed in inequitable control of the means of production, and *relations of domination*, expressed in inequitable control of the means of coercion that physically enforce decisions, and administration, that govern society.[40]

The means of coercion and administration are centralised in the state, controlled by state managers: senior officials, judges, military heads, mayors, parliamentarians. Capitalists are only *part* of the ruling class; those who run the state are always members of the ruling class; the ruling class is always a dominant, exploiting minority; the state is centralised in order that this minority can rule the majority. (Marxists have a different definition, but let's get clear about the anarchists.)

The popular classes' counterpower, for anarchists, *cannot* therefore be expressed through a state.[41] Anarchist anti-statism arises *from* recognition of the state's profoundly anti-popular class character.[42] In place of states and corporations, anarchists/syndicalists advocate that the means of production, coercion and administration be taken and restructured under genuine participatory democracy. When the "whole people govern", argued Bakunin, "there will be...no government, no state".[43] Wayne Price argues "*Anarchism is democracy without the state*".[44]

Paul cites Uri Gordon and George Woodcock, who insisted anarchism is against "democracy". But did they mean what Paul suggests? They defined "democracy" as imposing "collectively binding" decisions

---

38: Blackledge, 2010 , pp133-134, 136, 143-144.
39: Bakunin [1871b], p269.
40: van der Walt and Schmidt, 2009, p109.
41: Bakunin, 1990, p63.
42: Price, 2007, pp172-173.
43: Bakunin, 1953, p287.
44: Price, 2007, p172, emphasis in original.

on dissidents, and objected.[45] They did not oppose collective decisions—only this supposed coercion. Theirs is not an argument most anarchists would accept; nor do most anarchists think consensus decision-making preferable.[46] This is not, however, to deny that the Gordon/Woodcock line has a profoundly *democratic* intent.

There is nothing "difficult to understand" about Bakunin praising the 1871 Paris Commune as "practical realisation" of anarchist ideals.[47] Anarchists played a central role in communalist risings in France, Spain and Italy at this time; with Proudhonists, they were a large bloc on the Commune's Council.[48] The Commune's basic project was anticipated in Bakunin's 1870 open "Letter to a Frenchman", and by Proudhon, revolutionary anarchism's immediate precursor.[49] Bakunin's and Kropotkin's only critique of the Commune was that it did not go *far enough* in collectivisation and self-management, leaving too much power in the Council.[50]

Anarchism, syndicalism and specific political organisations

Paul suggests that anarchism denies the need for revolutionary political organisations that can link struggles, and fight for ideological clarity and revolution.[51] He is correct that there is an anarchist current that argues against specific political organisations. He is incorrect to present this current as *representative*.

Many key anarchists/syndicalists advocate specific political organisations, working with mass organisations like unions. Flores Magón stresses "an activating minority, a courageous minority of libertarians".[52] Bakunin, Flores Magón, Kropotkin, Makhno, Oiticica and Shifu also insist on "organisations of tendency", based on political unity and collective discipline (others favoured looser structures).[53]

"Organisations of tendency" include the International Alliance of Socialist Democracy, Spain's FAI, Mexico's *La Social*, China's Society of Anarchist-Communist Comrades, the postwar Uruguayan Anarchist Federation, etc. These were to fight the battle of ideas and promote self-activity, counterpower and counterculture, not to replace or rule the popular classes.

45: Gordon, 2008, pp69-70.
46: van der Walt and Schmidt, 2009 , pp70-71, 240-242, 244-247, 256-257.
47: Blackledge, 2010, pp131-132, 148.
48: Avrich, 1988, pp229-239.
49:   Bakunin [1870], pp184, 186-187, 189-192, 197, 204.
50: Kropotkin [1880], pp123-124.
51: Blackledge, 2010 , pp136, 139, 142.
52: In Hodges, 1986, pp83-84.
53: Bakunin [1865], p138; see van der Walt and Schmidt, 2009, chapter 8.

Anarchists/syndicalists are not "opposed to the political struggle" for rights, but stress it "must take the form of direct action".[54] Rights should be won *from below* by mobilising counterpower; participation in the state is ineffective, corrupting. All stress the importance of revolutionary ideas for a revolutionary change, a "new social philosophy".[55]

Do anarchists misunderstand the "Marxist tradition"?

Rejection of Leninist parties arises from a different concern: the argument that these parties created dictatorships. Paul thinks anarchists have a "massive misunderstanding of Marxism", and Leo that *Black Flame* caricatures "classical Marxism" in calling it reductionist and authoritarian.[56]

But Paul admits the "rational kernel" of the anarchist critique is "that the most powerful voices claiming to be Marxists in the 20th century were statists (of either the Stalinist or Maoist variety) who presided over brutal systems" of "bureaucratic state capitalism".[57] Leo admits that the anarchist critique is valid *if* "you include Kautsky, Stalin and Mao in the Marxist canon".[58]

That suffices. According to *International Socialism* and IST writers, Kautsky was long "the most prominent Marxist theorist"; Stalin represented "Soviet Marxism", Maoism a type of "Marxism-Leninism", etc.[59] By the IST's *own* admission, then, *mainstream* pre-Leninist Marxism was reductionist and statist; mainstream 20th century Marxism was "Stalinist or Maoist"; *all* Marxist regimes ended as state capitalist dictatorships, with even (the late Chris Harman stated) the Soviet Union a "Bolshevik dictatorship" by 1921.[60]

I am not sure why Paul confidently claims the "essence" of Marxism is "working class self-emancipation".[61] That's been rather *unusual* in Marxist theory and action, as Ian himself has shown.[62] Libertarian minority Marxist traditions like Council Communism and autonomism are the exception, not Leninism or "classical Marxism".

54: Rocker [1938], pp64, 74, 77.
55: Bakunin [1871a], pp249, 250-251.
56: Zeilig, 2009, pp221-2.
57: Blackledge, 2010, p133, note 15.
58: Zeilig, 2010, p222.
59: For example, Blackledge, 2006; Harman, 2004; Rees, 1998; Renton, 2002, 2004; Banaji, 2010, editor's introduction.
60: Harman, 1987, p18.
61: Blackledge, 2010, p132.
62: Birchall, 1974.

Leo claims *Black Flame* repeats the "daily clichés of the media".[63] I concede—*if* he means the mainstream *Marxist* media, mass papers like *Umsebenzi, L'Humanité, New Age, People's Democracy, Angve Bayan,* etc. This may be, by the IST's lights, mere "debased" Marxism—but why should anarchists accept the IST's judgement? Most *Marxists* do not.

We cannot claim that "the only significance of Christianity in history is to be found in reading unaltered versions of the Gospels", and ignore 2,000 years of the church and its offshoots. Marxism, too, must be judged by its history, not by selected quotes.[64]

The early "dictatorship of the proletariat" in the Soviet Union

Paul insists that Marxism's "dictatorship of the proletariat" merely proposes a "workers' state" to end "exploitative social relations".[65] Leo adds that this "most maligned concept" merely means "democratic defence of working class power".[66]

The problem is that it's not easy to find a real world example; this is pure assertion. Writers like Cliff looked hopefully at the early Soviet Union. Supposedly, "the land…was distributed to the peasants, the factories…taken under state ownership…run under workers' control" and "the oppressed nationalities got…self-determination". If "many hundreds of thousands" died, this was "not because of the action of the Soviet government".[67]

Regrettably, the facts show the Lenin-Trotsky regime to be the template for Stalin's. Land was nationalised, not "distributed", and "the action of the Soviet government" in forced grain requisitions killed millions. Peasant uprisings were crushed with fire and sword: iron dictatorship over 90 percent of the population. Industry was "under state ownership", not "workers' control": in 1919 state-appointed individual managers ran 10.8 percent of enterprises; by 1920, 82 percent.[68] Red Army elections were abolished in March 1918, command turned over to ex-Tsarist officers and party *commissars*.

Cliff condemned Stalin for Taylorism and piecework,[69] but Lenin

63: Zeilig, 2010, pp221-222.
64: Castoriadis, 2001, p77.
65: Blackledge, 2010, pp146-147.
66: Zeilig, 2010 , pp221-222.
67: Cliff, 2000 , pp66-67.
68: All figures unless otherwise stated, from Shukman, 1994, pp29, 166, 175, 177, 182, 184, 187.
69: Cliff [1964], pp30-34.

introduced these policies in 1918.[70] Unions, Harman claimed, enabled "workers' control".[71] Actually, these "unions" were state-run bodies by 1919, active in repressing strikes.[72] Rather than insist that "strikes were not to be suppressed",[73] the Bolsheviks routinely crushed them, also militarising industry.[74] The crushing of the Kronstadt revolt had numerous precedents.[75]

Harman claimed Bolshevism was the *soviet* "majority party". This was only true in a few cities, for a few months. Defeated in the 1918 urban elections, the Bolsheviks responded by dissolving, gerrymandering and purging *soviets*, repressing opponents.[76] Power was centralised in the cabinet *(Sovnarkom)* and Supreme Economic Council *(Vesenkha)*; a secret police *(Cheka)* and militarised Red Army; and a state bureaucracy heavily recruited from the old order. Thus an unpopular party of 600,000 ruled an empire of 90 million in 1920. The *Cheka's* mandate included watching the "press, saboteurs, strikers", and summary executions.[77] Besides 20 times more executions in five years than the Tsarist *Okhrana* in 50, it ran concentration and labour camps, "cleared from time to time by mass extermination".[78]

Cliff claimed the Bolshevik minority was nonetheless internally democratic. By 1919 the party was run from the top down, staffed with *apparatchiks*; factions were banned in 1921 and dissidents jailed.[79] The early 1920s saw Lenin's GPU operate a vast informer network; beatings, torture and rape were routinely used; left opponents were crushed; open *soviet* elections were prevented.[80] Rather than "self-determination," the Red Army installed puppet regimes in Belarus and Ukraine from 1919, Georgia (1921), Armenia and Azerbaijan (1922). The anarchist-led Ukraine saw its *soviets* banned, its communes smashed, its leaders executed—despite formal treaties of cooperation.[81]

70: Devinatz, 2003.

71: Harman, 1987, p43.

72: Pirani, 2010a.

73: Cliff [1964], pp28, 34.

74: For a summary see McKay, *The Anarchist FAQ,* section H 6.3.

75: Kronstadt argued for new, open elections to soviets; it never called for "soviets without Bolsheviks": Avrich, 1991, p181.

76: Avrich, 1967, pp184-185; Brovkin, 1991, p159; Farber, 1990, p22; Malle, 1985, pp240,366-367; Rabinowitch, 2007, pp248-252; Schapiro, 1977, p191.

77: Quoted in Daniels, 1985, p90.

78: Shukman, 1994, pp182-3.

79: Avrich, 1984.

80: Avrich, 1967, pp234-237; Brovkin, 1998, pp20-26, 44-46, 52-53,61-80,90-93; Bulletin[1923-1931]; Dubovic and Rublyov, 2009; Jansen, 1982; Pirani, 2010b.

81: For a recent debate on the "Makhnovist" anarchist movement, see McKay, 2007,

Delinking socialism-from-below from Bolshevism

It is precisely *because* anarchists and syndicalists defend socialism from below that they reject Bolshevism. Paul claims Bakunin's critique of the Marxist "dictatorship of the proletariat"—that it would end in a "barracks" regime of "centralised state capitalism"[82]—is "superficial" and "inept".[83]

By any reasonable measure, however, Bakunin's theory is "vindicated by the verdict of history".[84] *International Socialism* has tried to exonerate Lenin's and Trotsky's dictatorship by reference to difficult conditions: counter-revolution, "imperialism," economic crisis, etc. The "Bolsheviks had no choice", said Harman, but to rule alone: the "class they represented had dissolved itself while defending to fight that power". Power anyway rightly belonged to "only those who wholeheartedly supported the revolution…the Bolsheviks".[85] Cliff argued that "the pressure of world capitalism" later forced the Soviet Union's rulers to make the economy "more and more similar".[86]

This will not do. Leo objects to *Black Flame* suggesting classical Marxism tends to economic reductionism, but one would struggle to find a better illustration of exactly that tendency than these alibis.

It is contradictory to proclaim that Bolshevik ideology was *essential* to the revolution's supposed success, yet insist that it had *no* impact on the revolution's outcome. It is contradictory to condemn all anarchist experiences (as in Spain) as due entirely to ideology, not context, but to exonerate all Marxist experiences (as in Russia) as due entirely to context, not ideology.

Unless Leo embraces the "no choice" determinism he claims to reject, he must concede some *choice* is still possible when fighting faceless forces like "imperialism". If he does, he cannot deny Bolshevik culpability in destroying the "democratic defence of working class power". If he does not, he can hardly condemn Stalin, who faced the "pressure of world capitalism".

Bolshevik choices led straight to one-party dictatorship, even before the Civil War started (May 1918) and long after it ended (November 1920). This was *precisely* because the Bolsheviks insisted (as Harman revealed) that they alone deserved power: all rivals were automatically counter-revolutionary.[87] Faced with popular repudiation—by peasants, and by the embarrassingly not

---

pp30-32, 39.
82: Bakunin [1872], p284; Kropotkin [1912], pp170, 186.
83: Blackledge, 2010 , pp133, 146-147.
84: Compare Blackledge, 2010, p133.
85: Harman, 1987, pp19-20.
86: Cliff, 2000 , pp29-30.
87: See, for example, Lenin [1918], p599.

actually "dissolved" proletariat through the *soviets* and strike waves in 1918, 1919 and 1921—the party clung to power at all costs.

Despite some genuinely democratic elements in Lenin's thought, its overall thrust was simple: substitutionism.[88] Even *State and Revolution* is silent on political contestation in *soviets*: the "workers' party" will be "directing and organising the new system".[89] Unlike Leo, who hopes for democracy, Lenin insisted that "the dictatorship of the proletariat *cannot* be exercised through an organisation embracing the whole of that class... It can be exercised *only* by a vanguard".[90] This was, said Trotsky, "entitled to assert its dictatorship even if that dictatorship temporarily clashed with the passing moods of the workers' democracy".[91]

As for socialism, it would be top-down: "To organise the whole economy on the lines of the postal service...all under the control and leadership of the armed proletariat" (see above: meaning the party), "that is our immediate aim".[92] The "working masses" must "be thrown here and there, appointed, commanded", "deserters" "formed into punitive battalions" or sent to "concentration camps".[93] Lenin and Trotsky unapologetically opposed self-management,[94] and Trotsky's Left Opposition advocated forced industrialisation long before Stalin.[95]

Before anyone says I am picking quotations, note that the Bolsheviks acted on *precisely* the lines these quotes suggest; the *State and Revolution*'s council system existed only as words in an incomplete pamphlet.

To which tradition should we look for resistance today?

To defend the Russian Revolution against liberal and conservative critiques is commendable. To conflate this with a defence of the Bolshevik regime that destroyed the revolution is a serious error.

To reclaim socialism, we must reclaim its participatory democratic *and* revolutionary traditions, suppressed by Leninist Marxism. This requires that sincere Marxists seriously engage with—rather than arrogantly lecture to—the black flame of anarchism and syndicalism, and its alternative vision of libertarian communism, revolutionary process and radical democracy.

88: Price, 2007, pp128-129; Tabor, 1988, pp93-104.
89: Lenin [1917], p255.
90: Lenin, [1920], p21, my emphasis.
91: Trotsky, 10th Party Congress, in Farber, 1990, p203.
92: Lenin [1917], p273; also Lenin [1918], pp258, 269.
93: Trotsky, 9th Party Congress, in Brinton, 1970, p61; also Trotsky [1920], pp150-151.
94: Lenin [1918], pp258, 269; Trotsky [1920] 1921, pp150-151; also see Brinton, 1970.
95: Marot, 2006.

References

Abad de Santillan, Diego [1937], 2005, *After the Revolution: Economic Reconstruction in Spain* (Zabalaza Books).

Anderson, Benedict, 2006, *Under Three Flags: Anarchism and the Anti-Colonial Imagination* (Verso).

Avrich, Paul, 1967, *The Russian Anarchists* (Princeton University Press).

Avrich, Paul, 1984, "Bolshevik Opposition to Lenin: GT Miasnikov and the Workers' Group," *Russian Review*, 43/1.

Avrich, Paul, 1988, *Anarchist Portraits* (Princeton University Press).

Avrich, Paul, 1991, *Kronstadt 1921* (Princeton University Press).

Bakunin, Mikhail [1865], 1998, "The International Revolutionary Society or Brotherhood", in Daniel Guérin (ed), *No Gods, No Masters, Book One*, (AK Press).

Bakunin, Mikhail [1869], 1971, "The Programme of the International Brotherhood", in Dolgoff, 1971, http://anarchistplatform.wordpress.com/2010/06/17/the-program-of-the-international-brotherhood/

Bakunin, Mikhail [1870], 1971, "Letters to a Frenchman on the Current Crisis", in Dolgoff, 1971, www.marxists.org/reference/archive/bakunin/works/1870/letter-frenchman.htm

Bakunin, Mikhail [1871a], 1971, "The Programme of the Alliance", in Dolfgoff, 1971, www.marxists.org/reference/archive/bakunin/works/1871/program.htm

Bakunin, Mikhail [1871b], 1971, "The Paris Commune and the Idea of the State", in Dolgoff, 1971, http://flag.blackened.net/daver/anarchism/bakunin/paris.html

Bakunin, Mikhail [1872], 1971, "Letter to *La Liberté*," in Dolgoff, 1971, www.marxists.org/reference/archive/bakunin/works/1872/la-liberte.htm

Bakunin, Mikhail, 1953, *The Political Philosophy of Bakunin* (Free Press / Collier-Macmillan).

Bakunin, Mikhail, 1990, *Marxism, Freedom and the State* (Freedom Press).

Banaji, Jairus, 2010, "The Ironies of Indian Maoism", *International Socialism* 128 (autumn), www.isj.org.uk/?id=684

Birchall, Ian, 1974, *Workers against the Monolith: The Communist Parties since 1943* (Pluto).

Birchall, Ian, 2010, "Another Side of Anarchism", *International Socialism* 127 (summer), www.isj.org.uk/?id=663

Blackledge, Paul, 2010, "Marxism and Anarchism", *International Socialism* 125 (winter), www.isj.org.uk/?id=486

Blackledge, Paul, 2006, "The New Left's Renewal of Marxism", *International Socialism* 112 (winter), www.isj.org.uk/?id=251

Brinton, Maurice, 1970, *The Bolsheviks and Workers Control, 1917-1921* (Solidarity).

Brovkin, Vladimir, 1998, *Russia after Lenin* (Routledge).

Brovkin, Vladimir, 1991, *The Mensheviks after October* (Cornell UP).

Bulletin of the Joint Committee for the Defence of Revolutionists [1923-1931], 2010, *The Tragic Procession: Alexander Berkman and Russian Prisoner Aid* (Kate Sharpley Library/Alexander Berkman Social Club).

Castoriadis, Cornelius, 2001, "The Fate of Marxism", in Dimitrious Roussopoulus (ed), *The Anarchist Papers* (Black Rose).

Chaplin, R, [1933] 1985, *The General Strike* (IWW).

Cliff, Tony, [1964] 1988, *State Capitalism in Russia* (Bookmarks), www.marxists.org/archive/cliff/works/1955/statecap/

Cliff, Tony, 2000, *Marxism at the Millennium* (Bookmarks), www.marxists.org/archive/cliff/works/2000/millennium/index.htm

CNT [1 May 1936], *Resolution on Libertarian Communism as Adopted by the Confederacion Nacional Del Trabajo, Zaragoza, 1 May 1936* (Zabalaza Books).

Daniels, RV (ed), 1985, *A Documentary History of Communism* (I.B. Tauris), volume 1.

Devinatz, Victor G, 2003, "Lenin as Scientific Manager under Monopoly Capitalism, State Capitalism, and Socialism", *Industrial Relations*, 42/3.

Dolgoff, Sam (ed), 1971, *Bakunin on Anarchy* (George Allen and Unwin).

Draper, Hal, 1966, *Two Souls of Socialism*, www.anu.edu.au/polsci/marx/contemp/pamsetc/twosouls/twosouls.htm

Dubovic, Anatoly, and DI Rublyov, 2009, *After Makhno: The Anarchist Underground in the Ukraine in the 1920s and 1930s* (Kate Sharpley Library).

Engels, Friedrich [1873], 1972, "On Authority", in *Marx, Engels, Lenin: Anarchism and Anarcho-Syndicalism* (Progress Publishers), www.marxists.org/archive/marx/works/1872/10/authority.htm

Epstein, Barbara, 2001, "Anarchism and the Anti-Globalisation Movement", *Monthly Review*, 53/4.

Farber, Samuel, 1990, *Before Stalinism: The Rise and Fall of Soviet Democracy* (Verso).

Friends of Durruti [1938, 1978], *Towards a Fresh Revolution* (Zabalaza Books).

Goaman, Karen, 2004, "The Anarchist Travelling Circus: Reflections on Contemporary Anarchism, Anti-Capitalism and the International Scene", in Jonathan Purkis and James Bowen (eds), *Changing Anarchism* (Manchester UP).

Gómez Casas, Juan, 1986, *Anarchist Organisation: The History of the FAI* (Black Rose).

Gordon, Uri, 2008, *Anarchy Alive!* (Pluto).

Harman, Chris, 1987 [1968], "How the Revolution Was Lost", in Pete Binns and others (eds), *Russia: From Workers' State to State Capitalism* (Bookmarks).

Harman, Chris, 2004, "Pick of the Quarter", *International Socialism 104* (autumn), www.isj.org.uk/?id=17

Hodges, Donald, 1986, *Intellectual Foundations of the Nicaraguan Revolution* (Texas University Press).

Holloway, John, 2005, *Change the World Without Taking Power*, revised edition (Pluto Press).

Jansen, Marc, 1982, *A Show Trial under Lenin: The Trial of the Socialist Revolutionaries, Moscow 1922* (Springer).

Keffer, Tom, 2005, "Marxism, Anarchism and the Genealogy of 'Socialism from Below'", *Upping the Anti: A Journal of Theory and Action*, number 2.

Kropotkin, Pyotr [1880], 1970, "The Commune of Paris", in Martin Miller (ed), *Selected Writings on Anarchism and Revolution* (MIT. Press), http://dwardmac.pitzer.edu/anarchist_archives/kropotkin/pcommune.html

Kropotkin, Pyotr [1912], 1970, "Modern Science and Anarchism", in RN Baldwin (ed), *Kropotkin's Revolutionary Pamphlets* (New York: Dover Publications), http://dwardmac.pitzer.edu/anarchist_archives/kropotkin/science/toc.html

Lenin, VI [1917], 1975, "The State and Revolution," in *Selected Works in Three Volumes* (Progress), volume 2.

Lenin, VI [1918], 1962, "The Immediate Tasks of the Soviet Government", in *Collected Works* (Progress), volume 27.

Lenin, VI [1920], 1962, "The Trade Unions, the Present Situation and Trotsky's Mistakes", in *Collected Works* (Progress), volume 27.

Malle, Silvana, 1985, *The Economic Organisation of War Communism, 1918-1921* (Cambridge UP).

Marot, John Eric, 2006, "Trotsky, the Left Opposition and the Rise of Stalinism," *Historical Materialism*, 14/3.

Maura, J Romero, 1971, "The Spanish Case", in David Apter and James Joll (eds), *Anarchism Today* (Macmillan).

McKay, Iain, no date, *The Anarchist FAQ*, http://anarchism.pageabode.com/afaq/

McKay, Iain, 2007, "On the Bolshevik Myth", *Anarcho-Syndicalist Review*, 47, www.syndicalist. org/archives/asr41-50/McKay47.shtml

Meyer, Gerald, 2003, "Anarchism, Marxism and the Collapse of the Soviet Union", *Science and Society*, 67/2.

Paz, Abel, 1987, *Durruti: The People Armed* (Black Rose).

Pirani, Simon, 2010a, "Socialism in the 21st Century and the Russian Revolution", *International Socialism 128* (autumn), www.isj.org.uk/?id=687

Pirani, Simon, 2010b, "Detailed Response to Kevin Murphy", www.revolutioninretreat.com/ isjreply.pdf

Price, Wayne, 2007, *The Abolition of the State: Anarchist and Marxist Perspectives* (AuthorHouse).

Rabinowitch, Alexander, 2007, *The Bolsheviks in Power: The First Year of Soviet Rule in Petrograd* (Indiana University Press).

Rees, John, 1998, *The Algebra of Revolution: The Dialectic and the Classical Marxist Tradition* (Routledge).

Renton, David, 2002, *Classical Marxism: Socialist Theory and the Second International* (New Clarion Press).

Renton, David, 2004, *Dissident Marxism: Past Voices for Present Times* (Zed Books).

Rocker, R [1938] 1989, *Anarcho-Syndicalism* (Pluto).

Schapiro, Leonard, 1977, *The Origin of the Communist Autocracy: Political Opposition in the Soviet State First Phase 1917-1922* (Harvard University Press).

Shukman, Harold (ed), 1994, *The Blackwell Encyclopaedia of the Russian Revolution* (Wiley-Blackwell).

Tabor, Ron, 1988, *A Look at Leninism* (Aspect Foundation).

Thorpe, Wayne, 1989, *"The Workers Themselves": Revolutionary Syndicalism and International Labour 1913-23* (Kulwer Academic Publishers/ IISH).

Trotsky, Leon [1920], 1921, *The Defence of Terrorism* (The Labour Publishing Company/George Allen and Unwin).

van der Walt, Lucien, and Michael Schmidt, 2009, *Black Flame: The Revolutionary Class Politics of Anarchism and Syndicalism* (AK Press).

Zeilig, Leo, 2010, "Contesting the Revolutionary Tradition," *International Socialism 127* (summer 2010), www.isj.org.uk/?id=674

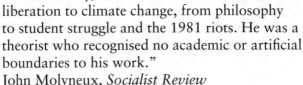

The social roots of "impairment"
Lee Humber

There was a lovely piece on capitalism and disability from Roddy Slorach in the last issue of *International Socialism*, with a very well balanced account of the social model of disability which, as Roddy says, "turned received wisdom on its head".[1] I thought it might be useful to add a short comment or two with regard to some of the implications of the dualism the model sets up between "impairment" and "disability", with specific reference to people with learning difficulties.

Many in the learning difficulties world feel that the social model has served them less well. Roddy alluded to some of the hierarchies experienced by disability activists generally, often with people with learning difficulties feeling excluded and unappreciated by the movement.[2] As Roddy clearly shows, we can understand these hierarchies primarily in terms of a politically weak movement that started relatively late and campaigned in large part during periods of political reaction and working class retreat. However, it may also be that some of the theoretical weakness of the social model, in particular the vaguely conceptualised nature of "impairment", didn't help.

The concept of "intellectual impairment" is problematic and is nowhere considered with precision by the social model's author, Mike Oliver. Numerous disability researchers and activists have expressed concerns about the ways in which "impairment" is left in the realms of medical discourse

---

1:   Slorach, 2011, p125.
2:   See, for example, Aspis in Campbell and Oliver, 1996, p97.

where it remains as a static, naturalised and individualised phenomenon.[3] The best of the learning disability academics—influenced by post-structuralism and the writings of Michel Foucault—seek to analyse "intellectual impairment" as a relational concept created through historically contextualised discourse (thus allowing for at least a partial consideration of the political —and personal—struggles that have informed the modern day identities of people with learning difficulties). As Dan Goodley argues, "The resistance of people with learning difficulties and their experiences of being disabled (where naturalised views of impairment are at the core of oppression) offer us lived examples that enable the re-socialising of impairment".[4]

I think much of this work is useful in as much as it represents a more fluid understanding of 'impairment' based on historically specific processes of social structuring. Where I think we might disagree is in the location of the continued oppression of people with learning difficulties in "naturalised views", that is, in the opinions and attitudes people with learning difficulties encounter daily. The oppression is more deep rooted.

In a—very small—nutshell, I think socialists can understand modern day learning disabilities as being historically rooted in the accelerated division of labour, characteristic of what Hobsbawm calls the "second industrial revolution", based on chemicals, electricity, and the internal combustion engine, of the late 19th century.[5] This is the period of the beginning of state education (the 1870 Education Act), bringing in its train the development of a system of segregated classes and schools for those falling behind in the mainstream education system. Marx's analysis of the reserve army of labour is useful here. He identified individuals belonging to the "relative surplus labour" grouping who were "unable to adapt" to the demands of industrial labour.[6]

Segregated schools were for those "unable to adapt" to the new demands of labour preparation through the new state school system. Reading, writing and arithmetic were historically new skills that working class children were expected to learn, and many struggled to do so. Some of these—overwhelmingly drawn from poorer urban areas—ended up in segregated schools with little expectation of finding regular future employment and very limited provision to support them doing so.[7] People with learning difficulties continue to occupy a position in the reserve army of labour—on the fringes of the labour market and as such serving capital by weighting

3: For example, Barnes and Mercer, 1996, and Wetherall and Potter, 1992.
4: Goodley and Rapley, 2001, p230. See also Fairclough, 1992, and Carlson, 2005.
5: Hobsbawm, 1969, p172 onwards.
6: Marx, 1979, p799.
7: Thompson, 1996, p226.

down average wage rates, but also available during times of labour shortage. For example, during World War Two tens of thousands of previously "unemployable", "mentally deficient" people found jobs in wartime factories.

The late Victorian early Edwardian period also saw—in the draconian 1913 Mental Deficiency Act—the first piece of legislation specifically designed to codify and administer the new social grouping, the "mentally (and/or morally) deficient". Rejected from mainstream schools, segregated in special provision, as adults most often found as inmates of workhouses, the new group was consigned to poverty from then until today (currently less than 7 percent of people with learning difficulties are employed). This period also saw—as Roddy shows—the development of the structures and ideology of eugenics, pioneered in Britain by Cyril Burt, father of the "11-plus", who succinctly summed up the eugenicist project to separate out those deemed mentally or morally deficient as "the natural elimination of the unfit stocks".[8] For unfit stocks read least valuable labour.

I would argue—and do at length elsewhere—that we can understand those bearing the label of people with learning difficulties primarily through their relationship to the labour market. Rejected from the mainstream as likely to provide below average rates of exploitation, the social and intellectual potential and the identity choices of millions of individuals have historically been delimited by segregated systems—of education, housing, and community. In these social structures and processes lie the roots of Goodley's "naturalised views" and ultimately the roots of "intellectual impairment" itself.

8:    Burt, 1909, p169.

References

Barnes, Colin, and Geoff Mercer (eds), 1996, *Exploring the Divide: Illness and Disability* (Disability Press).

Burt, Cyril, 1909, "Experimental Tests of Intelligence", *British Journal of Psychology*, 3.

Campbell, Jane, and Michael Oliver, 1996, *Disability Politics: Understanding Our Past, Changing Our Future* (Routledge).

Carlson, Licia, 2005, "Docile Bodies, Docile Minds", in Shelley Tremain (ed), *Foucault and the Government of Disability* (University of Michigan Press).

Fairclough, Norman, 1992, *Discourse and Social Change* (Polity Press).

Goodley, Dan, and Mark Rapley, 2001, "How Do You Understand 'Learning Difficulties'? Towards a Social Theory of Impairment", *Mental Retardation*, 39 (3).

Hobsbawm, EJ, 1969, *Industry and Empire* (Penguin).

Marx, Karl, 1976, *Capital*, volume I (Penguin), www.marxists.org/archive/marx/works/1867-c1/

Slorach, Roddy, 2011, "Marxism and Disability", *International Socialism* 129 (winter), www.isj.org.uk/?id=702

Thomson, Matthew, 1996, "Status, Manpower and Mental Fitness: Mental Deficiency in the First World War", in Roger Cooter, Mark Harrison and Steve Sturdy (eds), *War Medicine and Modernity* (Sutton Publishing).

Wetherall, Margaret, and Jonathan Potter, 1992, *Mapping the Language of Racism*, (Harvester Wheatsheaf).

Book reviews

We want rebel music
Lee Billingham

Ian Goodyer, **Crisis Music: The Cultural Politics of Rock Against Racism** *(Manchester University Press, 2009), £60*

Love Music Hate Racism (LMHR)—in tandem with Unite Against Fascism (UAF)—has played a key role in the movement to take on the British National Party (BNP) and the English Defence League (EDL), and face down a resurgent racism in Britain over the past decade.

The "Love Music Hate Racism" slogan was coined by David Widgery in the first issue of the Rock Against Racism (RAR) fanzine *Temporary Hoarding*. Widgery's book *Beating Time* (sadly out of print) brilliantly conveys the political excitement, creative energy and visual flair of RAR from the perspective of a leading participant. An analysis of RAR also forms part of Dave Renton's history of the Anti Nazi League (ANL), *When We Touched The Sky*.

Ian Goodyer's timely study of RAR aims for the first time to set the movement fully in its cultural and political context and particularly to examine the relationship between RAR and what he calls its "main political sponsor"—the Socialist Workers Party (SWP). He argues that RAR was a genuine mass movement comprising diverse and independent forces, but that the SWP's politics and ideological tradition were a crucial formative influence.

Most readers of this journal will be familiar with the history and political context of RAR, which is outlined very well in the book. The movement was formed in 1976 from a letter sent to the music press by Red Saunders and others following Eric Clapton's racist remarks praising Enoch Powell. It arose among the political and economic crisis of the mid-1970s with much of the left demoralised by the sell-outs of the Labour government and the National Front (NF) on the rise.

The movement reached a high point with the 1978 ANL/RAR Carnival in east London, which attracted around 100,000 people—many of whom marched the five miles from Trafalgar Square to Victoria Park. The 1978 Carnival's line-up has come to symbolise RAR's cultural achievements, combining punk (The Clash and Sham 69's Jimmy Pursey) with reggae (Steel Pulse and Misty). The two subcultures had much in common and a degree of cross-fertilisation and mutual respect had already begun. This was accelerated by punk and reggae bands and fans coming together for RAR gigs, a process that culminated in the Two Tone movement whose leading lights The Specials headlined the RAR Carnival in 1981.

Pursey himself was an example of the movement's ability not only to creatively blend the most radical popular music but also to influence musicians politically, having stood up to his band's section of skinhead followers in strongly backing RAR and the ANL. Tom Robinson (a top five artist at the time) and Misty were among a number of prominent musicians politically and organisationally involved in RAR beyond playing their part on stage. The 1978 Carnival also highlighted the movement's (and punk's) involvement with and ability to further other struggles against oppression— the Tom Robinson Band's anthem "Glad to Be Gay" and X-Ray Spex singer Poly Styrene's strident blow against sexism "Oh Bondage Up Yours!"

Goodyer argues that it was the coming together of nascent but exciting youth cultures with socialist ideology, and left wing activists involved with and steeped in the traditions of radical culture that made RAR possible. The movement's relationship with the SWP was "mediated" by three factors identified by Goodyer. First, the party's increasing emphasis on political rather than industrial struggles in the face of what later became known as "the downturn" engendered in activists a greater openness to and willingness to take part in campaigns like RAR and the ANL.

Second, the SWP's view of the USSR as a state capitalist society, in contradistinction to the Communist Party, the Labour left and orthodox Trotskyist groups, meant that its members tended not to have the distrustful attitude of much of the left to "Americanised" mass culture. The idea of "socialism from below" that followed from a "Neither Washington Nor Moscow" perspective meshed well with punk and reggae's DIY ethic and helped ensure (along with financial imperatives!) an emphasis on RAR being a grassroots, "bottom-up" campaign.

Third, the party's ideological commitment to the spirit of Trotsky's theory of the united front—as a means to unity in action around a particular issue without sacrificing political independence—helped give RAR "a powerful motive to take its message far beyond the pale of the organised left". This is a statement that could be applied more accurately to the ANL with its more formal structures

and political alliances between revolutionaries and reformists; nevertheless, argues Goodyer, the united front method applied by the SWP influenced their work in RAR. Overall, "the party's anti-Stalinist, humanist Marxism and the presence within its ranks of a number of young radicals, imbued with a commitment to cultural activism, were factors that shaped its ability to relate to a mass movement rooted in popular culture".

The book goes on to look at sharply contrasting examples of cultural-political campaigns that have followed RAR—Live 8/ Live Aid, and of course, LMHR. In the case of the former, Goodyer notes that Bob Geldof's aim for Live Aid to provide immediate famine relief in Ethiopia was achieved—to the tune of £150 million. But its other aim—politically to point the finger of blame at the failure of the Western powers to provide aid—was fatally undermined by the campaign's top-down nature.

Whereas RAR had sought to engage its audience and create activists, Live Aid was easily steered away from confronting power with awkward questions due to its emphasis on "punk diplomats" and lack of pressure from a genuine mass movement. Geldof's populism without wider political principle also led to Live Aid/8's sidelining of black and African musicians in favour of booking only acts with the broadest appeal.

If Geldof had found himself fronting a cause in 1985, he and the nauseating Bono rushed to put themselves at the head of an existing movement at the G8 in 2005, trying to mobilise its support for the very G8 leaders it was protesting against. As George Monbiot said at the time, "While the G8 maintains its grip on the instruments of global governance, a shared anthem of peace and love is about as meaningful as the Coca-Cola ad."

Conversely, Goodyer argues, LMHR "advances explicitly political aims whilst simultaneously exploiting the implicitly ...multicultural nature of modern music to exemplify its mission". Crucially, LMHR started from a position of being able to build on the success and experience of RAR and the ANL, particularly the far more integrated multiracial nature of both society and popular music. Goodyer rightly points out that this means "LMHR's appeal is potentially wider than RAR's." At the same time, the strategy employed by the Nazis during most of LMHR's existence, crudely put, had been forced to change from the NF's braces and boots, to the BNP's "Euro-fascist" turn to being "brutes in suits", as UAF joint secretary Weyman Bennet has put it. This has "necessitated a corresponding shift on the part of the anti-racist movement".

LMHR has reprised RAR's emphasis on audience engagement, grassroots organisation and close links to political anti-fascist campaigning while operating in a mainstream milieu which RAR only began to reach in its closing days. There have been more than 700 LMHR events in eight years. Over 110,000 people attended the 2008 LMHR Carnival in east London, and tens of thousands have attended other carnivals and gigs around the country.

In late 2007 the *NME* produced a special LMHR edition with a cover-mounted double-CD featuring a cover photo of six of the country's biggest acts (it was the magazine's best-selling issue of the year). Half a million copies of the NUT-sponsored CD were distributed to schools. And thanks to the band Hard-Fi's support, the "Love Music Hate Racism" slogan was emblazoned across ten million bottles of Becks beer.

LMHR's main sponsors throughout have been the trade unions, whose members have also been centrally involved as activists, with LMHR gigs and stages a common feature of May Day events, the Left Field at Glastonbury, national union conferences

and so on. These initiatives have brought thousands of young people into contact with the anti-fascist movement and helped take the movement into the BNP's "heartlands", doing the Nazis real damage.

The section of the book on LMHR does a good job of sketching in general terms the similarities and differences between the political and cultural contexts in which RAR and LMHR have operated. If I have a minor criticism it is that the book would benefit from a more concrete look at how the current movement has developed in different conditions to RAR and the ANL.

Much is often made, for example, of the apparent lack of similarly radical musical subcultures today to those which were concurrent with RAR. As Goodyer says, we should be wary of letting such comparisons "descend into a yearning for a more radical past, as if RAR provides a kind of 'gold standard' against which other movements must valorise themselves".

LMHR, too, for much of its time has relied heavily on two music scenes which, though certainly nothing like on the scale of punk and reggae, nevertheless have played a similar role among both music fans and in the movement. Grime, with a multiracial audience and mainly black MCs and producers, was rarely overtly political but was certainly a "DIY" culture open to even the least well off, and developed in reaction to its largely young exponents' lack of identification with the slicker, more moneyed-looking garage scene. At its best it was and is an eloquent expression of anger at poverty, racism and disenfranchisement.

The mid-noughties indie-rock scene, exemplified by major LMHR supporters The Libertines, was initially at least a reaction to the increasing corporate blandness of mainstream "indie" and was influenced by the anti-capitalist movement. It developed in east London and aimed to reduce the gap between audience and performer with its squat parties, impromptu gigs and pioneering use of online social networking. LMHR helped put these artists and audiences together, feeding into and off of the brief-lived vogue for "Grindie" music, but most importantly encouraging a common and popular anti-racist sentiment in popular music culture that identified the Nazi BNP as an enemy to be confronted and beaten.

This sort of mobilisation of a broad, mass, anti-racist sentiment, feeding into an active, militant and explicitly anti-fascist campaign, will be even more vital in the years ahead. The crisis facing capitalism is more intractable than in the 1970s, and the political crisis and instability accompanying it are more pronounced. This provides fuel for Nazi organisation and racist ideas to endure and grow over a long period. In Britain the elections in May 2010 saw anti-fascists deal a massive blow to the BNP, but they still grabbed more than half a million votes. Tensions over strategy within the Nazis' ranks has seen BNP members joining the ranks of the racist street thugs of the EDL.

Crisis Music is an honest, sympathetic and nuanced look at "cultural politics" through the prism of RAR—with whole sections devoted to critical responses to RAR, its relationship to youth culture, and a potted history of the left's attitude to culture through the 20th century, from modernism to the New Left. There are some great examples of RAR's radical visual style, with reproductions of posters, stickers and *Temporary Hoarding* covers. It contains a wealth of well-argued theory and background history that will be a fascinating read for any anti-fascist looking to learn the lessons of how a mass movement to beat back the Nazis was built last time. Sadly, it's currently only available in an academic edition at an eye-watering price, so ask your university or local library to get a copy in.

Natural's not in it
Martin Empson

John Bellamy Foster, Brett Clark and Richard York, **The Ecological Rift: Capitalism's War on the Earth,** *(Monthly Review Press, 2010),* £14.95

The failure of the world powers to reach a substantial agreement on carbon emissions at the Cancún summit in Mexico at the end of 2010 tells us much about the real priorities of the capitalist system. It is possible that there will be no binding international agreement on climate change to replace the Kyoto protocol in 2012. This is despite overwhelming evidence for global warming, the increasingly extreme weather worldwide and genuine fear from leading climate scientists that we are heading for a tipping point that could lead to runaway climate change.

In this context more radical arguments about the relationship between the natural world and human society will increasingly get a hearing. Those critiques that locate the problem within the capitalist system and urge a revolutionary solution to the problem are particularly useful.

As with many of their previous books, the authors do not shrink from arguing that international summits have failed because of the nature of the capitalist system. Rather than criticising particularly obnoxious multinationals or governments for whom "change becomes a matter of adjusting values and developing the proper eco-ethics", the authors discuss how ,"since the late 15th century, an economic system propelled by the accumulation of capital has been the dominant force shaping human society" (p261).

This drive to accumulate, Marx argued "gives capital no rest and continually whispers in its ear: 'Go on! Go on!" (p203). In this analysis, society's ecological problems are not simply ethical, nor are they technological. Rather the problems exist because the system's "treadmill of production" can only exploit the world's natural resources for raw materials, or use it as a dumping ground for the waste of the production process. The authors argue that we can only begin to develop solutions to this problem by building on Marx's work. For them, a "full understanding of nature is best realised through a materialistic, dialectical and historical lens" (p261).

The capitalist system doesn't simply destroy the natural world in the interest of production for production's sake; it also creates a "metabolic rift" between humanity and nature. This concept is explored in depth, starting with Marx's studies of the German chemist Liebig's work on soil degradation in the 19th century.

The authors also demonstrate how technological solutions alone cannot solve environmental crises. For instance, the Jevons Paradox has been known since the 1860s when the economist William Stanley Jevons explained how improved efficiency in the burning of coal in steam engines made it more cost effective as a fuel and hence more desirable. "Greater efficiency in resource often leads to increased consumption of resources" (p141). This has parallels with modern times where increasingly efficient petrol engines do not reduce the amount of fuel burnt by road vehicles. So calls for efficiency do not necessarily help reduce carbon emissions.

There are other related issues in a useful section looking at the "Paperless Office Paradox". The authors show how introduction of computer technology actually increases the requirements for older technology. Consumption of office paper in the US for instance, increased

by almost 15 percent between 1995 and 2000 (p189). The conclusion is that the development of a substitute for a resource can lead to an increased use of the original resource. This means that purely technical solutions—such as the replacement of fossil fuels with renewable energy—may not result in a reduction of carbon emissions from the burning of coal and oil, particularly in the short term.

The authors should be congratulated for producing an accessible introduction to these ideas. Unfortunately there are problems. Some of the chapters, particularly the one on "The Sociology of Ecology" seem needlessly academic and refer, often without explanation, to ideas and writers which the lay reader may not have encountered. This reflects the origin of most of these chapters in articles from other publications—only two of the 18 chapters are original, the others are abridged or revised articles from elsewhere. This shouldn't be a problem, since many of these sources are obscure journals, but it also leads to duplication and repetition—for instance, the Jevons paradox is explained seven times.

That aside, there is much to be gained from reading this book. All the arguments point towards the urgent need for revolutionary solutions to the question of climate change. Here, however, lies the problem. The authors call for an ecological revolution to stop capitalism destroying the world. Yet their vision of revolution seems to be flawed and limited. They seem to be moving away from a classical Marxist explanation of where change can come from.

What is needed, they argue, is "the organisation on socialist principles of an ecological and social counter-hegemony, deriving its impetus from various social actors. A new ecological materialism arising in the revolt against the global environmental crisis must merge with the old class-based materialism of socialism.... Such a new historic bloc...would draw on various classes and class fractions (including the critical intelligentsia), but would depend fundamentally on the working class(es)—though not so much today on the industrial proletariat as such, but on a wider environmental proletariat" (p398).

Nowhere is there any detailed explanation of what the "wider environmental proletariat" is. Elsewhere they argue that the "main historic agent and initiator of a new epoch of ecological revolution is to be found in the Third World masses most directly in line to be hit first by the impending disasters" (p440). But while the developing world will be initially hit hard by climate change, the impacts on the more developed world will not necessarily just come later—witness the destruction of New Orleans by Hurricane Katrina. We must argue against the implication that workers living in the developed world have less to fear from climate catastrophe.

According to the authors, the proletariat was the revolutionary agent because it had "nothing to lose" (p439). But, for Marx, the working class can bring about socialism both because it has the economic power to overthrow capitalism and because in the process it can "succeed in ridding itself of all the muck of ages and become fitted to found society anew".[*] This is particularly important if we are looking at building a sustainable world—workers will have to re-evaluate their conception of the natural world and production within it.

This weakness on the question of agency persists with the authors looking solely to developments in South America as a model. There is no doubt that the governments of

Chávez and Morales have made important steps in moving towards a more sustainable society. The mass movements that have developed in the region have ecological questions at their core, but to narrow down the question of ecology and socialism to what is going on there limits the excellent analysis developed by the authors.

This is a useful book, but if we are to put ecological questions at the centre of the struggle for revolution today we need to develop an alternative linked to a vision of a different kind of society. In part this requires the raising of transitional demands, such as the call for "One Million Climate Jobs" in Britain, which can form a bridge between the struggles against austerity and wider social transformation.[†]

But ultimately we need to re-examine the way in which revolutionary movements of the past have thrown up mass democratic organisations that can place the organisation of production in the hands of the producers. This mass involvement of workers and peasants in the revolutionary transformation of society is the only way we can start to heal the metabolic rift.

State of the union
Chris Bambery

*Perry Anderson, **The New Old World** (Verso, 2009), £24.99*

Given the crisis that has gripped Europe over the last year, exposing deep faultlines within the EU, there is no better time for a Marxist examination of the union to appear.

---

[*] Karl Marx, *The German Ideology*, www.marxists.org/archive/marx/works/1845/german-ideology/ch01.htm

---

[†] See www.climate-change-jobs.org

That it's written by Perry Anderson, former editor of *New Left Review*, ensures it's written with panache, is hugely enjoyable and that it provides a broad historical sweep. That said, it is not without some question marks.

The book brings together essays written in publications such as the *London Review of Books* and *New Left Review*, but that's no bad thing. It provides a concise history of the EU's formation and development which is a tour de force. Anderson draws on the work of economic historian Alan Milward, to whom the book is dedicated.

For Brits whose eyes glaze over whenever matters European are discussed, this book provides the antidote. This indifference to Europe has meant that throughout the last decade hundreds of thousands of European trade unionists, from east and west, have marched against neoliberal measures being proffered by the EU Commission but their British counterparts have stayed at home. Talk of the EU being "boring" plays into the hands of those who want it run in secrecy at an elite level, with EU citizens being told its affairs are too complex to be grasped.

Anderson's starting point is the correct one. How come the EU, whose economy is greater than the United States, Japan or China, has so little political clout? The obvious answer is because it is not a state. This is underlined in this recession by the fact that each bailout and rescue plan, for the banks and the car industry, has been implemented on a national level.

Anderson follows Milward in stressing the economic realities that drove the EU project forward. For France it had the advantage of containing Germany. The latter might be the economic powerhouse of Europe but France was the key military and diplomatic power. That was reflected in Paris's abandonment of its alliance with London in the wake of the Suez debacle in 1956.

The US also encouraged the project because it would help contain Russia. The Eisenhower administration put military and diplomatic considerations before economic ones. That changed in the Nixon-Kissinger years with the first great post-war depression when Europe was seen as a rival.

The "father" of the EU, Jean Monnet, looked towards the creation of a single European state, but the EU evolved through closed door deals done between different governments. The fact that it rested on nation states also ensured the survival and regeneration of those states in the immediate post-war years.

The New Old World contains essays on Germany, France and Italy, the key EU states, and on two fault lines, Turkey and Cyprus, both hot potatoes for the EU club. All are fascinating, though all will create debate.

This book begins with a calculated snub: Anderson says he does not regret the omission of any analysis of Britain because its "history since the fall of Thatcher has been of little moment". The great mobilisations against the Iraq war are thus ignored.

Despite his critique of the EU Anderson remains a supporter of the project. This is accompanied by a deep pessimism about the left in Europe and the ability of class struggle to shape events. Yet the European ruling classes are nervous over the possibilities of resistance. EU-wide resistance cannot be predicted, but the left and the working class remain players who can help determine the outcome.

The race to the bottom will go on across the EU, with the Channel providing no barrier to protect us. That, not the threat to "our" pound, is the biggest danger the people of this island face. It is the same danger faced by our brothers and sisters across the EU.

The political tradition associated with this journal opposes the EU as a bosses' club. Others on the European left support membership of the EU. That should not stop us resisting attacks together or striving to get the best social and economic conditions within the EU extended to each member state, east and west.

The New Old World contains a good explanation of what the EU is and should be read for that alone. Anderson seems to swing between wanting to expose how undemocratic and pro free market the EU is and advocating the creation of a European state. The book does not offer a way forward but, in truth, I was not expecting this. Do not let Anderson's pessimism stand in your way of enjoying his book—I didn't.

Forgotten famine
John Newsinger

Madhusree Mukerjee, **Churchill's Secret War: the British Empire and the Ravaging of India during the Second World War** *(Basic Books, 2010), £18.99*

The Bengal Famine of 1943-44 is one of the most terrible episodes of the Second World War. According to Madhusree Mukerjee's new book, the death toll has to be revised upwards from the generally accepted figure of 3.5 million men, women and children to over 5 million. Certainly, it was, as the Viceroy, Lord Wavell, put it, "one of the greatest disasters that has befallen any people under British rule". And yet it has almost completely disappeared from the history books.

One can read any number of the many biographies of the prime minister of the

time, Winston Churchill, without coming across any mention of the catastrophe that he presided over. Similarly with biographies of the deputy prime minister, Clement Attlee, the millions who died of starvation and disease while he occupied that post go unmentioned. Even more incredible is the way the famine is routinely ignored in histories of the British Empire.

Professor Denis Judd, for example, in his acclaimed one-volume account, *Empire*, does not so much as mention the Bengal Famine. More surprisingly perhaps, he does not mention it in his history of the British Raj, *The Lion and the Tiger*. And most astonishingly, he does not mention it in his biography of the Indian nationalist leader, Nehru, even though Nehru himself described the famine quite correctly as "the final judgement on British rule". The immensely prestigious multi-volume *Oxford History of the British Empire*, the summation of Anglo-American scholarship on the subject, also manages to ignore the episode.

Why this historical amnesia? The reason is quite simply that the majority of British historians of the empire have a benign view of British imperialism. While they will often accept that there were some abuses, even occasional crimes, overall the empire was a force for good. The Bengal Famine poses a serious threat to this benign paradigm, indeed it makes it untenable. Consequently, the famine has been airbrushed from the picture. It raises too many uncomfortable questions about the nature of British rule in India and therefore is either marginalised or ignored altogether. If this was the work of Russian historians during the Communist period, covering up the famine in the Ukraine in the early 1930s, their work would be quite correctly dismissed as Stalinist apologetics. They would, however, have at least had the excuse that their lives depended on the cover-up!

With the publication of *Churchill's Secret War* one can only hope that such a convenient lapse of historical memory will become impossible in the future, although, of course, one cannot count on this. Mukerjee provides a very useful introduction to the place Bengal occupied in the empire from the 1770s on, before going on to focus on the Quit India revolt launched by the Indian National Congress in July 1942 and on the famine. The Quit India revolt, itself a neglected episode, was put down with great brutality (shootings, beatings, villages burned down, rape and torture), and, as she shows, this repression continued even when the country was in the grip of famine. She chronicles Churchill's fury at the Indian challenge to British rule.

The indictment of the British Empire is that the famine was the product of Indian involvement in Britain's war and that the authorities completely failed to mount an adequate relief effort. Indeed, grain continued to be exported from India even while millions starved to death. Mukerjee estimates that if these exports had been diverted to Bengal, some two million lives would have been saved. The British government also decided, despite pleas from the authorities in India, not to organise the shipment of sufficient foodstuffs to alleviate the situation in Bengal.

Mukerjee develops a number of rationales for the British failure: the need to ensure adequate food supplies in Britain (Indians starving to death were politically preferable to the *possibility* of shortages in Britain) and to stockpile food for the liberation of Europe. As Churchill put it, Indians were used to starving! This brings us to Churchill's role in events, something most of his biographers have failed to confront. As she observes, with considerable restraint, "Churchill's broad-brush loathing of the natives might have added impetus to the other rationales."

Indeed, with Australian wheat flour being sent "to Ceylon, the Middle East and southern Africa—everywhere in the Indian Ocean area but to India", it is hard to avoid concluding that there was "a will to punish". In just about every War Cabinet discussion of India in 1943, Churchill displayed what she describes as an "inchoate rage". It is absolutely clear that the famine deaths of 1943-44 lie at the door of the British government.

The publication of *Churchill's Secret War* is to be wholeheartedly welcomed. Hopefully it signals the start of a debate about the responsibility for the Bengal Famine and what this tells us about the nature of the British Empire. Certainly, the fact that we have had to wait so long for such a book tells us a great deal about the British historians of the Empire. A paperback edition is urgently needed.

Africa's opening
Andy Wynne

Issa G Shivji, **Accumulation in an African Periphery—a Theoretical Framework** *(Mkuki na Nyoto Publishers),* £15.95

Professor Shivji of the University of Dar es Salaam has been writing in the Marxist tradition since the 1970s when, for example, he wrote the classic *Class Struggles in Tanzania*. His latest project, of which this booklet is the first chapter, is an analysis of the place and role of Africa in the global political economy of neoliberalism. The central message of the booklet is that the crisis of recent years has provided an opening for the Global South to refuse to play the capitalist imperialist game, whatever the rules. He argues it is time to rethink and revisit the direction of development and dominant strategies.

The two core sections of the booklet provide an analysis of the global economy in general and the Global South in particular. Starting with Marx's identification of accumulation as the motive force of capitalism, he goes on to consider the contributions of Lenin, Rosa Luxemburg and others in developing the theory of imperialism. He then considers how "accumulation by dispossession", a phrase coined by David Harvey, has shaped the historical geography of capitalism, particularly in the Global South.

Shivji briefly indicates how the Asian crisis of 1997-8 destroyed the myth of the Asian Tigers. They had previously been held up as the success story of the International Monetary Fund's neoliberal policies which Africa leaders were cajoled to follow. He argues that the recent financial crisis and subsequent global recession have shattered many illusions in the efficacy of global capitalism.

Shivji argues that it is the system of super-exploitation of the rural peasantry and the informal sector in the cities of the Global South that lies at the centre of "accumulation by dispossession". This allows a surplus to be produced in the Global South, or periphery, which is then accumulated at the centre. Various mechanisms achieve this, unfavourable terms of trade, debt servicing and profit repatriation (through manipulation of transfer prices, for example). But there is not a simple dichotomy between the periphery and the centre. Accumulation also occurs in various sub-imperialist centres, for example, Nairobi in East Africa, Lagos in West Africa, and South Africa.

The boom in prices of African raw commodities over the last few years has led to a series of perverse results rather than the economic development. In Dar es Salaam a multibillion dollar project was proposed to reclaim hundreds of square kilometres of the Indian Ocean to create a new city centre of shopping malls and offices. This would do nothing to serve the chronic demand for housing from the slums and the ghettos. While many "middle class" homes of Dar es Salaam are decorated with cheap plastic flowers imported from China, fresh flowers are exported from East Africa to Europe. Neoliberalism is also "heralding a new wave of commodification and expropriation of land" across Sub-Saharan Africa in which the "fist of the state... will be deployed freely".

Shivji concludes his booklet by saying that answers to such problems "cannot be answered in the abstract. They require a concrete analysis of the agency of change in the context of the state of international and national class struggles, which we hope to do in the ongoing study of the political economy of Tanzania." Given the nature of Shivji's previous work, we can look forward to this analysis providing a further contribution to our understanding of the Global South and our arguments for the necessity of collective action to effect real change. Meanwhile this booklet provides an excellent introduction to such an analysis.

Pick of the quarter

The accidents of publishing schedules mean that two issues of both *New Left Review* and *Historical Materialism* have appeared since *International Socialism 129* came out. They also mean that *Historical Materialism* 18.3 posthumously publishes an article by Chris Harman. Chris was contributing to a symposium on *Lenin Rediscovered*, Lars Lih's mammoth study of Lenin's *What is to be Done?* While welcoming Lih's book, Chris takes issue with his argument that Lenin, far from beginning to break with the orthodox Marxism of the Second International in this text, remained a loyal follower of the political and intellectual tradition developed by Karl Kautsky, chief theoretician of the German Social Democratic Party (SPD). Chris argues that, even though Lenin undoubtedly "*believed* he was a conventional follower of Kautsky", his practice as leader of the Bolsheviks increasingly diverged from that of the SPD. Paul Le Blanc takes a broadly similar approach in his contribution to the symposium. In his lengthy reply Lih rejects this fundamental objection, and also takes issue with the interpretations of Lenin provided by two other writers in the *International Socialism* tradition, Tony Cliff and John Molyneux.

One of Cliff's many acts of iconoclasm was to criticise Lenin's theory of the labour aristocracy. Charles Post in the lead article of *Historical Materialism* 18.4 offers a systematic critique of different versions of this theory, which seeks to explain the hold of reformism on workers in the North by their participating in the exploitation of the Global South. Post shows that this doesn't hold up economically—foreign direct investment is only a small fraction of total world investment, and most of it goes to the North. The theory also doesn't fit the history of the Western workers' movement, since often some of the best-paid sectors have shown the most militancy. The same issue contains two reviews of Andrew Kliman's interpretation of Marx's theory of value. Fred Moseley's displays a clarity and balance all too rare in such discussions.

There's quite a lot of meat in *New Left Review* 66—an interesting (though depressing) account by Richard Walker of how neoliberalism has changed California for the worse, Hung Ho-fung on Hong Kong, and Asef Bayat on Tehran. The latest issue leads with an article on Ireland by Daniel Finn whose focus on Republicanism seems a little misjudged, despite Sinn Féin's electoral successes in the South. Benno Teschke's review article of a new biography of the German legal and political philosopher Carl Schmitt offers a valuable critique of "an authoritarian and part-time fascist thinker" who is often presented these days, as Teschke points out, as "a radical—even critical—voice against a world-historical conjuncture characterised by liberal imperialism".

Finally, a special edition of *Socialism and Democracy* from November 2010 contains a collection of articles which survey Marxist writings from various parts of the world. Alongside Paul Blackledge's survey of the past decade of Marxism in the Anglophone world are articles which discuss works that have not been translated into English.

AC & JJ